From Copyright to Copperfield

From
Copyright
to
Copperfield

The Identity of Dickens

ALEXANDER WELSH

Harvard University Press
Cambridge, Massachusetts
London, England
1987

Publication of this book has been aided by a grant from the Hyder Edward Rollins Fund

This book is printed on acid-free paper, and its binding materials have been chosen
for strength and durability.

Library of Congress Cataloging-in-Publication Data

Welsh, Alexander.
From copyright to Copperfield.

Includes index.
1. Dickens, Charles, 1812–1870—Criticism and
interpretation.   2. Self in literature.   3. Fiction,
Autobiographic.   4. Identity (Psychology) in literature.
I. Title.
PR4592.S38W44   1987   823'.8   87-7614
ISBN 0-674-32342-4 (alk. paper)

For Doug Welsh

Preface

This book can be thought of as an assault on Warren's Blacking warehouse. For about fifty years, interpreters of Dickens's life and writings have invested heavily in the episode in which he was set to work as a child, putting up shoeblacking in bottles in a shop near the Strand in London. While I would not deny that the episode was traumatic in some sense, I am expressly denying that a trauma in childhood provides the best ground for biographical criticism. This book is devoted to the time in early middle life when Dickens *recalled* his traumatic experience, to his sense of identity as a writer of literature, and to the three novels he produced in this period: *Martin Chuzzlewit, Dombey and Son,* and *David Copperfield.*

By copyright, I refer specifically to the cause of international copyright in which Dickens was briefly embroiled during his first visit to America—a journey that contributed importantly to his self-recognition, his development as a novelist, and especially his humor. But this is far from my only concern. We should take for granted Dickens's material interests as a writer and also his ambition to associate himself with the greatest writers. The originality of the man should not be allowed to obscure the degree to which, in the course of shaping his life and transforming his work, he was engaged with earlier literature. So enamored have we become of the blacking warehouse, that we scant his adoption of the profession of writing itself, which included not only his predecessors among the novelists but such as Shakespeare, Molière, and Milton.

With a revised biographical criticism—wary of trauma and alert to literature—I have attempted substantial interpretations of *Chuzzlewit, Dombey,* and *Copperfield,* three grand novels named for heroes who progressively embody more constrained and tidy projections of Dickens himself. (They are the last novels named for heroes until *Our Mutual Friend.*) Though it will be apparent that the first is my personal favorite, I have given the most exhaustive attention to the third, in recognition of its popularity and its manifest autobiographical intent. Still, I try not to go over quite the same ground as earlier critics, who almost all have agreed that the first quarter or so of *Copperfield* brilliantly recreates the experience of childhood; not surprisingly, this was Freud's as well as Dickens's favorite. I emphasize Copperfield's adult life and in any case insist that Dickens and other nineteenth-century novelists did not learn the value of make-believe from Freud. It can only be the other way around.

A short book with a revisionary thesis must acknowledge a long debt to previous scholarship and criticism. Recently it has become possible to restudy the career of Dickens, up to the writing of *Copperfield,* because of the splendid Pilgrim Edition of his letters—the labor of Madeline House and Graham Storey, as well as Kathleen Tillotson, K. J. Fielding, and others. The three novels in question have also been made newly available by the Clarendon Press, in definitive editions by Margaret Cardwell, Alan Horsman, and Nina Burgis. My responses to some of these new materials first appeared in the *Yale Review* from 1975 to 1981, and I wish to thank the editor, Kai Erikson, for permission to use a portion of the last review here. On the three novels, an immense amount of thought and research has been brought to bear by other Dickensians over the years. Though I have tried to be conscientious in the argument and notes about all my published sources, I am sure I have forgotten or repressed others, and to those I must be especially indebted. As might be expected in a book of this nature, the authority I cite most frequently is John Forster—Dickens's literary friend, adviser, and biographer. Two of his expressions I have borrowed, perhaps a little mischievously, for chapter titles: but if Forster was indeed the model for the great Podsnap in *Our Mutual Friend,* then it only seems proper to let him speak for what is or is not "English" in Dickens.

It is a pleasure to thank Philip Collins, Donald Fanger, K. J. Fielding, Philip Koch, and Barbara Packer for their ready replies to my inquiries, and Jeanette Gilkison and Joan Maltese for their expert typing. Once again I am especially grateful to Ruth Bernard Yeazell for her encouragement and her critical reading of the manuscript.

Contents

Illustrations

The drawings are all by Hablot K. Browne, known as Phiz.

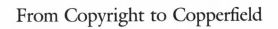

From Copyright to Copperfield

I

Charles Dickens

*T*his book about three pivotal works in the Dickens canon, *Martin Chuzzlewit, Dombey and Son,* and *David Copperfield,* offers no facts about the novelist that are strictly speaking new. It does propose to shift attention from the formative years of Dickens's childhood to his mature development, from the family romance to his writing career, and from the claim of originality to his creative use of earlier literature. In some of these respects, the burden of the argument is Eriksonian rather than Freudian.

Almost too much is known about Dickens, and his literary output is far too rich and rewarding of study, to establish such a revisionary thesis in anything less than several volumes. Nevertheless, I believe that this shift in emphasis might be salutary for biographical criticism in general and that some of its results may be demonstrated within a short compass. A biography may take either an epochal or a serial form, and the first generally has more explanatory power. By seizing on this or that epoch in the life—schooling, independence, marriage, and so on— the biographer tries to show cause for the person's subsequent history. Yet even a serial arrangement of achievements, travels, friendships, and the like conveys some interpretation of how the life was lived. Since Dickens was a famous novelist, his biographer could hardly register any more significant fact about him than the series of novels he wrote, from *The Posthumous Papers of the Pickwick Club* to the unfinished and posthumous *Mystery of Edwin Drood*. Such a biography, which might be compressed into one long sentence, would still provide a useful check on conclusions derived from the epochal form.

In our time, to explain a life usually means arranging the incidents around certain episodes that were arguably traumatic. This design is a type of epochal biography, but one for which the significant epoch is supposedly unknown at the outset of the inquiry. The narrative suspense thus differs from that of the predictable epochs of life, from birth through death. The biographer proposes to reveal what was hitherto concealed, very possibly concealed even from the subject. In the latter case, the concealment itself has meaning, for it was almost certainly motivated. If the gauge of importance is the purely personal, then what was concealed is likely to have been more important than what was not. Besides this marked bent toward the private, the method favors a passive construction of the epoch in question. Something happened *to* the person, when he or she was in a defenseless state. This model of explanation—which may be called the psychoanalytic model, though it did not originate with Freud—helps to make specific and thereby manageable the distress of being subject to those many conditions we moderns believe we are subject to, usually with good reason. From all these points of view, the idea of traumatic beginnings is attractive and modern, while it also resembles ancient myths of the birth of heroes.

As it is usually recited, the life of Dickens is no exception to the rule. Any reasonably attentive student of literature believes that the single most important event in the life of Dickens was not the writing of any novel, or his attaining of independence, or his marriage and the births of his children, but the four months he spent in Warren's Blacking warehouse at the age of twelve. As Edmund Wilson argued fifty years ago, appealing loosely to a psychoanalytic model, "these experiences produced in Charles Dickens a trauma from which he suffered all his life."[1] This way of thinking, in fact, is somewhat older than psychoanalysis, for Dickens himself believed much the same thing about his experience: its importance was not something dreamed up by Wilson. Just briefly, it is necessary to summarize what we know about the famous blacking warehouse.

Dickens's friend and first biographer, John Forster, claimed to have stumbled upon the secret memories of those childhood days in "March or April of 1847," when the novelist would have recently celebrated his thirty-fifth birthday—the biblical and Dantean midpoint of his life.

Forster, curious about his friend's childhood, asked him if he remembered meeting an older friend of theirs, who claimed to have been introduced to the young Dickens by his father, in the warehouse near the Strand. Dickens did not respond immediately, but "very shortly afterwards," according to Forster, "I learnt in all their detail the incidents that had been so painful to him, and what was then said to me or written respecting them revealed the story of his boyhood."[2]

The writing that Forster refers to is the famous autobiographical fragment, from which he quotes in his *Life* after the subject's death— twelve years before the appointed seventy years, in 1870. As with letters of Dickens for which Forster is the only source, we do not know how much of the fragment he printed or what he changed, though the temptations must have been severe in presenting this "picture of tragical suffering, and of tender as well as humorous fancy, unsurpassed in even the wonders of his published writings." Apparently, until the idea of treating the same material fictionally in *David Copperfield* occurred to Dickens, he intended to write a sizeable autobiography. *If* it is the case that he meant to publish what he had written, "as fact, before he thought of any other use for it," he may have changed his mind from a belief that his confession of feeling was too strong. His rhetoric, in the fragment, insists that he "cannot" write of the shame of having to work with common boys, pasting labels on jars of shoeblacking, while his father languished in jail for debt:

> No words can express the secret agony of my soul as I sunk into this companionship; compared these everyday associates with those of my happier childhood; and felt my early hopes of growing up to be a learned and distinguished man crushed in my breast. The deep remembrance of the sense I had of being utterly neglected and hopeless; of the shame I felt in my position; of the misery it was to my young heart to believe that, day by day, what I had learned, and thought, and delighted in, and raised my fancy and my emulation up by, was passing away from me, never to be brought back any more; cannot be written. My whole nature was so penetrated with the grief and humiliation of such considerations, that even now, famous and caressed and happy, I often forget in my dreams that I have a dear wife and children; even that I am a man; and wander desolately back to that time of my life.

In this acute misery, the child toiled six days a week for six shillings; a lodging was found for him, and he rejoined his family on Sundays in the Marshalsea Prison, where he was careful not to lead Bob Fagin or the other boys with whom he worked. Hardly believing that he had been "cast away at such an age," he suffered the shame of his abandonment as well as the loneliness and hunger he could so vividly recall. Despite some spare sympathy for him that he is able to record in the fragment, he swears that he received "no advice, no counsel, no encouragement, no consolation, no support, from anyone that I can call to mind, so help me God."[3]

The secret memory of the blacking warehouse explains a great deal in Dickens's life and fiction. It partially explains why, in the midst of his success with *Pickwick*, he should begin a fairy tale of the workhouse child, *Oliver Twist*. It explains the vein of self-pity that crops up again and again in the novels, and particularly the childlike sentiment that if he had died or turned bad, it would have served the grown-ups right. Thus the pitiful Oliver Twist has an even more pitiful workhouse comrade, named Dick, who does not survive; David Copperfield has an infant half-brother who is buried in their mother's arms and "was myself"; Esther Summerson lives, but her mother, by a series of extraordinary displacements, is still "the mother of the dead child"; and Richard Doubledick, in the story called "The Seven Poor Travellers," dies and comes to life again. In the late novels, when doublings and replacements have become a routine hedge against death, the strain of self-pity seems as strong as ever, whether it is the little surrogate John Harmon dumbly beseeching and actually dying, like little Dick, or the actual John Harmon pretending to die and consulting the reader on the question in his long soliloquy. Dickens was more aware of his own memories, perhaps, than of the intensity with which he projected his feelings even in characters who did not suffer as he had.

The psychoanalytic model adds two further dimensions to the interpretation of the blacking-warehouse days. Besides this commiseration of the self with the self, which finds its expression in fictional parallels, the wisdom of psychoanalysis suggests that suffering calls forth aggression in the subject, which in turn induces guilt. Indeed, if Dickens kept the episode a close secret, that was not merely because of his shame but because of his own reaction against those who made him suffer. In the autobiographical fragment, in fact, he just touches on his aggressive feelings toward his parents by denying any such thing: "I do not write resentfully or angrily: for I know how all these things have worked together to make me what I am: but I never afterwards forgot,

I never shall forget, I never can forget, that my mother was warm for my being sent back."[4] Resentment and anger are clear possibilities, then, and the guilt of harboring so much indignation becomes a kind of tertiary result of the episode. Aggression and guilt, usually unconscious, fuel the so-called dark side of Dickens's fiction, to which Wilson called attention. Wilson has been perhaps the only critic to take the interpolated tales in Dickens's first novel more seriously than the adventures of Mr. Pickwick and Sam Weller, and surely he exaggerated the importance of the most coherent of the tales, "The Story of the Queer Client"—a story that seethes with aggression against parental figures, but which is very uncharacteristic of the novel as a whole. Yet just as self-pity can be traced in the novels to the very end, so can parricide and guilt. Many critics since Wilson have succeeded in tracking down guilt in Dickens, and the motif of parricide remains closer to the surface than might be supposed.[5]

The method of inquiry in psychoanalysis often implies that less is more. Because the theory embraces a general assumption of repression and selective revelation, the evidence of hidden emotions need not be proportional to their hidden effects. A slightness or indeed lack of evidence may merely indicate the strength of the forces arrayed against its revelation. Thus unconscious motives account not only for the dark side of Dickens's fiction, comprised of mental suffering, aggression, and guilt, but for the bright side of humor as well. Wilson went so far as to suggest that the bright side did not shine of itself. The novelist's laughter he put down as "an exhilaration which already shows a trace of the hysterical" in *Pickwick*.[6] Since the terrain of secret thoughts extends so widely, the explaining power of secret memory can be extended indefinitely. In truth, Wilson was not formally committed to psychoanalysis, or he might not have placed so much stress on an episode that occurred when the subject was twelve years old and which *he* could remember very well, though he concealed it from his friends: lasting traumas are supposed to occur much earlier, before the age of six. Steven Marcus, better versed in the theory, is tempted to interpret the blacking warehouse as a screen memory of a still earlier primal scene. Though such a secondary and hypothetical construction seems far-fetched, Marcus is able to support it with careful readings from *Oliver Twist*.[7] What is hidden, we have learned, can be brought to light; and in the nearly one hundred years since Freud's discoveries, primal scenes have become for some analysts traditional epochs like independence and marriage. Yet unlike these epochs, the primal scene is significant because scarcely remembered.

Caution is called for here, because the method originally seemed useful in searching out the trauma unique to the subject of the biography. Present-day psychoanalysts, in fact, tend to care less about traumatic events than about the ways in which patients think about them, and as Albert D. Hutter has urged, the blacking warehouse itself ought to be placed in "a developmental framework."[8] Dickens was at least thirty-five when he wrote the fragment of autobiography, which Forster may or may not have tampered with when he himself was sixty. That sometime in the course of writing *Dombey and Son* Dickens prepared to reveal his secret is just as important to consider as his reasons for concealing it for the previous twenty years. The confession to Forster and the writing of *David Copperfield*, and the two in conjunction, were gestures of partial revelation. Shame was probably a sufficient motive for concealment,[9] without the effect of guilt; and pride played a certain part in the revelation. At *this* time of life, Dickens wanted someone to know about the blacking warehouse, because from his current point of view the episode did him some credit. He almost, apparently, published an autobiography that would have featured the experience as an epoch in his life. His twofold compromise—the fragment handed over to Forster and the fictional recasting of the episode in *Copperfield*—enable us to read the episode, as Dickens foresaw and Forster concurred, as something sensational, a secret to be shared. There was almost a boast in Dickens's complaint that, "but for the mercy of God, I might easily have been, for all the care that was taken of me, a little robber or a little vagabond." I am not and never have been a vagabond, he is saying, but that is to my credit and no one else's. In part, his is a story of conscious pride, consciously conveyed to the reader:

> But I held some station at the blacking warehouse, too. Besides that my relative in the counting-house did what a man so occupied, and dealing with a thing so anomalous, could, to treat me as one upon a different footing from the rest, I never said, to man or boy, how it was that I came to be there, or gave the least indication of my being sorry that I was there. That I suffered in secret, and that I suffered exquisitely, no one ever knew but I. How much I suffered, it is, as I have said already, utterly beyond my power to tell. No man's imagination can overstep the reality. But I kept my counsel, and I did my work.[10]

Dickens believed, at the time of the telling, that the episode contributed not only to the dark side but to all sides of his character—"for I know how all these things have worked together to make me what I am." As Edgar Johnson has suggested, if there is one very direct and probable result of his suffering as a boy, it was to fire his ambition not to suffer as a man.[11]

If I am exaggerating slightly the upbeat of this well-known narrative, it is because the present argument concerns the work of the period in which it was written—the period, that is, from the first American journey to *David Copperfield*. "I did my work"—if there is a major theme both personal and moral that runs throughout Dickens's life, it is that of self-sufficiency through work, against which the repeated note of self-pity is a minor, complementary theme. During the writing of *Martin Chuzzlewit* and *Dombey and Son,* he was conscious of having to apply himself to the task as he had not needed to earlier. The writing of the autobiographical fragment, with its confession of self-pity, was one means he used—besides throwing himself into amateur productions of *Every Man in His Humour* and *The Merry Wives of Windsor*—to climb out of a mild depression. His "*Chuzzlewit* agonies," as he called them, and the writing of *A Christmas Carol*—approximately three years *before* the gesture toward autobiography—coincided with what Forster calls "the turning point of his career." It is not precisely clear what Forster meant by this turning, and his pinpointing of it is a little too precise. But he seems to have meant something within the range of possibilities—of personal resolve and financial reward—that Johnson traces to the childhood experience. Forster ascribes it to the exigencies of the moment and the nature of the man:

> His temperament of course coloured everything, cheerful or sad, and his present outlook was disturbed by imaginary fears: but it was very certain that his labours and successes thus far had enriched others more than himself, and while he knew that his mode of living had been scrupulously governed by what he believed to be his means, the first suspicion that these might be inadequate made a change necessary to so upright a nature. It was the turning point of his career; and the issue, though not immediately, ultimately justified him.[12]

Forster admits that he need not have worried so much about Dickens's restlessness and travels at the time, probably because he worried mainly about his friend's ability to meet the considerable expenses and obligations arising from his early success in the world. In retrospect that question, at least, was taken care of.

We do not have to depend on Forster, or on anyone's theory, to be sure that the journey to America begins a new epoch in Dickens's life. The way to confirm this is to revert to the simpler form of biography and review serially his achievements up to this time. Dickens was twenty-four when, because of the minor success of the short pieces collected as *Sketches by Boz,* he was approached by the publishers Chapman and Hall to write the story for an illustrated work, a burlesque in monthly installments, which became *The Posthumous Papers of the Pickwick Club.* When the illustrator, Robert Seymour, committed suicide, he was replaced by the twenty-year-old Hablot Knight Browne. The long collaboration between "Boz" and "Phiz" had begun, and Dickens assumed control of the new work. Though the early sales of *Pickwick* were unspectacular, sales soared to 40,000 a month after the introduction of Sam Weller. Before Dickens had completed this novel, he had begun *Oliver Twist;* and before *Oliver Twist* was complete, *Nicholas Nickleby* began to appear. Meanwhile a periodical was planned, which Dickens would edit and for which he would supply copy. This periodical rapidly became the frame to the next novel, *The Old Curiosity Shop,* which appeared week by week and was followed in the same fashion by *Barnaby Rudge.* Then Dickens slowed down; before his thirtieth birthday a pause between novels occurs for the first time; and the period we are concerned with has arrived.

The early output spanned six years, in which Dickens drove on from one novel to the next. His reputation for humor was fixed for all time by *Pickwick* and, for pathos, by the death of little Nell in *The Old Curiosity Shop.* Through all this activity, Dickens can be said to have planned in advance only one novel, the last of the five to be published, which he had conceived as "Gabriel Vardon, the Locksmith of London" and contracted for when *Pickwick* was under way. As one can see, the completing of this "first" novel, which became *Barnaby Rudge,* took some pains. Some of the energy Dickens might have devoted to it was drained off by fierce disputes with three publishers, which have been excellently told by Johnson and by Robert L. Patten.[13] The young novelist had contracted for work at a much lower rate than—within a matter of months—his fame warranted. He was determined not to honor com-

8

mitments made in entirely different circumstances, and he angered busi-ness associates and embarrassed friends in the process. But these strug-gles apart, Dickens had still come to a kind of stopping place. Having written no fewer than five novels, he faced the ordinary novelist's prob-lem of writing his "second." Having no other plans, he decided to go to America.

Except for this pause in his production, it is not clear why Dickens decided to leave his children in the care of friends, the actor William Macready and his family, and travel with his wife to America. Forster did not really approve of the journey any more than Catherine Dickens did—though Washington Irving had assured the novelist of welcome in the United States. The friend and biographer can only record a few swift stages of the decision: the subject's motives he does not spell out. On 19 September 1841, Dickens wrote "to astonish" Forster with the news that, "after balancing, considering, and weighing the matter from every point of view, I HAVE MADE UP MY MIND (WITH GOD'S LEAVE) TO GO TO AMERICA." Three days later he gave more details, but offered as reasons merely "advantages of going . . . so great, that I have come to persuade myself it is a matter of imperative necessity."[14] He had already arranged with Chapman and Hall for a year's respite before beginning another novel, with an advance on the profits to be paid by them in the meanwhile. On 4 January 1842 he sailed from Liverpool for the New World, and by June he had returned as planned, though with a very different idea of America from that he had set out with. His *American Notes for General Circulation* was published, and *Martin Chuzzlewit* begun, at the end of 1842. But the restlessness of these years did not cease with the commencement of the new work. Dickens still experienced difficulties in settling down to write, and because *Chuzzlewit* sold poorly, he was also under some financial strain. The first and most famous of his Christmas books, *A Christmas Carol*, ought to have eased this problem at least, but it too was not immediately popular. As soon as the last number of *Chuzzlewit* was finished, in the summer of 1844, Dickens picked up his family—children and sister-in-law as well as Catherine—and moved to Genoa. The Christmas books, five in all, continued to get written, but the restlessness was still very evident. Not until the autumn of 1846—the longest interval between novels before his last decade—did he begin *Dombey and Son*.

What I am proposing, in the present biographical and literary essay, is that Dickens experienced in his late twenties and early thirties a moratorium in his career that, while it did not alter his vocation, influenced his work in important ways. The term "moratorium" is Erikson's and is especially useful because, though a psychoanalyst, Erikson has turned from emphasis on early traumas to stress the crucial passing of every stage in life and a person's interaction with the particular customs of a society. A stage of life, whether of infancy or old age, is always "psychosocial," therefore, and a so-called moratorium is common—for males at least—in the twenties. Erikson sometimes writes of the moratorium as "a second period of delay"—comparable, that is, to the latency between infancy and adolescence; or he may describe it more conventionally as "prolonged adolescence."[15] But the most striking use he makes of the concept is in his study of Luther, where he defines it as "a means of marking time" in the life of a person with a particular historical contribution to make. There he writes of Luther's and others' monastic commitment, "before they come to their crossroad, which they often do in their late twenties, belated just because they gave their all to the temporary subject of devotion."[16] Certain institutions—such as monasteries, certainly, or studying for the bar or perhaps graduate schools today—accommodate individual moratoria very well. Among English families who could afford it, travel on the Continent once provided another way for young men to mark time. One unspoken reason for Dickens's going to America, surely, was that other successful writers had taken the same course—that particular journey was a highly special institution in this sense, as well as a suitably vague extension of his purpose to make his fortune, he knew not how.

Dickens did not, like some of the great men Erikson has in mind, arrive at a crossroad and change direction, but it is worth noting some signs of uncertainty before the reaffirmation of his vocation at the close of this period. Forster, obviously, was made uneasy by his friend's behavior. The arrangement with Chapman and Hall to provide a year's leave, to begin with, drew from Forster "some fear as to the use he was likely to make of the leisure it afforded him." Dickens was hardly one to be idle in any circumstances, yet the plan for a journey, presented as "a thing that somehow or other, at no very distant date, *must be*," was disturbing to his friend.[17] It is sometimes hard to assess the judgment of the ever prudent Forster, who was exactly Dickens's age but always writes as if he were much older—an effect partly of Forster's personality and partly of his looking back on these scenes thirty or more years from the time of writing. But some of the compulsiveness of his subject shows through, and there are plenty of other indications of Dickens's restlessness. As in the Eriksonian model of identity confusion, he even flirted with different careers after his return from America. For a short while in the winter of 1845–46, he determined that he would be editor of the *Daily News,* a new undertaking of Bradbury and Evans and other backers. "I will take that Post of Editor which is marked in the little statement as having a Salary of a Thousand Pounds attached to it—for double that Salary," he wrote to the publishers; and they apparently never balked at the price, though Dickens himself began backing away from the agreement rather quickly.[18] In the spring he was off to the Continent once more with his family, and shortly thereafter he addressed Lord Morpeth about possible ways he might serve his nation in other than a literary capacity:

> I have an ambition for some public employment—some Commissioner-ship, or Inspectorship, or the like, connected with any of those subjects in which I take a deep interest, and in respect of which the Public are generally disposed to treat me with confidence and regard. On any questions connected with the Education of the People, the elevation of their character, the improvement of their dwellings, their greater protection against disease and vice—or with the treatment of Criminals, or the admin-istration of Prison Discipline, which I have long observed closely—I think I could do good service, and I am sure I should enter with my whole heart. I have hoped, for years, that I may become at last a Police Magistrate, and turn my social knowledge to good practical account from day to day . . .[19]

It seems odd to think of the successful novelist shopping about for other roles to play. There is also to be considered the literary evidence of the Christmas books. The short form was less daunting, for one thing, than an ambitious novel; but the Christmas books also typically posed, by means of a dream vision, an alternative life for the protagonist, who thereby could test himself and start anew. As Steven Marcus has argued, Dickens projected in these stories some of the confusion he was experiencing and which he laid to rest by composing the autobio-graphical fragment and *David Copperfield.*[20]

What happened, finally, is that Dickens inwardly took new bearings and recommenced his career as a novelist. The trauma of the blacking warehouse explains relatively little about this epoch; the journey to America, I believe, explains a great deal. In the childhood episode that he was about to recount, Dickens was a victim; in the American adventure, he was both victim and perpetrator of his difficulties. He drifted into that experience, but the resistance he met over the issue of international copyright—which he raised shortly after his arrival in Boston—forced him to resist and reflect in turn. He was a famous young man, who had departed for the New World in that faith, but having arrived there he discovered another face of fame. As Jerome Meckier suggests, the vulgar curiosity of strangers in America left Dickens feeling exposed. If he had imagined himself something of a radical, the trip made him an Englishman again.[21] The novelist had arrived at a stopping place in his career before he went to America. He may vaguely have supposed that he would profit from the trip by advancing the cause of copyright—though he vehemently denied this. Some few newspaper attacks on him in America put him rapidly on the defensive. If his sense of identity and moral worth was shaken, however, it was in the long run strengthened. He obviously did not suffer an "identity crisis" of debilitating proportions. On the contrary, he suffered just enough identity confusion at this time to have a valuable and lasting effect on his fiction writing. His disappointment with America and Americans was a formative and lasting experience but hardly traumatic. In some words of Barbara Packer on Emerson, a "bitter lesson we learn from experience is the soul's imperviousness to experiences. The traumas are not traumatic."[22] The years that produced *Martin Chuzzlewit* and *Dombey and Son* may usefully be regarded as a moratorium for Dickens, and—if it is permissible to modify Erikson's concept in this way—a moratorium provides an opening for inward reflection rather than trauma. This is not to say that such an experience can be wholly conscious, for experience never is wholly conscious. But it may be partly the result of conscious reflection, and in Dickens's case it was instructive and constructive of his art.

In the chapters that follow, I do not pretend to be uncovering a new theme in Dickens, for nearly thirty years ago J. Hillis Miller introduced "the theme of the search for a true and viable identity" in the novels.[23] But my approach to the texts and concept of personal identity are quite different from Miller's. I am frankly interested in the radical dispersal of Dickens himself in *Martin Chuzzlewit,* the answering unification of

Dombey and Son, and the fictional autobiography of *David Copperfield.* These novels tell us a good deal, in fact, about the novelist; but more important, approaching the first two via the author, and especially the journey to America, demonstrates a coherence not otherwise obvious in the first as well as the relation of all three. *Dombey and Son,* almost everyone agrees, marks the beginning of Dickens's mature work; the three together, I would argue, represent a beginning-over-again as a determined novelist. Dickens did not spin these fictions solely out of his own experience, or out of a metaphysical space where identity is defined. In beginning over again he drew upon major works of earlier literature, just as he had drawn upon *Don Quixote*—seemingly without even thinking about it—when he was commissioned to plot adventures for the Pickwick Club.[24] Dickens was such a brilliant satirist and man of his time that we fail to consider the degree to which, at crucial turnings, he shaped his work along lines suggested to him by great literary models. He chose to model *Chuzzlewit* on *Paradise Lost,* but so ironically and laughably that the ur-text is scarcely recognizable. His construction is mock-Miltonic, prepared for by the clowning of Milton's great contemporary, Molière. The novel gestures in the direction of a serious quest romance as well, but the stronger pull is toward the impositions of the infamous Pecksniff, inspired by the equally infamous Tartuffe. For *Dombey,* the novelist halted his wild parodic swing and deliberately wrote tragedy, producing his most concerted imitation of Shakespeare's *King Lear;* and even in *Copperfield,* his autobiographical novel, he continued to revise the relation of Lear and Cordelia. That Shakespeare's play had particular meaning for Dickens has long been recognized. At this juncture in his life, his strong literary response to it served to pull together his feelings about himself and the world around him.

Projection was hardly new to Dickens's fiction at the time. The hero of his first novel he perceived from the outside, as Cervantes and generations of readers perceived and loved Don Quixote from the outside; the hero of his second novel, an original fairy tale—if there is such a thing—Dickens identified with from the inside. Projection of the author, it may be said, took over Dickens's fiction with *Oliver Twist* and never let go of it again. But after the American experience, the projection flows much more wonderfully in characters who are at the same time targets of scorn and laughter than it does in thin resemblers of the author such as the younger Martin Chuzzlewit. Dickens learned to identify with the outrageously wicked of this world, as well as those pitifully helpless and dangerously vengeful people, like Oliver and Sikes, who were also himself. Who shall say that the writer does not relish the characters of Pecksniff and Scrooge as he relishes his own? Such supposedly objective portrayals of "the other" are the products of self-examination at a deeper level, and the joy with which such characters are exposed was a happiness that Dickens earned for himself by enduring America—or, to put it another way, we Americans reacted to his visit with such unexpected blows to his ego that we deserve credit for deepening the impulses, and broadening the achievement, of a man never noted for conscious self-criticism.

Let me try to demonstrate this fresh self-critical capacity in Dickens by instancing a small part of Mrs. Gamp's performance in *Martin Chuzzlewit*, since I do not call upon this character in the argument about Pecksniff and others in the novel. Gamp is of course a subversive character, who is rebuked for her intervention by old Martin Chuzzlewit only less sternly than Pecksniff is rebuked for more villainous behavior. Dickens does not for a moment intend to lose control of such creatures of his storied humor. They are to be each and severally put down, much as *Dombey and Son* will later serve to rebuke *Chuzzlewit* as a whole. Yet despite, or because of, the exerted control some very disarming things come to be said indirectly, by such characters, about the novelist himself. "By providing a constant parody of moralistic depression," James R. Kincaid suggests of Mrs. Gamp, "she is a walking rebuke to those who do not bear up."[25] As it happens, the words "moralistic depression" describe quite well something of Dickens's mood after America and call to mind also another character of the novel, Mark Tapley, who is always countering depression with his determination to gain "credit"; and although Tapley is more like a puppet of the novelist, Gamp is a formidable voice who speaks at times from so deep within Dickens that she is virtually her own man. Woe to the novelist who creates a Gamp and then affects to neglect her. When that character feels herself neglected, in the ensemble scene near the end of *Chuzzlewit*, she pushes to the fore and without being asked tells the following anecdote. The pronouns and syntax require a little getting used to, but the speech is reproduced here in its entirety:

"Which, Mr. Chuzzlewit," she said, "is well beknown to Mrs. Harris as has one sweet infant (though she *do* not wish it known) in her own family

14

by the mother's side, kep in spirits in a bottle; and that sweet babe she
see at Greenwich Fair, a travellin in company vith the pink-eyed lady,
Prooshan dwarf, and livin skelinton, which judge her feelins wen the barrel
organ played, and she was showed her own dear sister's child, the same
not bein expected from the outside picter, where it was painted quite
contrairy in a livin state, a many sizes larger, and performing beautiful
upon the Arp, which never did that dear child know or do: since breathe
it never did, to speak on, in this wale!"[26]

Mrs. Gamp thus interrupts the conversation with information she
feels will interest anyone present, and her gratuitous anecdote happens
to be about one of those still-born or dying children who populate
nearly every novel of Dickens, in images that invoke self-pity as much
as they evoke pity. Is it possible that Gamp, in order to call attention
to herself, is charging that the novelist has too often grotesquely called
attention to himself by placing such babies on display, as in a Victorian
freak show? Does the signboard image, larger than life, of the child
performing on the harp, for which it had no skill or opportunity,
travesty the frontispiece of the novel, which had just been completed
by Hablot Browne at Dickens's direction and in which Tom Pinch,
much larger than the other figures in the piece, performs more beau-
tifully on the organ than the novelist could do? That the materials for
the anecdote, both living freaks and bottled embryos, can be traced
independently in the record of early nineteenth-century London is one
thing.[27] An explanation of why these particular words spring from
Dickens's pen—the question of the specific target of the anecdote—is
quite another. I know of no way to explicate Gamp's impertinence,
which calls down a scolding from old Martin, *except* as a humorous hit
at all the pitiful dead children of his imagination who are Dickens
himself, and hence as effective self-criticism.

The eruption of Mrs. Gamp in the scene is rather startling in its
immediate narrative context, brilliant in what it says of the life of the
author after his American experience. If such is a fair reading of her
anecdote, there can be no greater compliment to Dickens than this
evidence of self-knowledge. He was not one ever to criticize himself
directly, yet just as *Martin Chuzzlewit* surpasses most books in the
language in laughter, it surpasses in self-knowledge, once allowance has
been made for its astonishing indirections.

II

Our English Tartuffe

*O*ur therapy works by transforming what is unconscious into what is conscious," Freud affirmed in his *Introductory Lectures*. "From what I have so far said a neurosis would seem to be the result of a kind of ignorance—a not knowing about mental events that one ought to know of. This would be a close approximation to some well-known Socratic doctrines, according to which even vices are based on ignorance."

Freud's reference to Socrates is a calculated defense of his own talking-cure. Socrates and psychoanalysis both insist on the value of self-knowledge: if the first can attribute even vices to a failure of self-knowledge, then the second not unreasonably can explain neurosis as an analogous failure. By transforming what is unconscious into what is conscious, psychoanalysis aims at a new kind of self-knowledge, the proof of which is the disappearance of neurotic symptoms. As the argument proceeds, moreover, Freud has to meet an objection that has been made to the Socratic method as well, even though by this point he has dropped the analogy. How can we be sure that the philosopher has not wholly dominated the dialogue or that, in "relieving the patient of his pathogenic ignorance," the analyst has not supplied his own ideas in its place? Freud is well aware of the charge that psychoanalysis insinuates its own explanations everywhere. "*Our* knowledge about the unconscious material is not equivalent to *his* knowledge," he says of the patient in a subsequent lecture, but it helps to overcome his re-

16

sistance "if we have previously given him the appropriate anticipatory ideas."[1]

In the first lecture, something quite exceptional happens. Freud paints himself into a corner explaining how psychoanalysis deals with pathogenic ignorance, and as he does so he deserts Socrates for Molière, and science for comedy.

> Knowledge is not always the same as knowledge: there are different sorts of knowledge, which are far from equivalent psychologically. "Il y a fagots et fagots," as Molière has said. The doctor's knowledge is not the same as the patient's and cannot produce the same effects. If the doctor transfers his knowledge to the patient as a piece of information, it has no result. No, it would be wrong to say that. It does not have the result of removing the symptoms, but it has another one—of setting the analysis in motion, of which the first signs are often the expressions of denial. The patient knows after this what he did not know before—the sense of his symptom; yet he knows it just as little as he did. Thus we learn that there is more than one kind of ignorance. . . . But our thesis that the symptoms vanish when their sense is known remains true in spite of this.[2]

Freud's allusion to Molière, even if intended as a joke, seems peculiarly self-damning. The play is *Le Médecin malgré lui*—conventionally translated as "The Mock Doctor"—and the speaker is the mock doctor himself. In a completely farcical situation, the mischievous plot of his wife Martine, Sganarelle is forced to assume the role of doctor. When he utters this line early in the play, he is still engaged in his usual employment of gathering fagots. "Il y a fagots et fagots"—Sganarelle is merely boasting of the quality of his fagots and justifying his price, though *fagot* could also mean an idle tale and the expression is one of memorable impertinence. Moreover, the mock disease that this mock doctor sets out to cure happens to be female hysteria, which can be cured in any case, he says, by marriage. That sly particle of psychoanalytic wisdom might be Freud's reason for invoking Molière, if it were not that Sganarelle enacts in the course of the play a stunning satire on the ignorance, not of patients, but of the medical profession. He mistakes the location of the heart and the liver in the body, for example, and brushes aside his error with the still more memorable expression, "nous avons changé tout cela, et nous faisons maintenant la médecine d'une méthode toute nouvelle."[3] It is hard to believe that Freud does not consciously or unconsciously implicate himself in alluding to this comedy.

Yet as Freud would be the first to admit, the unconscious need not send up a single message. The founder of psychoanalysis must have recalled that Sganarelle was famous in his own right, as the complacent but stalwart antiheroic clown played by Molière, the actor-manager, in at least six of his comedies: the allusion, in short, imputes both self-defense and a form of boast. Moreover, if the author of *Jokes and Their Relation to the Unconscious* can allude in this way to Molière's unwilling and, so to speak, irreproachable impostor, it is scarcely surprising that the author of *Martin Chuzzlewit* could borrow from Molière's infamous criminal impostor for the invention of the great Pecksniff, whom Forster characterized as "our English Tartuffe."[4]

The only explicit allusion to Molière in the novel, to be sure, has to be read in the illustration by Hablôt Browne for the last number, in which several books are scattered by the caning that Pecksniff receives from old Martin and two titles are visible in the lower left—*Paradise Lost* and *Le Tartuffe*. This happens, indeed, to be one of the illustrations for which the author's instruction to the artist survives: "The old man in a transport of burning indignation, rises from his chair, and uplifting his stick, knocks the good Pecksniff down; before John Westlock and Mark who gently interpose (though they are very much delighted) can possibly prevent him. Mr. Pecksniff on the ground. The old man full of fire, energy and resolution."[5] The caning takes place in the private rooms where Tom Pinch has been cataloguing old Martin's books, but the author makes no mention of specific books or titles. *Paradise Lost* and *Le Tartuffe* were possibly Browne's idea—an illustrator's interpretation of the novel as well as the scene. If so, Dickens agreed to let the titles stand in the illustration for all to read, and there is ample evidence of both inspirations, Milton's and Molière's, in the novel as a whole.[6]

The critics have often protested Dickens's handling of this scene in the narrative as strained and rather humorless. Chesterton, especially, complained of the treatment of Pecksniff, who was otherwise "the best thing in the story."

His fall at the end is one of the rare falls of Dickens. Surely it was not necessary to take Pecksniff so seriously. Pecksniff is a merely laughable character; he is so laughable that he is lovable. Why take such trouble to

unmask a man whose mask you have made transparent? Why collect all the characters to witness the exposure of a man in whom none of the characters believe? Why toil and triumph to have the laugh of a man who was only made to be laughed at?[7]

One answer, as far as the scene itself is concerned, is that *coups de bâton* are not unknown to comedy and puppet shows, and that Pecksniff goes out of the novel just as he came into it, with a tumble.[8] But Chesterton and other readers have sensed that Dickens was not fully in control of the character or the plot. The straining in the punishment may tempt us to substitute some of our knowledge for his knowledge and move us to ask just where the character is coming from. If Freud could indirectly—and rather sweetly—imagine himself as Sganarelle, could not Dickens, via Pecksniff, have fleetingly supposed himself a hypocrite like Tartuffe? Any identification of the character with Satan can be addressed separately, in connection with the extensive play on the fortunate fall in *Martin Chuzzlewit*. Suffice it for now to say that Tartuffe and the arch-hypocrite Satan also have something in common, and that Molière's comedy has sometimes been thought sacrilegious because of the pretended piety of the title character and the exalted calm with which Orgon worships him.[9]

The smooth piety, apparent disinterestedness, and concealed lasciviousness of Tartuffe would seem to be the inspiration of the very same qualities in Pecksniff. In fact, Edgar Johnson, contrasting Molière with Shakespeare and Tartuffe with Falstaff, associates Dickens's sharply restricted characterization with Molière's method generally. Johnson is also one of those who complain of Dickens's treatment of Pecksniff at the end.[10] His observation about characterization is fair enough, but *Le Tartuffe*'s aura of implication is much wider than its typed characters or farcical situations might suggest, and the role of greatest interest is really that of Tartuffe's victim, Orgon. The latter is both dull and imaginative, passive and aggressive in his attachment to the hypocrite. Not surprisingly, since Molière also played this character on the stage, Orgon is a little like the Sganarelle of *Le Médicin malgré lui*, though the action of *Le Tartuffe* traces the disillusionment of the clown rather than his accession to unexpected powers. Obviously there is no directly equivalent character in *Martin Chuzzlewit*, but the closest is Tom Pinch. As Michael Steig reminds us, "the character of Pecksniff is developed in relation to Tom Pinch."[11]

Tartuffe's breathtaking disclaimers of self-interest have been studied from the Sermon on the Mount. The riches of the world are nothing to him, and he can readily forgive his enemies. When confronted by Damis, who has hidden in the closet while Tartuffe offers love to his mother, the hypocrite abruptly pleads his own sinfulness, turning the factual charge against him into a pretense of self-abnegation. The urging of Jesus against the show of religiosity this ingenious hypocrite is able to redouble for his own benefit. Jesus advises, "let not thy left hand know what thy right hand doeth," and when you pray or give alms, "do not sound a trumpet before thee, as the hypocrites do in the synagogues and in the streets" (Matthew 6:1–6). Tartuffe boldly inverts this gospel exhortation of secrecy and adopts it to his would-be seduction of Elmire:

> Le scandale du monde est ce qui fait l'offense,
> Et ce n'est pas pécher qui pécher en silence.[12]

These same "Christian" paradoxes are what appeal to Orgon, who blindly intends to marry his daughter to Tartuffe, while the latter is trying his best to cuckold him. Orgon's name connotes both pride and subservience, and he is a fool on both counts; but his foolishness is also a little quixotic, since the pride is accompanied by devotion to an imagined ideal—which is only a mask for Tartuffe, to be sure, but is validated in itself by the teachings of Jesus. Orgon has elected to be the mouthpiece of a hypocrite, in other words, and what the hypocrite says is gospel. Except for his mother, Orgon is the only character in the play to believe in Tartuffe: besides Damis, Elmire, and Mariane, and Mariane's fiancé Valère, there are Cléante, the brother-in-law who speaks with conspicuous good sense, and Dorine the maid, who incessantly directs her barbs against the hypocrite. As a result of such vociferous opposition, Orgon becomes something of a martyr to the faith. His loyalty—however mistaken to begin with and fortunately diverted to the state by Monsieur Loyal at the end—is strangely the most positive note of the comedy. The foolish Orgon, after all, has no selfish motives as these are usually understood. He has been a good Samaritan to the despised Tartuffe, and no wonder the final statement of Molière's comedy is so hard to pin down.

Readers who find Tom Pinch's selflessness offensive or at best unbelievable—and that apparently includes most readers of *Martin Chuzzlewit*—might reflect that Orgon's act is a hard one to follow. Dickens tries to make the character *more* sympathetic, by substituting hopeless bachelorhood for threatened fatherhood and boundless modesty for arrant pride, but Pinch remains something of a clown, and recalling Molière's clown helps keep Dickens's in perspective.[13] Pinch's loyalty to Pecksniff is designed to be offensive for what Pecksniff is, but creditable for what Pinch is. The novel, like the play, is full of characters who see through the hypocrite, and these characters include every moral stamp from Jonas Chuzzlewit to John Westlock; but the more decent ones, including Westlock, respect Pinch for his devoted spirit. As in Orgon's case, Pinch's disillusionment begins with the demonstration of the hypocrite's improper sexual advances: Orgon accedes to the marriage of Tartuffe with his daughter and is only upset when he witnesses the attempt on his wife; Pinch, who loves Mary Graham from afar, concedes first place to young Martin and reacts only when she tells him (as discreetly as possible) of Pecksniff's sexual liberties and plans to force her to marry him.[14] After the revelation of Pecksniff's sexual interest, Pinch never altogether deserts "that Great Abstraction" who has preached to him Christian morality. "Pecksniff had gone out of the world—had never been in it—and it was as much as Tom could do to say his prayers without him. But he felt happier afterwards and went to sleep, and dreamed about him as he Never Was" (31.498, 503). To Westlock he later confesses his "folly" about Pecksniff, and Westlock is uncertain "whether to be glad or sorry, that you have made the discovery at last" (36.566). At the end of the novel, Dickens gives us a glimpse of "a drunken, begging, squalid-letter-writing" Pecksniff who asks and receives alms from Pinch, while denigrating him to others, and in his last apostrophe—a rhetorical stance that the novelist reserves for this character—he exclaims, "All known to thee, and yet all borne with, Tom!" (54.832), in order to assure us that Pinch will always be true to his faith even if Pecksniff is false.

In the *re*presentation of *Le Tartuffe*, a comedy in verse, within *Martin Chuzzlewit*, a sprawling novel of twenty monthly installments, some strange transfusions take place among the principal characters. Curiously, it is Pecksniff who takes over Orgon's role of paterfamilias, and at the end of the novel, when he has been trapped and beaten by old Martin, Pecksniff seems to borrow another leaf from Orgon. "To have been deceived," he says, "implies a trusting nature. Mine is a trusting nature. I am thankful for it. I would rather have a trusting nature, do you know, sir, than a doubting one!" (52.807). The rejoinder is brilliant, in fact, but its borrowing from the posture of Pinch-Orgon suggests a still deeper connection of these characters through Dickens's possible identification with both. Still more curiously, in his disillusionment, Pinch speaks aloud in the church in the manner of Pecksniff-Tartuffe:

> "I wouldn't have cared for anything he might have done to Me, for I have tried his patience often, and have lived upon his sufferance, and have never been the help to him that others could have been. I wouldn't have minded, Pecksniff," Tom continued, little thinking who heard him, "if you had done Me any wrong; I could have found plenty of excuses for that; and though you might have hurt me, could still have gone on respecting you. But why did you ever fall so low as this in my esteem! Oh Pecksniff, Pecksniff, there is nothing I would not have given to have had you deserve my old opinion of you; nothing!" (31.492)

This soliloquy is delivered within hearing of Pecksniff, who is concealed behind a pew as Orgon is concealed beneath the table in the play. And while Pinch is turning the other cheek, so unsuspecting of Pecksniff's presence, let us remember that he too has a strong, though suppressed, sexual interest in Mary.[15] In sum, *Martin Chuzzlewit* literally *re*presents the symbiosis of Orgon and Tartuffe: Tom Pinch is the understudy of the pious architect Pecksniff and the true receptacle of the latter's pretended virtue, but Dickens has also in some degree confused Orgon with Tartuffe.

As has long been recognized, Pinch has a privileged standing in the novel (so much so that many readers protest against this special investment of the character with inward virtue). The narrator's habit of apostrophizing Pinch implies that he has something like angelic stature. In the early chapters, the narrator "goes behind" only this character, mainly to demonstrate that his mistaken devotion to Pecksniff is sincere. The special connection between Pinch and the author was openly hinted at the completion of the novel, in the frontispiece by Browne for the first bound edition of *Martin Chuzzlewit*. The frontispiece, which was worked up according to Dickens's idea, shows Pinch extemporizing on his organ, surrounded by musical notes and scenes from the book, as

if he were the dreamer of the whole composition.[16] Obviously no one has this role in the action of the novel; only the author can be said to have an analogous role. The bald and white-fringed organist is depicted in all the illustrations as much older than he is said to be in the text—too old for either of the attractive young women of the novel, his sister Ruth and his conscious love object Mary. In the first number, "He was perhaps about thirty, but he might have been almost any age between sixteen and sixty" (2.16); in the fifteenth number, he is said to be "aged thirty-five" (39.601). Dickens was still thirty when he began *Martin Chuzzlewit;* at about the time he made the second reference to Pinch's age, he celebrated his thirty-second birthday, and in the manuscript he wrote "Thirty Two" for Pinch.[17] Dickens is obviously playing the age issue two ways: Pinch is precisely the same age as himself, but prematurely bald and stooped in order to forestall the supposition of direct sexual appeal.

If one adds the symbiosis of Pecksniff and Pinch to the identification of Pinch with Dickens, one comes up with some kind of association between Dickens and Pecksniff. The same conclusion can be, and has been, argued on other grounds, ranging from Chesterton's remark that Pecksniff is "so laughable that he is lovable," to observations about the character's articulateness, to comparisons of his style with that of the narrator, without taking into account his special relation to Pinch. At first it seems unlikely that the novelist would identify with the hypocrite of the story. A hypocrite is by definition two-sided, and it is theoretically possible to identify with the appearance *or* the reality of such a person, with the picture of virtue or the activity of self-aggrandizement. The objection to identifying with both at once is the moral objection to falsity or insincerity. Do away with that objection, however, as in unconscious or conscious play, and it becomes possible to be attracted to hypocrisy on its own grounds, for the powers of concealment and manipulation that two-sidedness confers. This amoral appeal of hypocrisy is undoubtedly what forces Dickens to come down on Pecksniff so heavily in the end. As we know from the reaction of Chesterton and other readers, it is possible to be swayed in the character's favor by his performance alone. According to Kincaid, "it is Pecksniff's positive values and not his moral failings that are important," and obviously Kincaid does not mean by "positive values" Pecksniff's healthy appetite or love of property but his sheer ability—"his dazzling display of artistic resiliency. Time and again he is confronted with impossible situations, and time and again he creates not only workable but triumphant responses." As Kincaid's terms imply, if readers can enjoy the two-sidedness, then the artist can certainly revel in the same power.[18]

Pecksniff's extraordinary verbal ability—often linked with that of the other virtuoso of the novel, Mrs. Gamp—provides too easy an identification with the novelist, since to say that no one but Dickens could have written his lines applies too widely to characters in all of the novels, as the same thing said of Molière applies to his characters. But some readers have tried to delve beneath this argument in broadly conceived psychological ground. Ian Watt has observed that Gamp and Pecksniff are "compulsively oral" in their eloquence as well as appetites. Their ability, through words, to rise above the moral rebuke that the novelist has in store for them suggests to Watt a persistent hunger that Dickens probably shared: "an anxious and hypocritical preoccupation with food and drink can be the result of the same loneliness that underlies the individual's basic drive to create an ideal image of himself through words and to impose this image on others."[19] Watt might have added that, before Pecksniff entered the language, with Tartuffe, to signify a hypocrite, his name itself had oral connotations. The first half suggests a bite at food or a grudging kiss, and the second half, moral disapprobation sounded through the nose. Moreover, "peck" has other, less respectable connotations that combine with "sniff" to create a still more mischievous image.[20] The names in Dickens's novels are often as intricate as the displacements among his characters.

The verbal connection that tells most against Dickens is a resemblance of the narrator's voice, in apostrophizing Tom Pinch, to the voice of Pecksniff in direct discourse with the same character. The resemblance was first noticed in 1845 by a reviewer unsparing in his prescriptive remarks on the language of the novel.[21] The implications of the case for comedy have recently been spelled out by Robert M. Polhemus: "Great satirists' targets are always somehow deeply rooted in themselves as well as their societies, and their satire works on a psychological principle of the scapegoat: they objectify in their imagination the traits they find most threatening in their own personalities and in the world, the traits they would most like to purge." Polhemus cites two passages, the first from Pecksniff and the second from the narrator, that betray an unmistakable similarity of these two artists with words:

"Old Tom Pinch!" said Mr. Pecksniff, looking on him with affectionate sadness. "Ah! It seems but yesterday that Thomas was a boy, fresh from a scholastic course. Yet years have passed, I think, since Thomas Pinch and I first walked the world together! . . .

"And Thomas Pinch and I," said Mr. Pecksniff, in a deeper voice, "will walk it yet, in mutual faithfulness and friendship!" (5.80)

And that mild figure seated at an organ, who is he? Ah Tom, dear Tom, old friend!

Thy head is prematurely gray, though Time has passed between thee and our old association, Tom. But in those sounds with which it is thy wont to bear the twilight company, the music of thy heart speaks out: the story of thy life relates itself. (54.831)

In the second passage, which was written to accompany the new frontispiece to the novel, the narrator poses as a sincere Pecksniff. The repetition of the voice must be inadvertent: Dickens deliberately repeats himself, for rhetorical effect, more than any novelist in the language, but here in saluting the story that "relates itself," he unconsciously echoes his hypocrite. As in Freud's indirect identification with Sganarelle, Dickens at once conceals and reveals a large self-criticism. He knew that moralizing "cost him nothing and usually resulted in immense personal profit," Polhemus suggests, and unconsciously created himself as Pecksniff: "some subversive, mocking side of him knew it and made sure that we would, too."[22]

A generation ago Hillis Miller argued that Dickens's novel was an inchoate study of personal identity. Miller offered to substitute, in effect, a broader theme of the definition of self for the expressed theme of selfishness. He called our attention to the shapes of hypocrisy, rather than its selfish motives, and to the degree to which the novel is concerned with hidden identities. "The novel is full of people who are wholly enclosed in themselves, wholly secret, wholly intent on reflexive ends which are altogether mysterious to those around them"—and a little mysterious to themselves as well. A line of Mrs. Gamp, he felt, "might serve as an epigraph" for the work as a whole: "we never knows wot's hidden in each other's breasts; and if we had glass winders there, we'd need to keep the shetters up, some on us, I do assure you!" (29.464). Miller's is still an important account of the definition of self in this novel, and the "two extreme dangers" to the self that he isolates, "the strain of sustaining an assumed identity" and "a passive submission to

27

other people," sound very much like reflections on Pecksniff and Pinch respectively.[23]

Though Miller was not concerned about tracing this division to any particular literary or biographical source, I am concerned with both. The formula of "assumed identity" in one character and "passive submission" in another is that of *Le Tartuffe;* the liveliest perception of self is almost certainly that of Dickens by himself. To this projection of the author we owe half a dozen principal characters in *Martin Chuzzlewit,* but the one most deeply hidden and at the same time authorized by a comic tradition is Pecksniff. In order to interpret the novel fairly, we should try to combine our modern understanding of identity and projection with Dickens's sensitivity to the charge of selfishness; and this effort further requires careful documentation of a controversy that arose during the novelist's first visit to America.

III

Hypocrisy and Copyright

*A*ccording to John Forster, the character of Pecksniff was the raison d'être of Dickens's new novel, the theme of which was the varieties and effects of selfishness:

> The first number, which appeared in January 1843, had not been quite finished when he wrote to me on 8 December: "The *Chuzzlewit* copy makes so much more than I supposed, that the number is nearly done. Thank God!" Beginning so hurriedly as at last he did, altering his course at the opening and seeing little as yet of the main track of his design, perhaps no story was ever begun by him with stronger heart or confidence. Illness kept me to my rooms for some days, and he was so eager to try the effect of Pecksniff and Pinch that he came down with the ink hardly dry on the last slip to read the manuscript to me. . . . And let me here at once remark that the notion of taking Pecksniff for a type of character was really the origin of the book; the design being to show, more or less by every person introduced, the number and variety of humours and vices that have their root in selfishness.

Subsequently, in his critical remarks on the novel, Forster refers to Pecksniff as "our English Tartuffe." If this "type of character was really the origin of the book," who or what besides Tartuffe was the origin of Pecksniff? Dickens himself, naturally, would tend to answer this question objectively rather than subjectively. Pecksniff is the hypocrisy one meets with everywhere. With the partial exception of the two

Martin Chuzzlewits, Dickens holds all the varieties of selfishness in his novel at arm's length, and at still greater distance in the case of the Americans. Forster claims that he had to dissuade his friend from including on the title page, as a motto, the line, "Your homes the scenes, yourselves the actors, here!"[1] Even without this aggressive use of the second person, the stiff irony of the novel's opening directs the satire well away from the author. Such willingness to attack, however, is not incompatible with suppressed anxiety about one's own vulnerability to criticism.

It is easy to feel that the Americans were the true inspiration of *Martin Chuzzlewit,* even though Dickens may not at first have intended to send his hero among them. The Americans, in the author's recent experience, were obviously two-sided: as the agents of his disillusionment with their country, in their fulsome disregard of his privacy while there, and in their determination to buy and sell his writings without ever paying him for them, as well as in their own social and political life. If Pecksniff and his friends are "lovable," in the Chestertonian phrase, the Americans of the novel are distinctly not—though Albert J. Guerard has pointed out how much closer they are to the imaginative center of the novel than is generally supposed.[2] Most often critics have judged those chapters as too strident and exaggerated: many of the Americans in the novel are worse than hypocrites; they are swindlers of the most obvious stamp. But his fiercely "objective" way of looking upon them in the novel has also its subjective ground in the novelist. By exaggerating his satire, Dickens is able to distance himself from his own naive hopes in America—whatever these hopes may have been. We do not know his side of the picture as well as we would like to, and are forced to judge by his silences as well as his letters and his satire.

The one possibility that seems worth reconsidering is that he actually went to America in the hope of making his influence felt on the issue of international copyright. There could be nothing intrinsically wrong with supporting this cause, which many besides himself regarded as just, but Dickens understood that he would profit greatly from an international copyright agreement, and at the same time he did not like to think that profit was an acceptable motive for advocacy of any kind. When a few American newspapers essentially accused him of seeking profit, he became bitterly unhappy with his proposal. Whether or not he behaved a little like a hypocrite on this occasion, he was distinctly accused of being one by the very lot whom he thought were hypocrites—and he seems to have had the better case, since American newspaper publishers were among those who profited most from British writing. Dickens was outwardly angry and perhaps inwardly conscience-stricken: his whole response to the American visit was not merely one of disappointment, but as if he had been thwarted somehow. It would not be surprising, in the circumstances, if the novelist discharged most of his anger at the enemy and some of his humor against himself, recalling Tartuffe in the process. As we have gathered from some of the best critics, the invention of Pecksniff is a proud one, in a way—and is he not worshipped by Pinch? In the end even Pinch must be disillusioned with his personal idol, and Dickens, we can be sure, learned about more than just the Americans from this episode in his life.

There are essentially two kinds of evidence of Dickens's involvement with the debate over copyright: his speeches and his silences. If we are to judge from his speeches and public activity in America, his was a reasonably straightforward advocacy of a just cause that touched him personally; he became indignant and angry, in his reports of this activity to his friends, when his efforts were resisted and his motives called into question by some native opponents of international copyright. What is odd are his silences before and after his visit to the United States. His letters betray no intention, before he departed England, to raise the issue of copyright. His published account of his travels, *American Notes,* makes no allusion to the subject afterward. Thus the evidence that Dickens intended to speak out on copyright is purely circumstantial: he arrived in America, and he spoke. On 22 January 1842 he landed in Boston, and on 1 February he addressed a dinner of distinguished men gathered in his honor as follows:

> I hope the time is not far distant when [your writers], in America, will receive of right some substantial profit and return in England from their labours; and when we, in England, shall receive some substantial profit and return for ours. Pray do not misunderstand me. Securing for myself from day to day the means of an honourable subsistence, I would rather have the affectionate regard of my fellow men, than I would have heaps and mines of gold. But the two things do not seem to me incompatible.

31

They cannot be, for nothing good is incompatible with justice. There must be an international arrangement in this respect . . .

At Hartford a week later, the day after his thirtieth birthday, Dickens resumed the subject at a second dinner in his honor:

> Gentlemen, as I have no secrets from you, in the spirit of confidence you have engendered between us, and as I have made a kind of compact with myself that I never will, while I remain in America, omit an opportunity of referring to a topic in which I and all others of my class on both sides of the water are equally interested—equally interested, there is no difference between us—I would beg leave to whisper in your ear two words, International Copyright. I use them in no sordid sense, believe me, and those who know me best, best know that. For myself, I would rather that my children coming after me, trudged in the mud, and knew by the general feeling of society that their father was beloved, and had been of some use, than I would have them ride in their carriages, and know by their banker's books that he was rich. But I do not see, I confess, why one should be obliged to make the choice, or why fame, besides playing that delightful *reveille* for which she is so justly celebrated, should not blow out of her trumpet a few notes of a different kind from those with which she has hitherto contented herself.[3]

It seems probable, therefore, that Dickens had thought about speaking in some such vein before he left England. If it is true that his "compact with myself" was not sealed before he arrived in New England, this may have been the caution of a man all too wary of the imputation of selfish motives, such as he glances at in these speeches, or the still deeper conviction that the cause was finally hopeless, hence foolish for him to think about or admit to himself.

After the Hartford occasion, Americans whose interests were threatened struck back, impugning Dickens's motives and implying that he was ungrateful for his fame and reception in America. Their attacks, in fact, seem to have blunted his intentions and broken his compact with himself, because his subsequent activity on behalf of copyright was private and political, as part of a collective effort of English and American authors to bring pressure on Congress.[4] Many things seemed to go wrong with his visit, but what soured Dickens and put him in mind of these wrongs was the swift and rather insulting response of a few newspapers to his plea. The very fact that he exaggerated their criticism of him suggests his sensitivity to the issue.[5] Just a month after his arrival, he wrote from New York to a sympathetic American, Jonathan Chapman, of his feelings: "I am sick to death of the life I have been leading here—worn out in mind and body—and quite weary and distressed." The reason, judging from the paragraphs that followed, was his bitterness about copyright:

> I have never in my life been so shocked and disgusted, or made so sick and sore at heart, as I have been by the treatment I have received here (in America I mean), in reference to the International Copyright question. I,—the greatest loser by the existing Law, alive,—say in perfect good humour and disinterestedness (for God knows that I have little hope of its ever being changed in my time) that I hope the day will come when Writers will be justly treated: and straightway there fall upon me scores of your newspapers; imputing motives to me, the very suggestion of which turns my blood to gall; and attacking me in such terms of vagabond scurrility as they would denounce no murderer with. I vow to heaven that the scorn and indignation I have felt under this unmanly and ungenerous treatment has been to me an amount of agony such as I never experienced since my birth. But it has had the one good effect of making me iron upon this theme; and iron I will be, here and at home, by word of mouth and in writing, as long as I can articulate a syllable, or hold a pen.
>
> I open my whole heart to you, you see! I write in such a spirit of confidence that I pour out all I have felt upon this subject,—though I have said nothing in reference to it, even to my wife. This is a foretaste of what you have brought upon yourself.[6]

The discrepancy between this vow to speak and write for the cause without stint and his confession that he has said nothing to anyone else about his feelings gives some idea of the shakiness of Dickens's position. To a comparative stranger he is able to write of "agony such as I never experienced since my birth," an agony of which he is unable to speak with those close to him. Or, at least, such is his rhetorical stance. Some years later he would write to Forster in similar terms about his feelings toward that other degradation he had experienced since his birth. Just as here he is accused "in such vagabond terms of scurrility as they would denounce no murderer with," so in the more famous account of the blacking warehouse, he might have become "a little robber or a little vagabond." As he has said nothing of his feelings in New York, "even to my wife," so he would write that he had never told anyone, "my own wife not excepted," of the infamous days of his childhood.[7] Remember that the autobiographical fragment, so frequently cited in modern accounts of Dickens's inward being, had not yet been written. Apparently the conceit about being thought a vagabond first occurred to him in New York.

Vagabonds abound in *Martin Chuzzlewit*. The conjunction of "a murderer and a vagabond" recurs in the satire of humankind with which the novel opens—again, well before the fragment was written. The first character to be addressed as "you vagabond" is Pecksniff, caught listening at the keyhole in the Blue Dragon (4.44), and the same hypocrite is the last to use the word, in his vain attempt to disperse the young people from old Martin's presence at the end (52.799). Mark Tapley affirms that Pecksniff is indeed "a wagabond, a scoundrel, and a willain" (43.660), but as Tapley also points out, it is Jonas Chuzzlewit who is the "murderin wagabond" of the novel (51.777). In the course of describing this character and attributing to him "a simplicity of cunning," the narrator has earlier been content to write him down as "a notable vagabond" (11.182). Jonas, like Pecksniff, also tries to turn the charge around and apply it to young Martin, the wanderer in America. And this last is perhaps the most curious application of "vagabond" in *Chuzzlewit*, since it so palpably upsets Tom Pinch and draws from him an excited reply. "You say very little, don't you?" Jonas challenges Pinch, and then gratuitously brings up the subject of Martin:

> "Ecod, I should like to know what goes on between you and a vagabond member of my family. There's very little in that, too, I dare say!"
> "I know no vagabond member of your family," cried Tom, stoutly.
> "You do!" said Jonas.
> "I don't," said Tom. "Your uncle's namesake, if you mean him, is no vagabond. Any comparison between you and him"—Tom snapped his fingers at him, for he was rising fast in wrath—"is immeasurably to your disadvantage." (24.390–391)

Not too much need be made of these charges and counter-charges except to point out that the vagabond business definitely predates the autobiographical fragment. In Dickens's letter from New York, obviously, "vagabond terms of scurrility" are employed by the Americans against Dickens, and in the novel, straightforwardly enough, the latter describes Hannibal Chollop as "a violent vagabond" (33.520). At the same time, the letter casts "murderer" as the object of the scurrility, hence as applicable in the comparison to Dickens.

Misery that is concealed is shameful misery. Thus the letter purports to describe a feeling that has been carefully concealed from others. No doubt very low Americans were responsible for Dickens's feelings (he would later warn people about such and pillory their newspapers in *Chuzzlewit*); but the most delicate feelings of shame, after all, are internalizations of what one believes to be the opinion of others, and there is bound to be pain when the others shoot at one with a blunderbuss. Though he insisted to Forster that "the shame was theirs, not mine,"[8] Dickens was obviously disconcerted. Outwardly, he took an increasingly high line of justice and personal resignation, as in a letter to another correspondent the same day:

> I do not expect that any alteration will take place in the Law of International Copyright, until I am past the sense of Justice or Injustice, and my children are fighting their own way in the World. Until the Law is altered nothing can be done through the General Honesty and Good Feeling. The absence of all Generosity, Honor, or Truth which distinguishes the gross assaults that have been made upon me, here, for alluding to the subject, sufficiently assures me of *that*.[9]

Yet even in this high-minded summary, the clause about his children and his foregoing results that might have been obtained *without* changing the law pretty well indicate the nature of Dickens's hopes and his material interest in raising the issue. Moreover, the language of his public speeches shows that he in part anticipated the reaction of his hearers. Both in Boston and in Hartford he carefully guarded against the charge of selfishness. With his "Pray do not misunderstand me" and his disclaimer, "I use [the words International Copyright] in no sordid sense," he handed the charge to the newspapers. Less consciously, in the second speech, he raised the question of hypocrisy by averring, "I have no secrets from you." In case the assurance failed of its mark, he then turned conspiratorial: "I would beg leave to whisper in your ear two words, International Copyright." That slight needling, with its hint that his hearers too might have something to be ashamed of, may well have been Dickens's undoing. There was an almost Pecksniffian delicacy in his discourse, and respect for all points of view. The Americans, or some of them, responded with a brutality like that of Anthony Chuzzlewit in the coach to London:

"Why, the annoying quality in *you,* is," said the old man, "that you never have a confederate or partner in *your* juggling; you would deceive everybody, even those who practise the same art; and have a way with you, as if you—he, he, he!—as if you really believed yourself. . . . You're not offended, Pecksniff?" (8.120–121)

Dickens promised to be "iron upon this theme" of copyright, and when he returned to England in June, he continued to justify himself as the champion of a lost cause. In a printed circular that he addressed to influential friends and sent around to the newspapers, he urged others to join him in refusing to sell advance proofs or otherwise to cooperate with American publishers. "Our common interest in this subject," he concluded, "and my advocacy of it, single-handed, on every occasion that has presented itself during my absence from Europe, form my excuse for addressing you."[10] He had, in his imagination, become a knight errant battling for Europe. This gesture effectively ended what was, after all, a fairly active campaign on his part for a copyright agreement with the United States, an agreement that did not come into being until 1891, twenty years after his death. He did not forget the Americans, on whom he took revenge in *American Notes* and in *Chuzzlewit,* but neither of these works mentions the cause of copyright, which he may have tried to forget. The one thing that Dickens insisted upon was that he had not gone to America with the *purpose* of advocating international copyright.

A last occasion for testing this purpose arose in connection with a review of *American Notes* in the *Edinburgh Review* for January 1843. Dickens's travel book was not noticed very favorably in general, and this intelligent but condescending review was no exception.[11] The reviewer went to great lengths to explain the weaknesses of *American Notes.* One excuse he offered for Dickens was that the popular novelist simply did not have the education to write a serious book about a foreign power. Another excuse, he ventured to say, was "that the study of America does not appear to have been his primary object in going, nor his main business while there."

He went out, if we are rightly informed, as a kind of missionary in the cause of International Copyright; with the design of persuading the American public (for it was the public to which he seems to have addressed himself) to abandon their present privilege, of enjoying the produce of

36

all the literary industry of Great Britain without paying for it;—an excellent recommendation, the adoption of which would, no doubt, in the end prove a vast national benefit. . . . In this arduous, if not hopeless enterprize, Mr Dickens, having once engaged himself, must be presumed, during the short period of his visit, to have chiefly occupied his thoughts; therefore the gathering of materials for a book about America must be regarded as a subordinate and incidental task—the produce of such hours as he could spare from his main employment. Nor must it be forgotten that in this, the primary object of his visit, he decidedly failed; a circumstance (not unimportant when we are considering his position and opportunities as an observer of manners in a strange country) to which we draw attention, the rather because Mr Dickens makes no allusion to it himself. A man may read the volumes through without knowing that the question of International Copyright has ever been raised on either side of the Atlantic.[12]

This was a shrewd, if gratuitous, argument. The anonymous reviewer, who was James Spedding, a man unacquainted with Dickens, had just spent four months in Washington and listened to the gossip about the latter's visit and his activities on behalf of copyright. He had observed the silence on the question in *American Notes* and argued—not quite psychoanalytically, but a little like the prosecutor in a criminal trial—that silence was an admission of some kind, most "decidedly" an admission of failure. If Dickens failed, of course, he must have intended to succeed.

The positive argument from circumstances, that since Dickens spoke on behalf of copyright he probably intended to speak, is a strong one. Much weaker is the argument, from his silence, about his state of mind. But Dickens himself reacted in such a way as to etch this argument deeper, by changing silence to fierce denial. On 14 January 1843 the *Times* quoted a sentence from Spedding's review, a sentence that glanced disparagingly at the English press. The *Times* leader-writer quoted it for his own purposes, not for anything it had to do with Dickens. But Dickens had seen the *Edinburgh Review* piece, and he wrote to the *Times* to reassure them that the English press was nothing like the American, and to deny at some length the argument from the review that the paper had neither quoted nor referred to. His letter was published the following day:

I am anxious to give another misrepresentation made by the same writer, whosoever he may be,—which *is* personal to myself,—the most public and positive contradiction in my power; and I shall be really obliged to you if you will allow me to do this through the medium of your columns.

He asserts "That if he be rightly informed, I went to America as a kind of missionary in the cause of international copyright." I deny it wholly. He is wrongly informed; and reports, without inquiry, a piece of information which I could only characterize by using one of the shortest and strongest words in the language. Upon my honour the assertion is destitute of any particle, aspect, or colouring of the truth.

It occurred to me to speak (as other English travellers connected with literature have done before me) of the existing laws—or rather want of laws—on the subject of international copyright, when I found myself in America, simply because I had never hesitated to denounce their injustice while at home; because I thought it a duty to English writers, that their case should be fairly represented; and because, inexperienced at that time in the American people, I believed that they would listen to the truth, even from one presumed to have an interest in stating it, and would no longer refuse to recognize a principle of common honesty, even though it happened to clash with a miserably short-sighted view of their own profit and advantage.[13]

Except for the weakness of "it occurred to me to speak . . . when I found myself in America," the statement of the final paragraph is a good one. Dickens does not quarrel with the reviewer's assessment of *American Notes,* as he might have, and he writes with a certain perspective on his adventure, once again admitting that he had "an interest" in copyright. What seems extraordinary is that he should go out of his way to reply in the *Times* to the paragraph he objected to in the *Edinburgh Review,* and the strenuous language of honor that he invokes—or elides—in the expression "one of the shortest and strongest words in the language." That is to say, the reviewer *lies,* "whosoever he may be." In Touchstone's terms, for the escalation of quarrels, Dickens has been handed the Lie Circumstantial, and he replies in language just short of the Lie Direct.

The quarrel was strictly over motive. The reviewer has tracked down the motive like a detective; the novelist sensibly changes the venue to the field of honor, where it was still possible in Victorian times to assert sole possession of one's motives. These Britons have no quarrel over copyright; all agree as to the desirability of international copyright, as is evident from the careful retraction published in the *Edinburgh Review* the following month:

In the . . . article we happened to state that Mr Dickens went to America as a "Missionary in the cause of International Copyright." We have since found that we were misinformed in saying so. We had no intention, however, to disparage a gentleman whose character and genius we alike esteem, by that statement. We thought the cause a good cause, and that we had sufficient authority for what was stated. But as it would be very wrong to ascribe Mr Dickens's visit to America to an erroneous cause, we willingly retract the statement, and regret that it was made.[14]

One wonders whether Dickens noticed that the editor used the word "cause" for both the political position and the motive, thereby turning the retraction into a kind of affirmation. Spedding went right on believing that he was right. He outlived Dickens by some ten years and thus was able to consult all of the letters from America in Forster's *Life*. In a long note to his collected reviews in 1879, he excerpted eight letters to show that, indeed, the novelist had been active in the cause: he was still a little irritated, perhaps, by Dickens's challenge in the *Times*. Dickens had also complained of the review, in a letter to Macvey Napier, as exhibiting him "as a traveller under false pretences and a disappointed intriguer." Spedding found no evidence of intrigue or false pretenses in the record of these events unless it was embedded in the novelist's own self-consciousness—his "fancy" or imagination.[15]

Essentially, Spedding conducted the same argument from circumstantial evidence that I am rehearsing here. Dickens seems to have been the only one who was deeply sensitive as to his motives. It was he who fended most anxiously in 1842 and 1843 against the imputation of hypocrisy. The evidence suggests that he probably did go to America with the idea of doing something about international copyright, and in any event he quickly came to understand that his motives might be questioned. Either way, he felt sufficiently uncomfortable to realize subjectively the great Pecksniff. It may not be finally important (as it is surely not possible) to fix the precise degree of Dickens's consciousness of what he was up to in America. He became indignant at Spedding's suggestion, I believe, because he had so prudently refused to admit this motive to himself. It is not clear that Pecksniff's hypocrisy is as consistently conscious in the novel as Anthony Chuzzlewit insists. The riotousness of the invented character results from his being brazenly deceitful on some occasions and marvelously self-deluding in others. Pecksniff is not fully in control of his doubleness, and Dickens solved that problem as Molière had solved it—by having a second character reflect the full sincerity of which some hypocrisy seems capable. Pinch's mistaken sincerity Dickens sometimes narrates directly; Pecksniff's false consciousness he does not. Whether his personal intervention in the copyright debate was premeditated or whether it merely occurred to him to speak when he found himself there is not finally as important as that he "decidedly failed," as Spedding remarks—fortunately failed, as far as readers of *Martin Chuzzlewit* and the great novels to follow are concerned. If Dickens had been a successful hypocrite, he would not have become sufficiently aware, consciously or unconsciously, of what two-sidedness was like.

It is possible to generalize about Dickens's predicament within a culture that persistently reproves selfishness and rewards the selfish. Both gentlemanly and Christian codes of behavior exact a selflessness that is still evident in the touchiness about motives that Dickens displayed throughout the American episode and on other occasions. Like many Victorians he was bent on making his fortune, yet too obvious ambition or success was not quite socially acceptable (notice the condescension of Spedding, a public school and Cambridge graduate, or the care with which his editor addresses the self-made novelist as "a gentleman whose character and genius we alike esteem"). The amalgam of commercial with gentlemanly and Christian pretensions in the nineteenth century is one of the glories of Pecksniff, through whom Dickens willingly expresses the contradiction.[16]

Likewise, it is possible to make a general case for projection in Dickens's treatment of the highly commercialized Americans. After all, the Americans were not and are not, on average, like those we meet in *Martin Chuzzlewit*. Dickens himself made many more friends among them than one would believe from the satire in the novel. The Americans we do meet there, Norman and Jeanne Mackenzie have suggested, are something like projections of the novelist:

> In quarreling with the Americans he was in a sense arguing with his own shadow. He saw them as bumptious and aggressive; they had a thrusting ambition; they were given to self-righteousness; they loved to drive a hard bargain and crow about it afterwards; though they were hospitable they were touchily proud and resentful of criticism; and, having come up in the world, insecurity made them crave admiration. At the heart of his angry discontent lay a strong element of self-deception.[17]

TO BE COMPLETED IN SEVEN PARTS, AT 6¼ CENTS, EACH PART CONTAINING THREE NUMBERS OF THE ENGLISH EDITION WITH TWO STEEL ETCHINGS

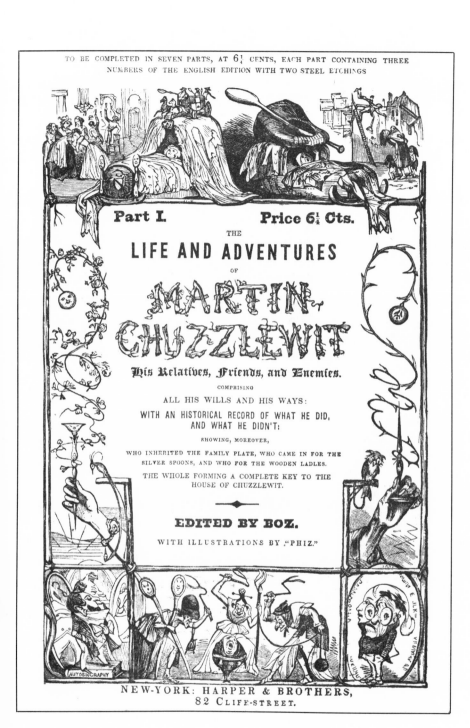

Part I.   Price 6¼ Cts.

THE

LIFE AND ADVENTURES

OF

MARTIN CHUZZLEWIT

His Relatives, Friends, and Enemies.

COMPRISING

ALL HIS WILLS AND HIS WAYS:

WITH AN HISTORICAL RECORD OF WHAT HE DID, AND WHAT HE DIDN'T:

SHOWING, MOREOVER,

WHO INHERITED THE FAMILY PLATE, WHO CAME IN FOR THE SILVER SPOONS, AND WHO FOR THE WOODEN LADLES.

THE WHOLE FORMING A COMPLETE KEY TO THE HOUSE OF CHUZZLEWIT.

EDITED BY BOZ.

WITH ILLUSTRATIONS BY "PHIZ."

NEW-YORK: HARPER & BROTHERS, 82 CLIFF-STREET.

If the Mackenzies are right, such thoroughgoing projection would be enough in itself to explain all the lambasting of selfishness in the novel.

The question of self-deception, however, is difficult to resolve. Dickens deceives himself on some levels of consciousness and discovers himself on others. There is at least as much insight into the whole man in *Martin Chuzzlewit* as there is in the autobiographical fragment that Dickens would write shortly thereafter, or even in *David Copperfield*— accounts of the life that are also in one degree or another blind. On the wrapper designed for the monthly numbers of *Martin Chuzzlewit,* in the lower left corner, a volume of "Autobiography" is clearly identified with Pecksniff. A caricature of that Christian gentleman and architect stands atop the volume so titled and gazes into mirrors. The design, whether Boz's inspiration or Phiz's, had to be completed for the first number, well before the rest of the novel was written. By the same token, too, this "Autobiography" antedates the famous autobiographical fragment.

IV

Chuzzlewit Madness

*O*ne of the many anomalies in the novel that most profited from Dickens's American experience is that there are two Martin Chuzzlewits. No harm, one may say, in having grandfather and grandson bear the same name, and some advantages in plot: since the main line of suspense concerns the reform and inheritance of young Martin, his bearing the same name as his grandfather anticipates a resolution of family differences. But as in the interpretation of Dickens's life in this period, a reading of the novel has to account for silences as well as outspokenness. The strategy of having two Martins produces confusion at first, as if Dickens were not fully aware of what he is up to. By convention, the title *Martin Chuzzlewit* should refer to the grandson, the hero who is involved in a courtship plot, who undergoes the most obvious conversion, and whose adventures occupy the greater number of pages. At the same time, Dickens seems to reserve part of the title role to the old man, who has a highly unconventional relation to the heroine, who apparently undergoes some conversion from his initial misanthropy, and who plans the fall of Pecksniff as if he were either God or the novelist. The novelist does not seem to have worked out just how the two Martins would share top billing, and neither achieves the central importance of Pecksniff or Tom Pinch, the popular fame of Mrs. Gamp or the notoriety of Jonas Chuzzlewit. Dickens strove to create some resemblance between the two Martins—both exhibit a mixture of good and bad qualities—but as Barbara Hardy remarks, old Martin's "dual role of selfish man and critic of selfishness" is one of the "glaring examples of contradictions left unreconciled, or of resemblances of which Dickens seems unaware" in the novel.[1]

The experiment cannot be faulted for lack of boldness. Dickens upsets both moral and speech conventions in his introduction of old Martin and his seventeen-year-old companion Mary Graham. The daring relation of two such persons of the opposite sex who are "not related" is quickly taken note of by Mrs. Lupin and others at the Blue Dragon inn. The two make a special point of addressing one another by their first names: Mary's "Did you call me, Martin?" is in fact the first indication that the old gentleman has a name (3.29). Dickens overlooks, in this instance, the degree to which conventions of novel writing depend on social conventions. Not only does he introduce old Martin, in tempting proximity to the heroine, before he introduces young Martin—the ostensible hero of the novel—but his narrator too addresses the old man as "Martin" in this chapter, and occasionally as late as the scene in which Pecksniff is finally punished while the other Martin stands silently by (chapter 48). In Victorian novels, forms of address reflect a character's age or status and to some extent control the reader's understanding of which character the narrator actually names. Pecksniff has the honor of first indicating, in direct discourse, the old man's full name. "You *are* Martin Chuzzlewit!" he exclaims at the Blue Dragon, and Chuzzlewit responds, "I *am* Martin Chuzzlewit!" (3.36). By these devices Dickens deliberately plays on the title of his novel, postponing his reader's realization that there is another Martin Chuzzlewit still in the wings. But the confusion that results from addressing both Martins by their Christian name is harder to explain as a conscious strategy.

Because the novel presents a whole clan of Chuzzlewits, each representing a different facet of selfishness, the novelist will occasionally need to distinguish them from one another by their Christian names: there are old Anthony and his son Jonas as well as old Martin and his grandson. Other characters—Tom Pinch, Mark Tapley, John Westlock—are addressed in the narrative by their first names for reasons of friendly intimacy. The first-naming of male characters establishes a circle of intimacy that apparently includes the murderer and would-be parricide Jonas but excludes the prime hypocrite Pecksniff, whom the narrator usually refers to with mock respect as "Mr. Pecksniff" and never as "Seth." Montague Tigg, alias Tigg Montague, the blackmailer and victim of Jonas, turns "upside down, and inside out, as great men have been sometimes known to be" (27.427). Thus there are many nuances of naming in *Martin Chuzzlewit,* mostly deliberate on Dickens's part. But the factor chiefly responsible for there being two Martins is the projection of the author that operates so unpredictably in this novel. Young Martin, through many implausibilities, inherits Dickens's experience as visitor to America; old Martin exercises Dickens's control over events in the novel, watches to see that his namesake unlearns his selfishness, and superintends the fall of Pecksniff; both Martins reenact the author's relation to his sister-in-law Mary Hogarth, one through the vaguest of courtships and the other with stern protectiveness and intimate acquaintance.

"Is there any other novel," Barbara Hardy asks, "where the characters are so made over for new roles?" And she instances not only Tigg and Jonas, and the latter's wife Merry-Mercy, but Chevy Slyme and young Bailey.[2] Is there any other novel, we might echo, in which Dickens himself turns up in so many different guises—and instance not only Pecksniff and Tom Pinch and the two Martin Chuzzlewits, but Mark Tapley and Jonas Chuzzlewit? Such multiple projection of the author explains the special intensity and often hilarious incoherence of the novel—the Chuzzlewit madness. *Martin Chuzzlewit* can boast neither of two usual shows of responsibility in traditional novels, a single protagonist and a coherent plot. Rather, a kind of irresponsibility holds sway, partly by design—Dickens intends to portray isolated selfish beings—and partly by projection of himself in protagonists and antagonists alike. The number of projections supports the argument that he is able to portray himself as the hypocrite Pecksniff and encourages one to ask what other evidence there is that he turned his American experience to account here: more than a few details in the novel would seem to have little justification *unless* they describe the author's own history. In sum, the hypothesis that Dickens's engagement in the copyright controversy influenced his creation of Pecksniff in particular and the wider hypothesis that this adventure occurred during a moratorium in his development, in which his sense of identity was already uncertain, should provide the best available guides to interpreting a novel that to many readers has seemed both brilliant and inchoate.

One way or the other, young Martin is a surrogate for Dickens the traveler to America. The novelist visited America in the spring of 1842; about a year later he determined to send his hero there. The strange thing about the fictional adventure is that Dickens hardly bothered to imagine what the journey would have been like for an impoverished young man like Martin, seeking his fortune in the New World. Often he simply substituted the kinds of experiences he was subjected to as a celebrity. Harry Stone long ago summarized the incidents, mostly in the ninth number of *Chuzzlewit*, that could only have happened to a person in Dickens's situation and pointed to the incongruities that result when Martin is said to have endured them. Thus, for example, the hero is forced to hold a levee, consulted as a literary authority, begged to share his influence with important people, and constantly grabbed by the hand or stared at.[3] Not omitted from his adventures, though totally incongruous for the unknown Martin, is the impudent attention of the press:

> Two gentlemen connected with the Watertoast Gazette had come express to get the matter for an article on Martin. They had agreed to divide the labour. One of them took him below the waistcoat; one above. Each stood directly in front of his subject with his head a little on one side, intent on his department. If Martin put one boot before the other, the lower gentleman was down upon him; he rubbed a pimple on his nose, and the upper gentleman booked it. He opened his mouth to speak, and the same gentleman was on one knee before him, looking in at his teeth, with the nice scrutiny of a dentist.

Just as the newspapers in America sometimes commented on Dickens's flowing hair, so with Martin, "contradictory rumours were abroad on the subject of his hair." Meanwhile the natives crowd in upon him, and the self-appointed master of ceremonies, Captain Kedgwick, calls out for order: "Gentlemen, you that have been introduced to Mr. Chuzzlewit, *will* you clear?" (22.366).

Obviously if Dickens had confined himself to what was strictly plausible in Martin's travels, we would not have made acquaintance with such marvelous literary personages as Mrs. Hominy or such politicians as Elijah Pogram. Among the hilarious offerings of the American chapters of *Chuzzlewit* are letters that would never have been written to Martin but might conceivably have been written to a celebrity like the author. A letter from one Putnam Smif, of 47 Bunker Hill Street, begins:

Sir,

I was raised in those interminable solitudes where our mighty Mississippi (or Father of Waters) rolls his turbid flood.

I am young, and ardent. For there is a poetry in wildness, and every alligator basking in the slime is in himself an Epic, self-contained. I aspirate for fame. It is my yearning and my thirst.

Are you, sir, aware of any member of Congress in England, who would undertake to pay my expenses to that country, and for six months after my arrival? (22.363)

In this instance Dickens uses his own experience subjectively as well as objectively. The letter is such that he might have received *or*, through unconscious projection, have written himself—as indeed he did write it. He too was young and ardent and, so to speak, aspiring for fame. Putnam Smif merely wants to get even with the English novelist by basking in *his* country for six months. To the distraction of Dickens in this period and the disillusionment of his journey, we owe a whole new dimension of his humor. Even Smif, who never appears in person, shares something of the quality of Pecksniff and Gamp, a quality that is generated from a kind of chagrin or disillusionment of Dickens with himself. As Forster wrote of *Martin Chuzzlewit*, rather more abstractly, "We have in this book for the most part, not only observation, but the outcome of it, the knowledge as well as the fact. While we witness as vividly the life immediately passing, we are more conscious of the permanent life above and beyond it."[4]

Just as Dickens never specified his own motives in going to America, he never fully explains Martin's intentions in the novel. When his hero finally reaches Eden, U.S.A., he hangs out a placard on which he has lettered the words "CHUZZLEWIT & CO., ARCHITECTS AND SURVEYORS," but that sign represents the sum total of Martin's professional activities and of the reader's knowledge of his plans (23.379). Dickens simply does not bother to fill in, before this, any practical discussion of purpose, and what purpose can be garnered from the text is contradictory: in parting from Mary Graham, the hero has spoken of an absence of "a few months" or "a whole year," never of emigrating to the New World (14.242), yet his purchase of some worthless property from the Eden Land Corporation and his carefully lettered sign imply a stay of some length. A vague statement of purpose, pronounced by the narrator, would seem to apply as much to Dickens personally as to the character:

It is an illustration of a very common tendency in the mind of man, that all this time he never once doubted, one may almost say the certainty of doing great things in the New World, if he could only get there. In proportion as he became more and more dejected by his present circumstances, and the means of gaining America receded from his grasp, the more he fretted himself with the conviction that that was the only place in which he could hope to achieve any high end, and worried his brain with the thought that men going there in the meanwhile might anticipate him in the attainment of those objects which were dearest to his heart. (13.226)

Since the narrator everywhere refrains from specifying the dejected hero's "high end," the curious biographer is bound to feel that "objects which were dearest to his heart" comes close to stating without naming Dickens's objects. What is there about trying one's hand as architect and surveyor, somewhere on the American frontier, "that men going there in the meanwhile might anticipate him"? If the passage is merely a screen for Dickens's hopes of the year before, it throws a positive light on his idealism, since the notion of outdoing rival champions beckons him more than the promise of material gain. One of the curious silences of Dickens on the subject of international copyright, in fact, surrounds his view of the efforts of others in this field. He never mentions anywhere, for example, the long and fervent speech on behalf of copyright by an American champion, Cornelius Matthews, who shared in the after-dinner ceremonies in New York, where Dickens himself contributed only the briefest of remarks.[5] But "doing great things in the New World," as a way of not saying what Martin would do there, is finally as frustrating as the silences of the novelist about his journey.

It took Dickens a few weeks at least, after debarking in Boston and addressing the copyright issue there, before he arrived in New York pretty well convinced that America was a disappointment. Dejection overwhelms Martin almost as soon as he sets foot in America. In a mere "twelve or fifteen hours" after debarking in New York, he feels "a strong misgiving that his enterprise"—still unspecified—"was doomed." He tries to cheer himself up, but "whatever thoughts he called up to his aid, they came before him in depressing and discouraging shapes, and gave him no relief" (17.295). Passing through "grim domains of Giant Despair," Martin reaches the nadir of his journey when he and Mark Tapley are deposited by the river boat in the hideous swamp and human swindle called Eden. Here in "a jungle deep and dark, with neither earth nor water at its roots, but putrid matter, formed of the pulpy offal of the two, and of their own corruption," the narrator pulls out all the stops of description and the hero and his companion attempt to set up housekeeping. Even in these grim surroundings, Dickens reminds us that disappointed hopes may be more painful than harm inflicted by others, since "many a man who would have stood within a home dismantled, strong in his passion and design of vengeance, has had the firmness of his nature conquered by the razing of an air-built castle" (23.375–379).

It is generally supposed that the Eden of the novel was modeled on Cairo, Illinois, and the Eden Land Corporation on a land swindle known as the Cairo City and Canal Company. Once it was even argued that Dickens had lost money by investing in Cairo back in 1837 and that he traveled to America in order to inquire after his investment—propositions that are patently untrue.[6] Eden, remember, functions not merely as an inverted paradise for purposes of satire. The swamp is a locus for grievances against the Americans, to be sure, but also for the reform of Martin Chuzzlewit. Martin falls ill in this dismal place, which is the physical nadir but spiritual zenith of his American experience. The example of Mark Tapley's care for him, and the necessity of caring in turn for Tapley, effects a conversion from his habitual selfishness. "It was long before he fixed the knowledge of himself so firmly in his mind that he could thoroughly discern the truth; but in the hideous solitude of that most hideous place . . . he felt and knew the failing of his life, and saw what an ugly spot it was." Such is the central recognition on the hero's path toward selflessness in *Martin Chuzzlewit*. The romance convention, which is now dominant over the satiric, does not preclude the symbolic place from having personal significance for Dickens, who both moralizes and indulges himself in this death-bed conversion. For one thing, just as Martin has never really divulged his reasons for coming as far as Eden, U.S.A., so he is careful to keep his conversion to himself—a caution somewhat unnecessary for a fictional character. "He was so doubtful (and with justice) of his own character, that he determined not to say one word of vain regret or good resolve to Mark, but steadily to keep his purpose before his own eyes solely: and [the casuist in Dickens keeps probing and excusing] there was not a jot of pride in this; nothing but humility and steadfastness: the best armour he could wear. So low had Eden brought him down. So high had Eden raised him up." This all-important action takes very few words to narrate, and to tell the truth there is not a great deal of outward proof of Martin's conversion in the rest of the novel. The nature of the quest remains as obscure as ever, in the words that the hero does address to his companion (who continues to behave as a servant and to be treated as such). "We left home on a mad enterprise, and have failed. The only hope left us . . . is to quit this settlement for ever, and get back to England" (33.525–526).

We have no reason to suppose that Dickens suffered from depression, as Martin Chuzzlewit did during his visit to America. If there was such a thing as a mild depression of the author, it was of longer duration and associated with his general uncertainty of purpose in the five or six years prior to the success of *Dombey and Son*. Even for this longer period, the evidence is varied and suggests nothing very drastic: the conscious desire for a respite from novel writing after completing *Barnaby Rudge;* a restlessness that did not cease with America but prevailed upon him to take his family to Italy and Switzerland; money anxieties and lower than expected sales of his books; difficulties in writing that we do not hear of earlier in his career; the sentimental review of selfish lives in his Christmas books and their general theme of cheering oneself up; even a new and more serious tone in regard to social problems. The American visit, I take it, was sufficient to bring such feelings into focus, at least in his art, in the deep depression of Martin in the fanciful Eden. It was certainly not an investment that turned sour in Cairo, Illinois, that jarred Dickens into projecting this state of mind; it was more likely the failure of "an air-built castle," the idea of doing something heroic about international copyright and the chagrin of admitting defeat and possible selfishness. Great dramatic writers characteristically amplify their sensitivities in their fictions, and any check to Dickens's normally high spirits may have produced very low spirits in young Martin. In a period of greater than usual questioning and introspection, the "outpourings of vulgar curiosity" in America—to use Jerome Meckier's phrase—may have affected Dickens more deeply than we know.[7] A general feeling of exposure to criticism, I believe, reinforced specific self-criticisms and provided a subjective basis for the attack on selfishness.

To grasp fully the treatment of depression in *Martin Chuzzlewit*, we need to regard not only the despair of the hero in the most dismal of settings but the agent of conversion who is Mark Tapley. This very odd person, with his tediously repeated formula for seeking merit in adversity, is only a figment of character at most, though he too is a surrogate for Dickens—the figment of a Christian and moralistic response to depression that can only be retrospective of the American journey. Since in the fiction Mark so evidently anticipates Martin's disappointment, his foresight is equivalent to the novelist's hindsight. Though the conception of Mark Tapley is fixed from the beginning and he is more or less wound up like a toy, the conception is far from simple. Morally, he is a foil for the hero; psychologically, a complement. Whereas Martin is blithely unaware of anyone's feelings but his own, Mark is attracted by suffering and serves others; whereas Martin is easily depressed, Mark is endlessly manic—or, as he says, jolly. The tediousness and repetitiousness of his message, which have often put readers off, are best understood as the nagging demand by one half of a personality that the whole personality cheer itself up. Dickens is obviously pleased with this demon of gospel spirits whom he invented to ride his hero's back, but he is even more pleased with the irony of the basic conception: Mark Tapley is so helplessly disposed to be jolly that he can award himself no "credit" for his state of mind unless he voluntarily subjects himself to scenes of suffering and a selfish master. This irony begins to warp the conception toward an aggressive parody of Christian morality.

As Mark explains near the end of the novel, in case the reader has failed to get the point after numerous repetitions, "My constitution is, to be jolly; and my weakness is, to wish to find a credit in it." So irredeemably committed to joy is he that he has no choice, no moral life of his own. His happiness, he feels, ought to be tried by suffering, but so steadfast is it that it cannot be tried and be found wanting. Only his credit can be affected a little, in conjunction with others' moral failure or suffering. Thus he latches on to young Martin, as an exemplar of weak moral being, and befriends the steerage passengers and others who suffer real hardship and loss. Mark's love, his care for others, and his usefulness are "real" enough, in the fictional world of the novel; but his defensive patter about credit, which is his hallmark, performs a kind of doubletake on the gospels.

"Lookin on the bright side of human life in short, one of my hopeful wisions is, that there's a deal of misery a waitin for me; in the midst of which I may come out tolerable strong, and be jolly under circumstances

51

as reflects some credit. I goes into the world sir, wery boyant, and I tries this. I goes aboard ship first, and wery soon discovers (by the ease with which I'm jolly, mind you) as there's no credit to be got *there*. I might have took warning by this, and gave it up; but I didn't. I gets to the U-nited States; and then I *do* begin, I won't deny it, to feel some little credit in sustainin my spirits."

After this hit—worthy of Sam Weller—at the United States as a place where the most cheerfully disposed person in the world might have to struggle a little to keep up countenance, Mark retells the story of Martin's conversion there as it affects him. He had counted on America from the beginning, and found it much as he expected, but he had also counted on Martin's selfishness and has now been frustrated by the latter's moral turn for the better.

> "What follers? Jest as I'm beginnin to come out, and am a treadin on the werge [of feeling a little credit], my master deceives me."
> "Deceives you!" cried Tom.
> "Swindles me," retorted Mr. Tapley, with a beaming face. "Turns his back on ev'rything as made his service a creditable one, and leaves me, high and dry, without a leg to stand upon. In which state, I returns home. Wery good. Then all my hopeful wisions bein crushed; and findin that there an't no credit for me nowhere; I abandons myself to despair, and says, 'Let me do that as has the least credit in it, of all; marry a dear, sweet creetur, as is wery fond of me: me being, at the same time, wery fond of her: lead a happy life; and struggle no more again the blight which settles on my prospects.' " (48.733–734)

Look at it this way, Dickens seems to be saying through this figment of his imagination: the Americans are swindlers and without credit, but if one plays a little game with oneself and thinks of the moral credit of not giving in to the mood with which their rapaciousness and one's own innate selfishness should affect one, then one can outswindle the swindlers and return home contented. The time has come for Martin Chuzzlewit to reflect on his own shortcomings and turn the other cheek.

At the same time, Mark Tapley's own conversion, as announced in this same passage, betrays his role in the game. Inwardly, Mark and Martin part company after Eden because they no longer have any need for each other. The converted hero is no longer the object of Christian compassion, and discharging his manic servant signals the end of his tendency to depression. As a figment of Dickens, Mark has stood for Christian desperation tactics from the beginning—the trick of accepting humiliation or suffering by willing it, of being jolly, as he says, "under circumstances as reflects some credit." His actions as a "real" person in the novel can only be applauded, but as a clown and partial projection of Dickens his words need to be attended to as carefully as those of Pecksniff or Tom Pinch. His ironic inversions of every self-interested stance toward life provide more fun than Martin's conversion, to be sure, but the obsessive recourse to these locutions does not logically (or psychologically) entail his own conversion, which Dickens gets over so lightly in the proposed marriage to Mrs. Lupin. In the end, the material and sexual demands of the clown are uppermost, as in the case of Shakespeare's Touchstone or Lavatch. Mrs. Lupin is the one overtly sexual woman in the novel, just as her Blue Dragon is the one truly comfortable interior; Mark Tapley's particular comeuppance, therefore, is something of a comedown for any who have put stock in his Christianity. Dickens intends the reversal, obviously, to take the opposite course of Martin's, but then the jokes about "hopeful wisions bein crushed" and "abandons myself to despair" have to be taken seriously, since the reader has been urged to value Mark's irony throughout. His rather nutty advocacy of surrendering the self in order to find it is one religious stance in the novel that we have learned to trust, but now he is humorously admitting defeat. The Christian vision of self-sacrifice and the Christian avoidance of despair *have* been abandoned at this point, as they are abandoned every day in what Gamp refers to as this "wale" of life.

Mark Tapley's characteristic disguising of his good deeds as unsuccessful forays for "credit" obeys the injunction, "Let not thy left hand know what thy right hand doeth." Insofar as he really desires credit, of course, he disobeys the same injunction. Dickens invented the character as a sort of mirror for Martin Chuzzlewit to see himself in and then let him escape through the looking glass. In his happy combination of spiritual and material values, he is also a foil to Pecksniff's wicked combination of the same; they are both "hypocrites," but Dickens has only good feelings about Tapley. Hippolyte Taine wrote that there were no Pecksniffs in France because his countrymen had "ceased to affect virtue," and that "the only chance for the French modern Tartuffe is to confess and exaggerate weaknesses." Forster, whose paraphrase this is, thought that the English had "something of an advantage here."[8] But in the interplay of Martin Chuzzlewit and Mark Tapley, Dickens had already foreseen the advantages of confession and exaggerated weakness in his manifold descriptions of selfishness. Moreover, Martin and Mark slip back into the idealized English landscape of the novel— in which it is better to marry than to burn—more comfortably than either Pecksniff or Tom Pinch can abide there.

One other possible surrogate for the author, the "murderin' waga-bond" who is Jonas Chuzzlewit, is only partially connected to the American adventure. Insofar as Jonas is a mighty exemplar of selfishness, he fits the scheme for the whole novel inspired by Dickens's recent experience, but insofar as he is a murderer and a parricide, he harks back to an earlier fantasy of killing. In a sense, the fascination with murder as such begins and ends with Sikes's murder of Nancy in *Oliver Twist*, since Dickens's strenuous readings of that scene in the eighteen-sixties may well have contributed to his own death.[9] From what he revealed in the autobiographical fragment a few years after the completion of *Martin Chuzzlewit*, it can certainly be presumed that he harbored some resentment against his parents—as long as it is acknowledged that he also took more than usual care of them. Jonas Chuzzlewit is both murderer and would-be parricide. Both he and his blackmailer, Tigg Montague, believe that he has poisoned old Anthony out of sheer impatience to come into the property. The aborting of the parricide and displacement of the murder upon the blackmailer merely underline the fantasy nature of the whole design. Jonas is a thor-oughly despicable character, quite evidently capable of violence, and has already gone to the trouble of poisoning his father, but Dickens pulls back from the completion of this crime. "It was foul, foul, cruel, bad," in old Chuffey's words; "but not as you suppose" (51.779). Old Anthony dies a natural death, and Jonas kills the deserving Montague instead.

This is not to depreciate the violence of these English scenes—violence that is, after all, merely boasted of by Hannibal Chollop and his admirers in America. I would only ask Freudian interpreters to allow that, if the novelist could project in his fiction unconscious fantasies of parricide, then he most certainly could project conscious and unconscious admissions of selfishness. At least since Edmund Wilson, critics of Dickens have made Jonas Chuzzlewit a more popular study than

Pecksniff, and that is clearly a mistaken emphasis for understanding the novel as a whole. In some ways Jonas is most interesting for his sub-terranean relations with the other representative of the younger generation among the Chuzzlewits, Martin. Thus Jonas accuses Martin of being a "vagabond" (24.390–391); the two are momentarily confused by John Westlock, who asks "in what degree of relationship they stood towards each other, being different persons" (39.617); and their paths cross in Wiltshire, as Jonas descends on Pecksniff coincidentally with Martin's return from America (43.673–674). Especially curious is the dreamlike role that Martin plays as bystander in the discovery of Jonas's intended parricide. The confession of Lewsome, the surgeon's assistant who sold the poison to Jonas, at once repels the hero and renders him helpless, in a scene that is awkwardly narrated to say the least. " 'What do you mean?' demanded Martin, sternly. 'Do you know he is the son of the old man of whom you have spoken?' " As the story unfolds, "Martin was so amazed, so shocked, and confounded by what he had heard, that it was some time before he could reduce it to any order in his mind, or could sufficiently comprehend the bearing of one part upon another, to take in all the details at one view." A regular con-sortium of the younger generation in the comedy—Tapley, Pinch, Westlock—supports the hero in this scene, but the group is utterly at a loss as to how to respond to the charge of parricide. The narrator, also at a loss, seems to conspire with the characters to do nothing: "Besides, there was the great difficulty and responsibility of moving at all in the matter. Lewsome's story might be false; in his wretched state it might be greatly heightened by a diseased brain; or admitting it to be entirely true, the old man might have died a natural death"—the solution to the quandary that is finally chosen by the novelist. All are agreed that this dreadful charge ought to be old Martin's responsibility to investigate, but he at this time is supposedly in the thralls of Pecksniff. Still more awkwardly,

> [young] Martin could not endure the thought of seeming to grasp at this unnatural charge against his relative [Jonas], and using it as a stepping-stone to his grandfather's favor. But that he would seem to do so, if he presented himself before his grandfather in Mr. Pecksniff's house again, for the purpose of declaring it; and that Mr. Pecksniff, of all men, would represent his conduct in that despicable light; he perfectly well knew. On the other hand, to be in possession of such a statement, and to take no

measures of further enquiry in reference to it, was tantamount to being a partner in the guilt it professed to disclose.

If all this mental churning seems more like a dream of parricide than the criminal fact, so it is, and obviously more young men than Jonas are wrapped up in the dream. "In a word, they were wholly unable to discover any outlet from this maze of difficulty, which did not lie through some perplexed and entangled thicket" (48.737–740). The upshot of the discovery is that the young men troop off in search of Mrs. Gamp, to get her assistance in finding out what old Chuffey knows!

Fortunately, Jonas does not succeed in poisoning his father, and the old man dies a natural death after all, which earlier and in itself provides an effective centerpiece for the satire on money in the novel. "Plunge him to the throat in golden pieces now, and his heavy fingers should not close on one," the eighth number of *Martin Chuzzlewit* concludes (18.310). This demise of Anthony Chuzzlewit competes for the attention of the nurse, Mrs. Gamp, and the undertaker, Mr. Mould; it is fully and splendidly accessible to the reader as satire. The death as intended parricide is a much dreamier affair, with no body to it in the text, though it involves besides the principal actor, Jonas, the titular hero and his friends, and has wider ramifications in the plot as a whole— the life-insurance business, detection and blackmail, murder and pursuit of the murderer, and eventually suicide.

One additional affective center of the novel, though more conventional than parricide, is as mysterious as this and as nearly without body, and that is the passion for Mary Graham. Not that dreams of parricide and dreams of Mary are necessarily linked in any way thematically: it is enough that these two affective centers function alike, by drawing the principal surrogates for Dickens together in the action. Except for the mild titillation of her relation to old Martin when they first appear, and the less agreeable titillation of her squeezing and bullying by Pecksniff, and despite the noble unrequited love of Tom Pinch and the stuffy requited love of young Martin, the ostensible heroine is almost never on the scene and has almost no convincingly imagined presence in the novel. Yet she is the love object of all four of these gentlemen, and I dare say would have been the love object of Jonas Chuzzlewit as well, if the novelist had not felt the need to make someone—namely, Mercy Pecksniff—really suffer for the latter's violence.

The common source of this widespread interest in the heroine is Dickens. She is very weakly present in the text because, as in the case of the hero's motives for visiting America and the rationale for his adventures there, Dickens was so closely involved with what he was writing that he did not see the need, or did not wish, or was unable to make the representation plain. Mary Graham is far less realized as a character than most of his heroines, yet her position in the action of the novel is quite prominent. It may not be finally possible to demonstrate that she is a reincarnation of Mary Hogarth, whose premature death in 1837 freed Dickens to fantasize about their love.[10] She is not much of a reincarnation, for one thing, and there is not a great deal of evidence linking the fictional and real women beyond the nearly too obvious similarity of names. Mary Graham is also seventeen, or the age of Mary Hogarth when she died; and Tom Pinch distinctly speaks of her to his sister as one who is precious to him and has died, a "departed spirit" with whom he dreams he is in heaven (50.763). That Pinch's longing for this shadowy heroine is the only interest in her that Dickens chooses to develop—in elegiac and somewhat fulsome tones—does suggest that she is a stand-in for Mary Hogarth. Dickens could not possess his pretty sister-in-law in death any more than he could in life: Tom Pinch cannot possess Mary Graham. But very noticeably the latter's marriage to young Martin, which has been the "design" of old Martin all along, is deflected, shunted to one side at the end, in favor of much sentiment about Tom's love and even Tom's sister's marriage to Westlock. What her position in the novel does prove is that her admirers, the two Martin Chuzzlewits, Pecksniff, and Pinch, all have something in common.

By such devious paths and despite its multiplicity of character and motive, *Martin Chuzzlewit* is a fiction highly egocentric. Martin's peevish depression and Mark's forced cheer, Jonas's parricidal longings and Pecksniff's arrant lust, Tom's everlasting self-abasement and devotion, all insist too much. The utility of each make-believe passion can always be referred back to Dickens, who in the same novel unabashedly substitutes some of his own adventures in America for his hero's. For some ways of thinking about literature, to suggest that a novel is more finely organized about the novelist's own projection than any other principle—that the self in the center of the work is no other than Dickens—is tantamount to declaring that the work fails aesthetically. Indeed this particular novel is often said to be without organization, notwithstanding Dickens's intention to concentrate on "selfishness." This lack is said to be a major difference between *Martin Chuzzlewit* and *Dombey and Son,* which many critics follow Kathleen Tillotson in declaring "the earliest example of responsible and successful planning" by Dickens.[11] Yet once an egocentric pattern has been perceived in the former novel, though the ego in question be the author's rather than a single hero's, it has value similar to that of any other "organic" unity pointed out by criticism. Very many of the forms admired by New Criticism, such as repeated imagery or parallel actions, are not readily perceived by readers unassisted: but such forms undoubtedly have their rhetorical effect, which it is the business of critics to discern. So also projections of the novelist, if they can be shown to organize seemingly disparate elements of the text, must be presumed to have their effect on the reader who is not fully aware of them. I would go further and argue that, unless the forms tell of some life—whether the author's or the community's—they are patterns of only potential interest and potential meaning. The partially hidden and partially displaced egocentricity of *Martin Chuzzlewit* is more rewarding of study than the novel's supposed absence of aesthetic form.

V

Paradise Lost

*T*he other title visible in Hablot Browne's illustration for the final number of the novel, besides *Le Tartuffe*, is *Paradise Lost*. We do not ordinarily think of Dickens as a student of English poetry, or as a poet himself working in the nearly inescapable shadow of Milton. Yet as most readers of *Martin Chuzzlewit* become aware, and as Stuart Curran has shown in some detail,[1] the novelist depends in a number of different scenes and for his overall plan on Milton's version of the Fall, both of Satan and of humankind. If Dickens's personal experience has been scattered and redistributed through a good many regions of the text, so have his literary borrowing and parody. But his design of using Milton surfaces most obviously in the climax of the action against Pecksniff.

From that scene the reader gathers that old Martin has been playing God all along. The exposure of Pecksniff, as we have noted, is a bit strained. The indignation, which the reader is noisily invited to share, is of the kind that must rapidly exhaust itself rather than be satisfied. Because of the carefully contrived suspense up to this point, a certain amount of the action has to be narrated over again, mostly by the old man himself while he is fuming about and attacking the hypocrite. It may be the most nearly humorless chapter in the novel, but the theology is surprisingly thorough. Old Martin has laid plans from the beginning, both "cherished projects" for his chosen friends and wary tests for Pecksniff.

Self; grasping, eager, narrow-ranging, over-reaching self; with its long train of suspicions, lusts, deceits, and all their growing consequences, was the root of the vile tree. Mr. Pecksniff had so presented his character before the old man's eyes, that he—the good, the tolerant, enduring Pecksniff—had become the incarnation of all selfishness and treachery; and the more odious the shapes in which those vices ranged themselves before him now, the sterner consolation he had in his design of setting Mr. Pecksniff right, and Mr. Pecksniff's victims too.

Because of his sure knowledge of how Pecksniff must behave, Martin has kept his plan to himself and left the will of his adversary entirely free—a point that he now makes several times in the process of upbraiding him. "He called upon Mr. Pecksniff (by the name of Scoundrel) to remember that there again he had not trapped him to do evil, but that he had done it of his own free will and agency" (52.790–791, 805). Although Martin Chuzzlewit is patently an angry God, he is concerned to state formal conditions befitting his power.

Martin has extended similar freedom of action to young Martin, it now appears. What has hitherto seemed ambiguous or hostile in his behavior was part of a plan to test his grandson's love and obedience. Young Martin "little thought" that the banknote he received in London, upon departing for America, was from his grandfather. In this case providence has operated a little too mysteriously, as old Martin explains to his namesake: "I hoped to bring you back, Martin, penitent and humbled. I hoped to distress you into coming back to me. Much as I loved you, I had that to acknowledge which I could not reconcile it to myself to avow, then, unless you made submission to me, first." Mary Graham was also to be tested: "he told them how, resolved to probe this Pecksniff, and to prove the constancy and truth of Mary (to himself no less than Martin), he had conceived and entered on his plan; and how, beneath her gentleness and patience, he had softened more and more." The coexistence of two Martin Chuzzlewits—and their adjunct Tom Pinch—has seemed most troublesome with respect to Mary. Old Martin has wanted young Martin to love her all along, but his own interest is such that he has tended to forget the principle of free will. He now explains "how it was little comfort to him to know that Martin had chosen Her, because the grace of his design was lost" (52.802–804). Thus a rich and powerful but less than perfect God has set the course of action, with the shadowy heroine first cast in a human role and then in that of divine intercessor. Except where Pecksniff and Gamp are concerned, old Martin is now a little contrite, just as young Martin became secretly penitent in Eden. The kind of criticism that modern readers are likely to level against Milton's God—that he finally need not have permitted evil in the world—has been accommodated within Dickens's text, in the initial selfishness and uncertain temper of the old man and in some slight criticism that Mark Tapley offers as this scene gets under way. Old Martin is partly to blame, Tapley hints, for young Martin's behavior. Chuzzlewit does not reply directly, but his rephrasing of the point shows that he appreciates it: " 'So you think,' said Martin, 'that his old faults are, in some degree, of my creation, do you?' " (52.793).

In the great scheme of things that is now unveiled before the reader, before young Martin and his friends, and before Pecksniff as well, the hypocrite is the devil and has been the devil from the beginning—though unlike the case of Milton's Satan, in this comic version hypocrisy has become visible to a good many men and angels, and not to God alone.[2] In *Martin Chuzzlewit* the romantic fall of man and his voluntary removal from Eden precede the fall of Satan at the end. After young Martin has learned the lesson of selfishness, and old Martin too has confessed to problems in that line, the blame can be shifted and a futile punishment administered to Pecksniff. If the shifts from one to the other of these characters seem rather quick and unwarranted, that is because poetic justice has been overdetermined by psychological displacement. Old Martin in the role of justicer is a stand-in for the novelist, but so are Pecksniff and young Martin, the hypocrite and the man chastened in America. The separate identities of the characters are a bit precarious, and some of the awkwardness of the scene is the result of this precariousness. Here we have Martin advising Martin to hold Mary's hand, and the narrator responding from the skies, "Hold it! If he clasped it half as tightly as he did her waist.——Well, well!" (52.805). But earlier, in the garden in Wiltshire, Pecksniff has seized Mary's hand and held her forcibly about the waist, and the narrator has commented ironically, with one of the many diffused allusions to *Paradise Lost,* "that she would have preferred the caresses of a toad, an adder, or a serpent: nay, the hug of a bear: to the endearments of Mr. Pecksniff" (30.482). Young Martin is largely passive during the fall of Pecksniff, but so is the hypocrite aggressively passive, as always: " 'I am not angry,' observed Mr. Pecksniff. 'I am hurt, Mr. Chuzzlewit: wounded in my feelings: but I am not angry, my good sir.' " One part of the dialogue accidentally identifies the young hero with the hypocrite, as both Martins share a confessional moment:

> "There is a kind of selfishness," said Martin: "I have learned it in my own experience of my own breast: which is constantly upon the watch for selfishness in others; and holding others at a distance by suspicions and distrusts, wonders why they don't approach, and don't confide, and calls that selfishness in them. Thus I once doubted those about me—not without reason in the beginning—and thus I once doubted you, Martin."
>
> "Not without reason," Martin answered; "either."
>
> "Listen, hypocrite! Listen, smooth-tongued, servile, crawling knave!" said Martin. "Listen, you shallow dog. What! When I was seeking him, you had already spread your nets; you were already fishing for him, were ye?" (52.800–801)

The mood of contrition does not prepare us for the sudden turning to the hypocrite, which on the stage would be clear enough but here seems to collapse identities, while the undifferentiated use of "Martin" has already made the dialogue sound like an interior monologue.

Though it remains obscure how Pecksniff hoped to prey on young Martin, or influence the grandfather by cultivating the grandson, the analogy between the hypocrite and Satan seems clear. He is the seducer and tempter, the inflated figure who holds Tom Pinch in thrall and attempts to win others to his side. Upon his discovery and exposure he appears to shrink, like Satan when he reports his dirty work to his comrades in hell. "Not only did his figure appear to have shrunk, but his discomfiture seemed to have extended itself, even to his dress. His clothes seemed to have grown shabbier, his linen to have turned yellow, his hair to have become lank and frowsy; his very boots looked villainous and dim, as if their gloss had departed with his own" (52.806). If he suffers only in appearance, remember that a hypocrite depends above all on appearances. The passage echoes another moment of shame that is more nearly parallel to the career of Satan, since it follows the attempted seduction of the woman in the garden: "He seemed to be shrunk and reduced; to be trying to hide himself within himself . . . His shoes looked too large; his sleeves looked too long; his hair looked too limp; his hat looked too little; his features looked too mean; his exposed throat looked as if a halter would have done it good" (30.483). In

Paradise Lost Satan's involuntary metamorphosis, surrounded by his fellows, is no less symbolic of shame. Amid scorn and hissing tongues,

> he wonder'd, but not long
> Had leisure, wond'ring at himself now more;
> His Visage drawn he felt to sharp and spare,
> His Arms clung to his Ribs, his Legs entwining
> Each other, till supplanted down he fell
> A monstrous Serpent on his Belly prone.
>
> (X.509–514)

Yet the argument from "design"—of old Martin's permissive will and his attempt to frustrate the hypocrite conclusively—becomes fully apparent only by the last number of *Martin Chuzzlewit,* and even there it is not very satisfactorily worked out. The novelist himself falls prey to the Chuzzlewit madness, the peculiar combination of hilarity and personal intensity that characterizes the novel as a whole. Before Dickens gave way to laughter at himself and Pecksniff by means of this fiction, he rebounded from the discomfort and (as he saw it) potential for shame in his American visit with an excessive irony still apparent in the opening chapter and elsewhere. This strong-arming, backed by self-criticism as well as contempt for the world, has the effect in the long run of heightening the marvelous laughter. It also tends to invert traditional roles, parody the fortunate fall, and scatter allusions to Milton throughout the text—though Dickens the romantic does not propose to justify the ways of God, but of man.

The Chuzzlewit madness began with the peculiar name—the most aggressive and baffling of any of the personal names that Dickens featured in the titles of his novels. Forster tells us—and surviving slips tend to confirm—that the name evolved from "Sweezleden, Sweezleback, and Sweezlewag" to "Chuzzletoe, Chuzzleboy, Chubblewig, and Chuzzlewig," thence to "Chuzzlewit."[3] A vague suggestion of animal species inhabits the names as a group, while the predatory connotations of one partial homonym, "weasle," give way to the oral connotations of "nuzzle," "muzzle," and "guzzle." The final result is a brilliant one, even more so than "Pecksniff," which seems to have been stable from its inception. Dickens preserved the idea of greed, but rendered it potentially more comic by making it passively satisfied. At the same time, in shifting sounds, he gave the first part of the name the force of a verb. Besides "nuzzle," "muzzle," and "guzzle," there is only one other

possible rhyme wtth "chuzzle," and that is "puzzle." The verbal sug-
gestions and especially "puzzle" probably dictated the change from
"wig" to "wit." The whole name, trailing animal associations from eons
of time, became more abstract and apt for development, appropriate
for an entire family of antiheroes (two of whom have the novelistic
grace to turn out heroes) and symbolic of a deliberately baffling humor
in the telling.[4] Dickens was pleased with the result and immediately
introduced the name in the history of origins that begins the novel,
and whose irony is directed both within and without, at the characters
and readers of the work:

> As no lady or gentleman, with any claims to polite breeding, can possibly
> sympathize with the Chuzzlewit Family without being first assured of the
> extreme antiquity of the race, it is a great satisfaction to know that it
> undoubtedly descended in a direct line from Adam and Eve; and was, in
> the very earliest times, closely connected with the agricultural interest.

The opening paragraph begins to unfold a sort of legal defense against
slandering these Chuzzlewits and is at the same time an elaborate spoof
or puzzle-wit, a confession of the need for a defense of humankind. In
the same high tone of mock defense, the second paragraph embraces
even the Jonas Chuzzlewits and what I take to be a glance at Dickens
and the rest of us as vagabonds. For "as there was, in the oldest family
of which we have any record, a murderer and a vagabond, so we never
fail to meet, in the records of all old families, with innumerable repetitions of the same phase of character."

The spirit of the opening is that of Milton's hell, the uncreating
creation that is a mockery both of true beginnings and of itself—or of
"universal self," as the first number concludes (3.42). A gathering of
the great Chuzzlewit clan, in the second number of the novel, resembles
the council in hell.[5] Pecksniff rises to his feet in this scene, which takes
place in his house, and starts to propose that the assembled envious
host can best get at the pocketbook of Martin Chuzzlewit senior by
investigating that gentleman's interest in his grandson. Pecksniff is all
the hypocrite; he is going to pretend "disinterestedness" (4.60). The
maneuver is like the proposal urged by Beelzebub, but first devised by
Satan, to subvert God's creation by attacking the rumored favorite, a
race called Man.[6] At this point Pecksniff is interrupted, however, and
it is never precisely clear what his designs on young Martin can be: as

architects, the master and apprentice are highly implausible, except in their general rivalry to the architects of the plot, old Martin and the novelist. Resemblances and associations seldom hold for long in *Martin Chuzzlewit*, as Dickens in his eagerness turns up this stone and that and finds an abundance of crawling things. As we look down upon the council scene, Montague Tigg claims to be "proud as Lucifer." It is he who has a "regular Satanic" moustache and invokes Shakespeare and Milton (4.44–47). Eventually this person will rival Pecksniff's special claims to providence and disinterest, by founding the Anglo-Bengalee Disinterested Loan and Life Insurance Company. That company in itself will constitute a brilliant stroke for Dickens, since the modern secular institution of insurance—fraudulent or otherwise—so evidently substitutes for religious faith in providence. All the same, the irony takes some twists and turns that lead nowhere.

The irony that fosters confusion and touches off mad laughter is also responsible for the significant parodies of the fortunate fall in the novel, the expulsions from a mock paradise in Wiltshire and the journey to America. Both young Martin and Pinch are expelled, one after the other, from the supposed pastoral innocence that imbues Pecksniff's home.[7] An inversion of the case of Adam and Eve is apparent in the situation itself, since Pecksniff is neither God nor angel. He regards, or pretends to regard, his "lowly" establishment in Wiltshire as a pastoral retreat, an ideal place for young men, whose parents or guardians can afford the fee, to study architecture on their own while absorbing virtue from himself. He is a poseur and on one occasion even presents himself as Adam: "It is an ancient pursuit, gardening. Primitive, my dear sir; for, if I am not mistaken, Adam was the first of our calling. . . . I do a little bit of Adam still" (24.384). But mainly Pecksniff does not dig (he is only pretending to dig on this occasion). He is paterfamilias in Wiltshire, proprietor of the garden. When he apprehends, earlier in the novel, that Martin Chuzzlewit and his grandson are estranged, he dismisses the young man for his sins:

> "I weep for your depravity, sir," said Mr. Pecksniff, "I mourn over your corruption, I pity your voluntary withdrawal of yourself from the flowery paths of inward peace;" here he struck himself upon his breast, or moral garden; "but I cannot have a leper and a serpent for an inmate. Go forth," said Mr. Pecksniff, stretching out his hand: "go forth, young man! Like all who know you, I renounce you!" (12.211)

In a parallel action, Pecksniff later dismisses a resident of longer standing in his house, the patient all-deserving Tom Pinch. This action is still more farcical and daring, because the hypocrite now has more at stake. Old Martin and Mary are staying with him, and Pinch has learned of Pecksniff's advances on Mary. The hypocrite boldly forestalls the sexual complaint by accusing Pinch of the same, and he performs his duty to society, as he says, by showing his rival the door. Pecksniff is pushing his luck, and Dickens the limits of farce:

> "I will not say," cried Mr. Pecksniff, shedding tears, "what a blow this is. I will not say how much it tries me; how it works upon my nature; how it grates upon my feelings. I do not care for that. I can endure as well as another man. But what I have to hope, and what you have to hope, Mr. Pinch (otherwise a great responsibility rests upon you), is, that this deception may not alter my ideas of humanity; that it may not impair my freshness, or contract, if I may use the expression, my Pinions. I hope it will not; I don't think it will. It may be a comfort to you, if not now, at some future time, to know, that I shall endeavour not to think the worse of my fellow-creatures in general, for what has passed between us. Farewell!" (31.497)

The wit of these two episodes is simple and effective. By turning over the garden to an impostor, the Satan of the novel, Dickens contrives that the expulsion shall be welcome to both young men and satisfying to the reader. By inverting the old story, he has ipso facto defined the fall as fortunate. For Pinch, especially, this is a turning point, though one that is typically predicated on his relations to others rather than experienced inside.

The false paradise of Eden, U.S.A., affords a much more elaborate and not so patently successful parody of the fall. The narrative carries young Martin as far as Eden, remember, and leaves him there for three full monthly installments (chapters 24–32) while attending to a good many other strains of action in England. Such a long absence of the hero from the pages of the novel signifies more than parody: the reader is inevitably made to imagine the effect of the passage of time upon Martin and Mark Tapley, even though the narrative eventually takes up again where it left off. So there develops a serious, romantic expectation of what will happen in America, even as there is gross parody for purposes of satire, already anticipated by the name "Eden" and the boast of General Choke: "What are the Great United States for, sir . . . if not for the regeneration of man?" (21.348).

As if apologizing for returning to Martin Chuzzlewit and America, Dickens makes his transition from the comedy in London as ostentatiously as possible. With more than a touch of the sarcasm with which he began the novel, he calls Eden "a terrestrial Paradise" and pastes the same label on the unknown interior of Augustus Moddle—the supposed lover of Charity Pecksniff, who has been the subject of the previous number.

> From Mr. Moddle to Eden is an easy and natural transition. Mr. Moddle, living in the atmosphere of Miss Pecksniff's love, dwelt (if he had but known it) in a terrestrial Paradise. The thriving city of Eden was also a terrestrial Paradise, upon the showing of its proprietors. The beautiful Miss Pecksniff might have been poetically described as a something too good for man in his fallen and degraded state. That was exactly the character of the thriving city of Eden, as poetically heightened by Zephaniah Scadder, General Choke, and other worthies: part and parcel of the talons of that great American Eagle, which is always airing itself sky-high in purest ether, and never, no never, never, tumbles down, with draggled wings, into the mud.   (33.514)

Things do not sound at all good for Miss Pecksniff—or for Mr. Pecksniff, for that matter, whose "Pinions" are threatened in much the same way as the wings of this American Eagle. The comparisons themselves are a scandal, a kind of smashed fruit of the Chuzzlewit madness: they could hardly be otherwise after cramming into this "easy and natural transition." But surprisingly, a conceit that at first reading seems wanton or expeditious, and not very funny, begins to ripen soundly on all sides. In the delicate question of Moddle's chances with Pecksniff's daughter, the novelist touches on private states of mind; in his evocation of "man in his fallen and degraded state," he prepares for his hero's inward conversion. Dickens's Eden is not the mythical Eden from which man has descended, but a mythical place to which he may return. The substance of the argument will be psychological rather than historical.

Two sets of distinctions need to be made in interpreting Eden, though the novel and the myth finally override these distinctions in practice. First of all, *Martin Chuzzlewit* uses Eden in two ways, for the satire of America and as a locus for the hero's conversion. Because the number begins with a sarcastic reference to "a terrestrial Paradise," the reader has every reason to expect more satire—"a reg'lar little United States in itself," as Mark Tapley calls the place (33.518). And indeed this chapter features a visit from the notorious Hannibal Chollop. But it also comprises the sickness and near deaths of first Martin and then Mark, the conversion of Martin, and their departure from Eden (a voluntary departure this time). So when Dickens announces the earthly paradise at last, he announces not only a continued satire but the moral and psychological turning point in the life of Martin Chuzzlewit—parallel to the disillusionment of Tom Pinch with Pecksniff. But, secondly, the myth of the earthly paradise that Dickens draws upon in the novel has two different aspects, as a place of origins, before time and history, and as a place of return, for the recouping of innocence.[8] History began with a fall from paradise, which is echoed in numerous ways at the beginning of *Martin Chuzzlewit* and in the pretenses of Pecksniff throughout: so much for origins and the knowledge of good and evil. But the journey of Martin Chuzzlewit to Eden—a reenactment of the journey of Dickens to America—is a quest romance, in which the hero typically experiences in the earthly paradise things not altogether expected.

Since Dickens persists in hinting that the United States is not for the regeneration of man, how can it be that his hero is regenerated there? Moreover, since Eden is nothing but a pestilential swamp, how can it serve as anything but a travesty of the earthly paradise of romance? Both psychology and literature can obviously assist us here. In no way would an Eden that was purely Edenic affect the conversion of the hero. Comfort and bliss in America would only confirm Martin Chuzzlewit in his selfish ways. He needs to be shaken, he has to suffer and accept suffering, before he can change inwardly, and at this crisis the satiric vision transmutes to romance. Students of the earthly paradises of earlier literature will recall that the concept has always been fraught with irony. Such paradises are bound to earth, and if bowers of bliss were truly blissful, heroes would hardly discover anything about themselves by visiting them. When the hero Dante, in the most famous of all quests, reaches the earthly paradise in the final cantos of *Purgatory* and encounters Beatrice there, he does not experience unmixed joy. On the contrary, in the midst of those lovely surroundings he has to confront his own sins; the climactic moment of his journey, the moment in which Virgil is left behind and the hero's own identity is affirmed

by Beatrice, is also the bitterest moment in *The Divine Comedy*. To paraphrase what Dickens says of his hero, so low has Eden brought the character Dante down, and so high has it raised him up. For all his romantic imagination, Dickens is a more literal-minded poet than Dante: he requires miserable surroundings and physical illness to make an impression on his hero. But almost all earthly paradises besides Dante's employ some unpleasant features of the landscape to bring pressure to bear on the necessary introspection. In this regard, it is worth citing A. Bartlett Giamatti's conclusion to his study of renaissance epic:

> It was precisely in those poems that "peace" and "bliss" were found to be empty desires, unobtainable ends; it was precisely in the gardens of those massive works that these two words first revealed their elusiveness. . . . Our modern skepticism in regard to peace and pleasure was shaped in the false earthly paradises; it was from Ariosto, Tasso, and Spenser that we learned what a "dreadful place" a false Eden was, and it was from Dante, and particularly Milton, that we finally understood how far we had fallen from the true paradise.[9]

Dickens is finally more concerned with the psychology than with the morality of the quest. Like so many other versions of the fall since the late eighteenth century, the journey of Martin Chuzzlewit illustrates what Harold Bloom has called the internalization of quest romance. In a sense, classical and renaissance heroes also set out to find themselves—or so it seems to us in reading of their adventures. What distinguishes the modern quest is chiefly the consciousness of some inward motive, or the consciousness of some motives and wariness of others. Bloom's corrective thesis about the romantic revival, that it was not a movement to embrace nature but away from nature and toward a definition of the self, applies well enough to *Martin Chuzzlewit*.[10] Though in his *American Notes* Dickens paid due respect to great natural sites such as Niagara, in the novel he merely ridicules the popular association of America with nature. His hero is not once moved by nature except negatively, and then toward an understanding of his true self. Martin strives involuntarily for some sense of personal identity, and this quest is dogged by selfishness. Eventually he renounces the Promethean aims of the expedition and comes to value the purgatorial trial of a peculiarly nasty Eden. We cannot be sure, from the text of the novel, what these Promethean aims were. But neither are we sure, from a reading of the historical record and the novelist's letters, what were the aims of Dickens's visit to America.

The Americans, in effect, wrote some of Martin Chuzzlewit's story before Dickens ever thought of visiting their country. The adoption of the old Adam as the quintessential American and the celebration of this nation as a vast garden were already features of a national mythology.[11] These ideas were current among the writers and politicians whom Dickens met in the spring of 1842, and they fitted easily with his own store of literary and biblical tradition. To dwell on prelapsarian man, on either side of the Atlantic, was to think most certainly of the fall of man. I believe that the inspiration for the quest romance in *Martin Chuzzlewit* was primarily Dickens's musings about his own identity in those years, but it is striking how close this aspect of the novel comes to the theme of Emerson's essay of 1844, "Experience." In that essay the fall is defined as nothing less than the discovery that we exist. To that critic—and precursor of Harold Bloom—the internalization of quest romance can be total. The mood that inspires Emerson's essay is one of conspicuous depression, and the act of writing serves in some degree to lift him out of mourning for his son. Though the writer is determined to accept his life, he is also impatient with its worldly aspect of nagging injustices. Emerson was also aware of the copyright controversy of the time, and this becomes one of the concerns he brushes aside in the essay: "Whilst the debate goes forward on the equity of commerce, and will not be closed for a century or two, New and Old England may keep shop. Law of copyright and international copyright is to be discussed, and, in the interim, we will sell our books for the most we can." I do not mean to suggest that Emerson had much in common with Dickens, whose semblance he rather disliked. Rather, the point is that two such dissimilar men could adapt the idea of the fortunate fall to their own purposes. The peroration of Emerson's essay is finally no more sophisticated than Dickens's public and private attempts to frame his American experience in terms of honor and justice, and the words can be made to apply to Dickens personally:

> in the solitude to which every man is always returning, he has a sanity and revelations, which in his passage into new worlds he will carry with him. Never mind the ridicule, never mind the defeat: up again, old heart!— it seems to say,—there is victory yet for all justice; and the true romance

which the world exists to realize, will be the transformation of genius into practical power.[12]

For all its rich inheritance of literature and myth, chapter 33 of *Martin Chuzzlewit* is nevertheless something of a disappointment, redeemed only by the tobacco-spitting and gun-toting Hannibal Chollop. The serious climax of the romance, it seems, is hardly more than a convenience—not much like the poems Bloom has in mind and certainly not like Dante and Milton. From what ought to be the main turning point of the novel, Dickens's pen scampers away as fast as he can make it go—though he has made up for this hurry in advance, in a way, by the previous long silence about America that allows us to imagine what we please. The fall of Pecksniff in chapter 52 is no more satisfying. In each case, a crucial dramatization of the chastening of selfishness falls flat—and this novel is nothing if not thematic in intention. Apparently Dickens works best in *Chuzzlewit* when he is least mindful of such necessary developments. Yet again and again we are presented with his brilliant intuitions. He knows better than to end the novel on so lame a note as the reproval of the great hypocrite.

Except for the final apostrophe to Tom Pinch, the novel concludes with a finely contrived nonstarter. Augustus Moddle lets his mind be known at last, and in a delightful letter from Gravesend, after failing to show up for his wedding to Charity Pecksniff, he laments, "Oh, Miss Pecksniff, why didn't you leave me alone!" (54.831). But since neither party to the wedding has had any love to spare for the other, this is a story of selfishness also. The novel concludes with a reversal of expectations but not of moral consciousness this time, and when Augustus runs away the novelist manages the stunt more successfully than he manages the caning of Pecksniff or the conversion of young Martin. We cannot suppose that Dickens could have known in 1844 that his younger brother Augustus, whose nickname "Boz" he had appropriated in 1833, would leave his wife in the lurch and run off to America in 1860.[13] But Boz, perhaps—what about Boz? Could Boz imagine himself in the shoes of the fictional Augustus? There is widespread belief among students of Dickens that Jonas Chuzzlewit, wifebeater and murderer, has something of the novelist in his makeup. Earlier in the novel Jonas has thought it a fine joke to hover between Mercy and Charity Pecksniff—Merry and Cherry, as they are called—wanting the first but pretending to woo the second, in an action perhaps remotely like Dickens in his daydreams between Mary Hogarth and Catherine Hogarth his wife. Now we have the plight of Augustus, wanting Merry but being forced to make do with Cherry against his will. Jonas is a favorite with the critics because of his violence, which the novelist must of course repress. But if murder and sadism belong to the Chuzzlewit madness, so may the instinct to cut loose altogether. Dickens seizes the double advantage of punishing the criminal and celebrating the last-minute courage of the bridegroom: Jonas he bears down upon with terrifying guilt, and Augustus he slyly whisks away. The monster of selfishness takes poison; the nitwit affords laughter to all.

Boz can be discovered almost anywhere in *Martin Chuzzlewit*, working things out, as in Augustus Moddle's farewell letter: "I love another. She is Another's. Everything appears to be somebody else's. Nothing in the world is mine—not even my Situation—which I have forfeited—by my rash conduct—in running away." Again, if Dickens indirectly made fun of himself in this manner, his self-recognition was neither hoarded nor wasted but spent on art. In the words of Charles Lamb, defending his role as an informal essayist in 1833, "If it be egotism to imply and twine with his own identity the griefs and affections of another—making himself many, or reducing many unto himself—then is the skilful novelist . . . the greatest egotist of all."[14]

VI

Dickens as Dombey

*D*espite the disappointing sales of *Martin Chuzzlewit,* halfway through its writing Dickens felt that it was "in a hundred points immeasurably the best of my stories," and he reaffirmed to Forster his faith in his power to "sustain my place in the minds of thinking men, though fifty writers started up to-morrow."[1] His judgment seems to me a sound one. He bested selfishness in that novel by lashing out in many directions and by laughing indirectly at himself; and in so doing he more than adequately addressed "universal self." *Dombey and Son,* immediately more successful with his readers and acclaimed by critics today as a new departure in novel writing, curiously boasts no such world-famous characters as Pecksniff and Gamp—nor even the equivalent of Augustus Moddle.

Thirty years ago Kathleen Tillotson explained the difference of the two novels in terms such as these:

Pecksniff exists mainly in the limelight of a series of superb scenes (and also as refracted in the contrasted natures of Tom and Martin); but under this continued exhibition, with its extravagantly comic dialogue, he becomes less not more repulsive. Dickens's comic inventiveness is still overflowing, neither subordinated to the general purpose nor fully contained by moral and social criticism. The resulting ambiguity is clearer still with Mrs. Gamp, who is almost extraneous to the plot. We are less aware of the horrors of her ministrations than of the private world she blissfully inhabits, "as light as any gash balloon," and which Dickens makes it seem a privilege to share. Contrast the continued yet unstrained harnessing of the comedy to the "general purpose and design" [a phrase Dickens applied to *Chuzzlewit*] in *Dombey*, where the absurd is on the side of the angels. Toots and Susan Nipper and Captain Cuttle and Miss Tox, all, by their natures and their share in the action, supply continuous moral comment on the evil represented in Mr. Dombey; and they do so naturally and implicitly, without the copybook pointedness of Mark Tapley.[2]

This is only part of the sustained comparison that found *Dombey and Son* superior both in art and in realism. The moral test that Tillotson brings to bear upon the runaway dialogue of Pecksniff and the horrors of Gamp accords perfectly with Victorian tenets of realism but is also congruent with Steven Marcus's estimate of the novels—though Marcus is somewhat more sympathetic to what may be called the free associations of *Chuzzlewit*.[3] The fact is that Dickens does rein in his humorous projection and displays greater social consciousness in *Dombey*, but the novel is not more representative of humanity by virtue of placing the absurd "on the side of the angels." The absurd in this world are frequently *not* on the side of the angels. Moddle is certainly not on the side of the angels, and he is no less foolish than Toots. And while Dickens—not very effectively, as Tillotson remarks—goes out of his way to rebuke Pecksniff and Gamp, he all but applauds Moddle's desertion of Charity. Novelist, character, and readers understand that Charity is not all love and kisses.

The widely accepted conclusion that, whereas *Martin Chuzzlewit* may be superior in wit and invention, *Dombey and Son* is superior in organization and serious depiction of society should not be allowed to obscure the close relation of the two. Unusually for Dickens, the two novels were devoted to themes that could be stated in a single word: the second, according to Forster, "was to do with Pride what its predecessor had done with Selfishness."[4] Pride and selfishness are related themes, in literature or in life, and both have to do with personal identity as well as morality. The two novels further resemble each other in the ambitiousness of their designs. Each aspires to a kind of mythic significance for the culture, and not to actions that matter for the characters' lives alone. Each presumes to follow, in very different degrees of seriousness, a powerful literary example—*Paradise Lost* in the first instance and *King Lear* in the second. And each proceeds to the enactment of its theme by means of a fall, the one purgatorial and the other tragic. Such aspirations, presumptions, and procedures were not so common with Dickens that they can be disregarded, and they involve these novels closely with each other. Though the received opinion—owing much to Tillotson's thoughtful comparison—is that *Dombey and Son* is the true harbinger of the novelist's later work, it might be better to say that the two achieve their effect together.

Both novels belong to that stretch of years in which Dickens's production noticeably slowed, in which he took himself to America, Italy, and Switzerland, in which he traveled a good deal and nothing seemed to satisfy. If anything, the felt difficulty in writing seemed to increase with the second novel. His generally depressed spirits were not incompatible with a great deal of activity, but his restlessness was conscious and worrisome to his friend Forster. The Christmas books that he undertook from 1843 to 1848 were toilsome to write in the main, and they too show Dickens involved with himself. Eventually, as this period came to some sort of resolution, he wrote his autobiographical fragment and conceived the idea of *David Copperfield*. From a biographical standpoint *Chuzzlewit* and *Dombey* can be viewed as a continuous meditation on selfishness and pride: the evidence of the American adventure suggests that, in this instance, conscious pride came after a fall—as indeed pride, or a renewed sense of dignity, must often be one's recourse in attempting a comeback from real or imagined injuries. The slight Dickens suffered in America he exaggerated somewhat, in order to burnish and whet his sense of honor; when James Spedding wrote that he had gone to America to lobby for international copyright, he bristled with challenges, as if to escalate a quarrel that was not really being offered him. Dickens seems to have been more critical than any of his acquaintances were of the possible dubiety of the episode. It can only be to his credit that, in a second phase of reflection upon his experience, he saw pride as a lonely and potentially tragic affair. In any event, after the Chuzzlewit madness he attended to the Dombey pride. Each experiment contributed to his development as a novelist—the first by liberating an ironic projection of the self that was not on the side of the angels, and the second by deliberately exercising control.

Dickens created two Paul Dombeys as well as two Martin Chuzzlewits, and this pairing is another feature that the novels have in common. In *Martin Chuzzlewit* the pair are grandfather and grandson. Each has an extracurricular resemblance to the author, as novelist and traveler to America respectively, though the plot is the fairly conventional one of atonement and inheritance. After some initial misunderstanding and rivalry—and confusion of reference in the narrative—the two Martins' interests coincide in the familiar extension of the mortal self that is known as a personal estate. This extension of the self, with its customary waiver of charges of selfishness, is silently affirmed by the end of the novel. In *Dombey and Son,* a concerted attempt at tragedy, Dickens repudiates such an arrangement for the course of two generations and restores it only at the very end, in the birth of a third Paul to Dombey's daughter. For the main and tragic portion of the action, he forgoes the prudent distancing of grandparent and child that he employed for the two Chuzzlewits and, in *The Old Curiosity Shop,* for Nell and her grandfather. Paul Dombey senior is at least the undisputed father of little Paul. But Dombey and Son is also the business firm ("Wholesale, Retail, and for Exportation") by which the father will be perpetuated and the son subsumed. In his plan for the novel Dickens proposed to deliver a "death-blow" to this scheme of inheritance; and faithful to this design, he killed off the second Paul in the fifth number. Patently *Chuzzlewit* and *Dombey* are concerned with selfishness and pride in their moral aspects and with the definition of self. Two Martins allowed for the continuation of the self by natural means, a survival that is offset in the earlier novel by satire and the mysteries of Gamp's profession but not foreclosed by the plot. The death of little Paul in the second novel does foreclose survival by this means, and the tragic recognition belongs to Dickens as well as to Dombey.

Naturally the novelist hoped for a greater financial success with *Dombey,* and this he rapidly achieved. The demand for the book raised the print run for each installment to 32,000, and by the time he was finished 40,000 of the first number were in print, a vast improvement over *Chuzzlewit.*[5] Dickens studied to achieve this success, Ada B. Nisbet has suggested, by deliberately introducing the death of the first Mrs. Dombey in the first number and the death of her child in the fifth number, in order to exploit the kind of pathos he had achieved with the death of Nell.[6] It might be argued that his plan was not only strategic in the market place but psychologically conservative and regressive. The novelist, after all, felt at home with this kind of pathos, and the elaboration of Paul's death is suspiciously like a renewed indulgence in the fantasy of Charles Dickens as dead child. But in the novel Paul behaves more as an angel, even a threatening familiar of death, than as a transparent image of self-pity; and if the character originates in part from the fantasy, now it is employed primarily to frustrate the father and to sanctify the sister as a second familiar of death. The plan was well thought out, as seen in the letter to Forster of 25 July 1846, which accompanied the manuscript of the first number:

> I design to show Mr. D. with that one idea of the Son taking firmer and firmer possession of him, swelling and bloating his pride to a prodigious extent. As the boy begins to grow up, I shall show him quite impatient for his getting on, and urging his masters to set him great tasks, and the like. But the natural affection of the boy will turn towards the despised sister . . . and when he is ill, and when he is dying, I mean to make him turn always for refuge to the sister still, and keep the stern affection of the father at a distance. . . . The death of the boy is a death-blow, of course, to the father's schemes and cherished hopes; and "Dombey and Son," as Miss Tox will say at the end of the number, "is a Daughter after all." . . . From that time, I purpose changing his feeling of indifference and uneasiness towards his daughter into a positive hatred. For he will always remember how the boy had his arm round her neck when he was dying, and whispered to her, and would take things only from her hand, and never thought of him. . . . At the same time I shall change *her* feeling towards *him* for one of a greater desire to love him, and to be loved by him; engendered in her compassion for his loss, and her love for the dead boy whom, in his way, he loved so well too. So I mean to carry the story on, through all the branches and off-shoots and meanderings that come up; and through the decay and downfall of the house, and the bankruptcy of Dombey, and all the rest of it; when his only staff and treasure, and his unknown Good Genius always, will be this rejected daughter, who will come out better than any son at last, and whose love for him, when discovered and understood, will be his bitterest reproach. For the struggle with himself, which goes on in all such obstinate natures, will have ended then; and the sense of his injustice, which you may be sure has never quitted him, will have at last a gentler office than that of only making him more harshly unjust.[7]

Obviously Dickens has a firm idea of how he will treat this hero in an ambitious twenty-installment novel. Dombey's "struggle with himself" is bound to be psychological and will evolve and affect him over time. In practice, the novelist does not attempt to represent Dombey's thoughts, except on certain occasions when he does so by means of prophetic rather than insightful language. Nor is little Paul portrayed from the inside: Dickens magnifies rather than penetrates states of mind in the novel and gives to the boy's dedication to death and the grown man's estrangement mythic proportions.

That useful index of selfishness in this world, money, is carried over directly from *Chuzzlewit* to *Dombey,* but with the difference between an outburst of laughter and a sharp intake of breath. In the former novel Dickens satirizes money-selfishness in the clamoring of the Chuzzlewits after old Martin's fortune and the machinations of Pecksniff—cynically also in Scadder's Land Corporation, splendiferously in Tigg's Anglo-Bengalee establishment, and cruelly in the grasping of Jonas Chuzzlewit in his father's counting house. All of these forms and occasions of satire are highly effective, and the truth that was also to confront Mr. Dombey—that you can't take it with you—is demonstrated with stunning force on the body of old Anthony, who lived and died for money. No sooner is that corpse wrapped for burial than a famous colloquy takes place between the nurse and the undertaker on the power of money, and whether charges for death or for birth ought to come dearer. "Everything that money could do, was done," according to Mr. Mould in that novel. "And what can do more, Mrs. Gamp?" (19.322). This rhetorical question is thoroughly transformed in the sequel, where it emerges as an abrupt inquiry by the younger of the two Dombeys:

> "Papa! what's money?"
> The abrupt question had such immediate reference to the subject of Mr. Dombey's thoughts, that Mr. Dombey was quite disconcerted.
> "What is money, Paul?" he answered. "Money?"
> "Yes," said the child . . . "what is money?"
> Mr. Dombey was in a difficulty. He would have liked to give him some explanation involving the terms circulating-medium, currency, depreciation of currency, paper, bullion, rates of exchange, value of precious metals in the market, and so forth; but looking down at the little chair, and seeing what a long way down it was, he answered: "Gold, and silver, and copper. Guineas, shillings, halfpence. You know what they are?"
> "Oh yes, I know what they are," said Paul. "I don't mean that, Papa. I mean, what's money after all."

It is but one lesson in the novel-long education of a father. " 'What is money, Paul?' he *answered*"? Dickens captures perfectly the reversal of roles in the dialogue. After a little more prodding from the son, the father comes out with "Money, Paul, can do anything"—the same ground upon which Gamp and Mould have agreed to disagree in the previous novel and which little Paul is about to open up again in two senses.

> "Anything, Papa?"
> "Yes. Anything—almost," said Mr. Dombey.
> "Anything means everything, don't it, Papa?" asked his son: not observing, or possibly not understanding, the qualification.
> "It includes it: yes," said Mr. Dombey.
> "Why didn't money save me my Mama?" returned the child. "It isn't cruel, is it?"[8]

By such methods as these, which Philip Collins has likened to the colloquies with the Fool in *King Lear*,[9] Dickens has no difficulty in arguing the powerlessness of money, which Paul's death shortly thereafter conclusively demonstrates. Satire claims that money both is and is not powerful; pathos proves that it is not. After the first five numbers of *Dombey,* money simply no longer poses the issue of selfishness that it did in *Chuzzlewit*. Not money getting but pride and a rear-guard action against losing face are what occupy the hero from now on. And more than face, his very being and identity: since money is not the end of life, how can Dombey acknowledge what he fears and suspects, that the end is death? He has not really seen the last of his foolish child, for his daughter—his "unknown Good Genius always," according to Dickens's plan—will constantly remind him of Paul. He will not strive for money but against this female child, who is "powerful where he was powerless, and everything where he was nothing" (47.628).

The considerable success of Dickens in carrying out his plan depends on the objectivity that he is able to maintain in the narrative. *Dombey* does not exhibit nearly the wanton—and inspired—projection of *Chuzzlewit*. The novelist does not closely identify with any of the characters, not even little Paul, and consequently they are never in danger of collapsing into one another without his knowledge. On the contrary, he consciously manages the necessary connections. After the death of Paul, Dickens's memorandum to himself reads, "Great point of the No. to throw the interest of Paul, *at once on Florence*."[10] Once this transition is attended to, the remaining three-quarters of the novel gets under way with Dombey renewing his futile effort to replicate himself, by means of a second marriage. Since Dickens does not narrate his thoughts for the most part, we can only presume that the hero hopes to create yet another Paul Dombey by these means. But in proceeding to the marriage market at Leamington in the company of Major Bagstock, Dombey encounters on the railway platform the husband of Paul's former nurse, with a bit of crape in his cap as a sign of mourning for the dead child. Again Dombey is forced to realize that he never exclusively possessed his son, since even this contemptible engine stoker can mourn for him. The earlier reticence in narrating Dombey's thoughts pays off, by enabling the novelist suddenly to dramatize this invasion of the hero's privacy.

> So! from high to low, at home or abroad, from Florence in his great house to the coarse churl who was feeding the fire then smoking before them, every one set up some claim or other to share in his dead boy, and was a bidder against him! . . .
> To think of this presumptuous raker among coals and ashes going on before there, with his sign of mourning! To think that he dared to enter, even by a common show like that, into the trial and disappointment of a proud gentleman's secret heart! To think that this lost child, who was to have divided with him his riches, and his projects, and his power, and allied with whom he was to have shut out all the world as with a double door of gold, should have let in such a herd to insult him with their knowledge of his defeated hopes, and their boasts of claiming community of feeling with himself, so far removed: if not of having crept into the place wherein he would have lorded it, alone! (20.275)

The sensation of a herd come "to insult him with their knowledge of his defeated hopes" resembles the feelings that Dickens experienced in America, but the context is so different and the narrative so dramatic that these thoughts are objectively portrayed in the character.

Hitherto Dombey's subjectivity has been largely concealed by the narrative, but now it bursts forth as Dickens allegorizes the railway locomotive as "a type of the triumphant monster, Death" (20.275). Strictly speaking, that is, Dombey's thoughts have been disturbed and his journey spoiled by the encounter with Toodles on the platform; but Dickens amplifies these thoughts at once naturalistically, through the speed and noise of the train, and mythically, by punctuating each paragraph with the words "monster, Death!" The rhetorical tour de force is such that the journey's purpose—enabling the second marriage of Mr. Dombey—is overshadowed by death before it is actually made known to the reader. The failure of Dombey's second effort to replicate his own being is guaranteed in advance by the same force, death, that put an end to his first effort. But now this force drags the mature hero toward his end, remorselessly. If there is any regression, in the death of Paul, to the pitiful death that Dickens so often entertained, the death that threatens here is not pitiful at all. Again, the effect is that of objective realization of the thought, despite the extraordinary rhetoric. The allegory of destructive death will eventually be borne out in the death of Carker, by then the only remaining managerial and aggrandizing arm of Dombey and Son, beneath the wheels of a second locomotive at the end of the novel.

For all the astonishing course of Dombey's thoughts, the railway does deposit him in Leamington, where he meets the statuesque widow who "seemed with her own pride to defy her very self" (21.288). Though Edith Granger does not appear in Dickens's initial plan, it is worth noting that Forster introduces the ruling passion of the novel as that "of Mr. Dombey and Mr. Dombey's second wife."[11] The lady is something of a caricature, much more obviously torn between good and bad impulses than Dombey himself. That she is conscious of her self-hatred makes her more interesting to watch than he, but less plausible in her actions. Something of a defiant feminist,[12] she employs suicide tactics against a man who values only her appearance and her proven capacity to bear a male child (since deceased, like Paul). Edith was designed by Dickens to be Dombey's nemesis and her own. Not only would the marriage be childless, but her self-contempt would provide the cutting edge of his self-recognition. Finally, she would drag the tragic hero down into disgrace by becoming Carker's mistress. When Lord Jeffrey protested against this last development,[13] Dickens devised the strange contretemps in which the second Mrs. Dombey disgraces her husband by running away but denies Carker his "voluptuous compensation for past restraint" (55.736). Both characters, the manager and the woman who defeats him, have been mainly enlisted against Dombey's pride. Carker gives over his personal ambitions, honest and otherwise, in hopes of destroying Dombey; Edith surrenders her remaining self-respect, except where Carker is concerned, to the same purpose. They are swept away by antagonisms that the tragedy requires of them.

Dombey is undoubtedly a great man, with reason to be proud of his standing in the world. Whatever the limitations of his character, he must be granted the stature of a tragic hero—greater than those about him and great enough to fall. He is not a king or a nobleman, obviously, but the head of a famous merchant house in the City. Dickens, his author, was undeniably a great man also and famous as a writer. But Dickens had learned a good deal that was new to him about fame, in America. The sheer crowds that he attracted were new to him and were not the same thing as a vast readership. The experience made evident to him some of the limitations of fame: being famous, after all, meant being known by people one did not really want to know; it could swell one's pride without in the least satisfying particular and personal longings. Indiscriminate fame, showing no respect for Dickens's person or privacy, was more discomforting than anonymity; nor had fame made his plea for justice to authors any more palatable or persuasive. In some of these respects, renown was very little different from notoriety. Dickens was able to use what he had learned in conceiving of Dombey and the fall of that great man. He did not attribute to his hero, as in *Martin Chuzzlewit*, experiences that only a famous novelist could have had. But Dombey is not just anyone either, and at the turn of his fortunes, when Edith has eloped and he has driven out Florence, he is acutely conscious of what Dickens calls "the world."

> The world. What the world thinks of him, how it looks at him, what it sees in him, and what it says—this is the haunting demon of his mind. It is everywhere where he is; and, worse than that, it is everywhere where he is not. . . . and is always the busiest, he knows, when he has gone away. When he is shut up in his room at night, it is in his house, outside it, audible in footsteps on the pavement, visible in print upon the table, steaming to and fro on railroads and in ships; restless and busy everywhere, with nothing else but him. (51.682)

Note that the world, even in Dombey's time of defeat, is not equated with revilement. The force of opinion of which he is conscious is far more general than that, and it is not something he merely suffers but a potential motive to action. Just as Dickens resolved not to permit the crowd to get the better of him, or opponents to stop him from being "iron upon this theme" of international copyright, so Dombey's perception of the world stirs him to action once more. "Prying and tormenting as the world was, it did Mr. Dombey the service of nerving him to pursuit and revenge." Dickens saved his opinion of himself by coloring his quarrel with the Americans as an affair of honor; in *Dombey and Son*, however, he is critical of this motive throughout. Thus he continues to come down on Dombey's "exaggerated sense of personal importance" and his "jealous disposition to resent the least flaw in the ample recognition of his importance by others" (53.705).

The House of Dombey in the City is an allegory of the house of fame, and Dickens employs the second Mrs. Dombey and Carker the manager to pull it down. To a great extent, Edith's strong character and implausible actions have been dictated by the need to make her superior to Dombey—not morally superior but superior in experience of the world. "I am a woman . . . who, from her very childhood, has been shamed and steeled. I have been offered and rejected, put up and appraised, until my very soul has sickened." In her own eyes, we are to believe, she is a completely degraded person, like the prostitute Alice Marwood who shadows her and turns out to be her cousin. She has already been through it all; she has been defeated by the world and has become a free agent of sorts, prepared for a revenge that she knows in advance is meaningless. "Shamed and steeled," she has already endured the self-recognition that is in store for Dombey, and in this sense of anticipating the action of the novel, she is close to Dickens, who has invented her. "I stand alone in the world, remembering well what a hollow world it has been to me, and what a hollow part of it I have been myself. You know this, and you know that my fame with it is worthless to me" (54.724). The words are addressed, in fact, to Carker in Dijon, and Carker will bear the brunt of the fall that he has helped to bring about. In their implausible but powerful confrontation, the word "shame" is so freely bandied about by Edith that it sticks to Carker. His is an equivalent of the fall of the House of Dombey, displaced to France to make things a little less wretched at home. "Death upon the wing" comes after Carker at last. "Shame, disappointment, and discomfiture gnawed at his heart" (55.732, 737).

To be sure, Dombey is finally responsible for the fall of the house about a year later, after Florence has married and sailed away like Cordelia with the King of France. "The year was out, and the great House was down" (58.773); similarly, the Dombey household is emptied of its servants and furnishings, and the hero remains in darkness

and silence, free of the world at last. Only his sister, Mrs. Chick, is worried about him. She who chided the first Mrs. Dombey for not making an effort to live is now similarly concerned for Mr. Dombey. "How long is this to last! If my brother will not make an effort, Mrs. Pipchin, what is to become of him?" Mrs. Chick, remember, is a Dombey, and if her brother will not make an effort, "what is to be the end of it?" (59.791–793). The pretension to sheer will by a Dombey may also remind us a little of Dickens, who everyone agrees had an extraordinarily powerful will—but not sufficiently powerful to keep him alive indefinitely. The possible representations and glances at the author in *Dombey and Son* are typically self-critical. If they result from projection, then it is rarely uncritical projection. Thus the novel's control of its materials is justly celebrated.

VII

Dombey as King Lear

*I*n defending against Taine's criticism, that Dombey "becomes the best of fathers, and spoils a fine novel," Kathleen Tillotson takes note of "another proud father and banished daughter, Lear and Cordelia."[1] It is an exaggeration in any case to say that Dombey becomes the best of fathers, and unmistakably true that the reconciliation of father and daughter, as well as much else in the novel, is based on *King Lear*. In his darkest moment Dombey contemplates suicide—more like Gloucester in the play—when Florence returns "asking *his* forgiveness" (59.801). The emphasis is Dickens's but, before that, Shakespeare's: both stress the constancy of the wronged daughter, whose loving ministration and forgiveness bring some peace to a defeated father.

When Tillotson observes, in contradistinction to *Chuzzlewit,* that "the absurd" in *Dombey* "is on the side of the angels" and that certain of the foolish characters, "by their natures and their share in the action, supply continuous moral comment on the evil represented in Mr. Dombey," she inadvertently calls attention to another of the novel's debts to Shakespeare. Dickens adhered closely to the paradox of *King Lear* that every loyal and true character is either named a fool or behaves like one, whether it be Cordelia, the Fool himself, Gloucester, Edgar, Albany, or Kent. We have to remember that since the early seventeenth century *King Lear* had not appeared on the English stage as a tragedy, or as anything like Shakespeare's play, until the production by Dickens's friend Macready in 1838. During this long interval the theater knew only Nahum Tate's version of 1681, which made Cordelia and Edgar lovers, provided a happy ending, and omitted the Fool altogether. Macready restored Shakespeare's play and revived the Fool (a move that was made easier somehow by casting an actress in the part). Whenever Dickens required an exalted test of love and truth in his fiction, he tended to favor the Cordelia model of loyalty to a difficult father, but *Dombey and Son* is a special case.[2] Most of the important configurations of characters in the novel bear some relation to the play, beginning with the perturbed estrangement of the hero from his own immediate family, which has its source in the failure of male inheritance. (Though we are scarcely in danger of forgetting the irony of Dickens's title, we sometimes overlook the ancient irony that Lear has no sons.) Dickens does not shirk the question of sexuality as a means to acquiring male progeny. He is more decorous about such matters than Shakespeare, as his audience demanded, but he adopts from the play a crass abandonment to sexuality by others that is opposed to the hero's failure in it, as well as a melodramatic bafflement of this late turn in the action. It is true that Carker is much less amused by his situation than Edmund, but like Edmund he has an essentially good brother, John Carker, who suffers in disgrace beneath his control and contempt and whose goodness is finally rewarded.

The strong impression of *King Lear* upon Dickens's fiction first became apparent in *The Old Curiosity Shop*,[3] begun two years after Macready's revival of the tragedy and three years after Mary Hogarth's death. The combination of these two events was a potent one, resulting in the most morbid of Dickens's novels and his widespread reputation for pathos. The main action, the death of little Nell, has remained to this day more famous than the title of the novel. Everywhere Nell and her grandfather travel on their pilgrimage—the influence of Bunyan is also apparent—she is attracted to the dying and the dead, and she eventually predeceases the old man. That object of Nell's love is helpless from the beginning, and the action of the novel therefore like a deadly prolongation of the relation of Lear and Cordelia at the end of Shakespeare's play. Despite the premature reversal of the roles of parent and child, Dickens is in some respects more faithful to Shakespeare than are other adapters of the play. He does manage to convey a sense of loss and recognition of love in the old man at the last.[4] Still, *The Old Curiosity*

Shop has mostly to do with Nell, who is surrounded in the novel by no fewer than five old men—even the notorious Quilp is introduced as "elderly." Not only is her grandfather weak and dependent throughout, but Dickens does not even bother to give him a name. *Dombey and Son* shows a marked difference in this respect, for Mr. Dombey is a hero of name and substance. The novel fully engages the prospect of death for a mature individual, and not merely the pathos of death in the very young or of the old lingering too long.

In *The Old Curiosity Shop* Dickens concentrated on the pathos of the ending of *King Lear*. In *Dombey and Son* he concentrated on the father's motive for the rejection of his daughter. Florence, who is six years old at the birth of her brother and death of her mother, can be said to be ignored and rejected from the beginning, and Dickens is at great pains to implicate Dombey's overweening desire for the continuance of the firm of Dombey and Son—which is to say, of himself. When Paul dies, the father's neglect of the daughter turns to hatred: her survival rubs in his loss and nags at his guilt. The psychology of their relation is impressively handled by Dickens, who is more often complimented for his unconscious brilliance in this line than for his deliberate insights. The breaking point comes after Mr. Dombey's second marriage, which further exacerbates his jealousy of his daughter's love. Then he rejects her conclusively—with a blow to the face—and causes her to flee from the house, in the chapter entitled "The Thunderbolt" (chapter 47).

In *King Lear* the rejection occurs in the first scene, when Cordelia opposes love and truth to flattery and immediately suffers the consequences. But Dickens develops and postpones the final rejection of his Cordelia until, in "The Thunderbolt," he can superimpose this action upon Lear's own ejection out of doors by his other children, in the third act of the play. Florence, in effect, must absorb the feelings of Lear on the heath—hence the title of this chapter—as well as the implicit suffering of her father. Her recognition of Dombey's cruelty, a recognition that is now explicit, so far substitutes for his self-recognition. By making her conclusive rejection coincide also with Edith's elopement, Dickens is able to recapitulate the fierce condemnation of female sexuality that disturbs Lear's consciousness from the moment he is opposed. As John Butt and Kathleen Tillotson remark, "the second marriage is the real storm-centre of the novel,"[5] and when Dombey strikes Florence, "he told her what Edith was, and bade her follow her, since they had always been in league." This is as far as Dickens is willing to go in characterizing the sexual aspect of his hero's feelings, but the novel has already implicitly called Edith a whore, through her prostituting herself in the marriage market and by comparison to Alice Marwood. And now Florence, the chapter powerfully concludes, "was in the streets" (47.637). No one acquainted with Victorian euphemisms can mistake what it means for a homeless girl to be in the streets. Such compression may make it seem that Dickens is merely toying with Shakespeare, but in fact the overlaying of scenes from *King Lear* in this chapter involves even the social themes of the novel.

Dombey and Son has often been praised for its social consciousness. Dickens this time addresses the ills of society as a whole, and not merely those moral failings that seemingly could be put right by doses of indignation, laughter, or scorn. The novel in part reflects the sanitary movement of early Victorian England, and especially the belief that at least some moral failings are the result of physical causes. The concern for public health in the eighteen-forties helped inculcate the modern conviction that many people cannot be held responsible, as individuals, for the course of their lives. That some immorality as well as illness was due to wretched living conditions was especially apparent in large cities, where the life of one person could infect the rest. In *Dombey* the best-known passage on these matters—almost always quoted out of context by those interested in Dickens as a social historian—is also from the chapter called "The Thunderbolt." The famous paragraph beginning "Oh for a good spirit who would take the house-tops off" points to the connection of moral and physical ills in the modern city, "from the thick and sullen air where Vice and Fever propagate together, raining the tremendous social retributions which are ever pouring down." The argument differs markedly from the ironic reduction of the human family at the opening of *Chuzzlewit,* for here the novelist calls for reforms that would unite and display the strengths of that family. If people would only see the interconnected causes of things, they "would then apply themselves, like creatures of one common origin, owning one duty to the Father of one family, and tending to one common end, to make the world a better place!"(47.620).

As long as one has a general feeling for the urban history of the time, this social message by itself does not pose difficult problems of interpretation. Though the father deferred to is God, and neither a Chuzzlewit nor a Dombey, the message on the whole is not religious. But in point of fact the sequence of the arguments in the surrounding text is one of the most bewildering in all of Dickens, and the raining down of "tremendous social retributions" is not fully explicable without reference to *King Lear*, whose constant appeal from microcosm to macrocosm is reflected here in the shift from discussion of Dombey's case to the discussion of society, and from Dombey to "the Father of one family." The discursive portion of the chapter begins, not with the city and the sanitary conditions that are its main subject, but with the question, "Was Mr. Dombey's master-vice, that ruled him so inexorably, an unnatural characteristic?" The master vice is his pride, with its concomitant blindness and stubbornness, and the occasion of the question, the irreducible conflict with the second Mrs. Dombey. The answer to the question, which Dickens spells out for five paragraphs, is that "it might be worth while, sometimes, to inquire what Nature is, and how men work to change her, and whether, in the enforced distortions so produced, it is not natural to be unnatural" (47.619). This study of nature and the unnatural, in the chapter that tells of the break with Florence and with Edith, owes its inspiration to *King Lear* and especially to the climactic scenes on the heath, with their stress on uncovering and seeing through to the condition of humanity.

> Poor naked wretches, whereso'er you are,
> That bide the pelting of this pitiless storm,
> How shall your houseless heads and unfed sides,
> Your loop'd and winnow'd raggedness, defend you
> From seasons such as these? O, I have ta'en
> Too little care of this! Take physic, Pomp,
> Expose thyself to feel what wretches feel,
> That thou mayst shake the superflux to them,
> And show the heavens more just.[6]

The impress of Shakespeare explains the play on "natural" as between what is and what ought to be, the reconstitution of a superhuman Nature however vaguely defined, the emphasis on seeing and judging humanity truthfully, and the transition from personal suffering to social justice.

In Shakespeare's tragedy both Lear and the bastard Edmund invoke the goddess Nature. On the one hand "natural" refers to everything in the world as we know it, and on the other hand—especially in the negation "unnatural"—the word refers to moral conclusions about the kinds of behavior regarded as viable in the community. Meanings of the first kind are used to lever meanings of the second into positions of unassailability. Whereas Edmund boasts of his freedom from the "custom" of human convention, Lear deliberately confuses nature with bonds of filial gratitude and rightful authority. The king's most blistering charges of unnatural behavior are directed at his daughters, especially at Goneril and Regan, whose defiance of him is material and self-centered. Those two, whom he has engendered, he prays Nature will ungender. "Is there any cause in nature," he asks in the mock trial of Goneril and Regan, "that make these hard hearts?" (III.vi.77–78). In the novel, which excises the two unnatural daughters from the action, Dickens turns this charge around to ask whether his hero's behavior, unnatural in the moral sense, may not be defended on the grounds that it is naturally caused—analogous to the vices of people who dwell in urban squalor. *His* recognition, the novelist's, becomes parallel to Lear's growing awareness that morally unnatural conduct cannot be judged apart from nature, and he asks the reader to share in this recognition as preparation for witnessing Dombey's most degrading act.

> Alas! are there so few things in the world about us, most unnatural, and yet most natural in being so! Hear the magistrate or judge admonish the unnatural outcasts of society; unnatural in brutal habits, unnatural in want of decency, unnatural in losing and confounding all distinctions between good and evil; unnatural in ignorance, in vice, in recklessness, in contumacy, in mind, in looks, in everything. But follow the good clergyman or doctor, who, with his life imperilled at every breath he draws, goes down into their dens . . . Look round upon the world of odious sights . . . Breathe the polluted air . . . And then, calling up some ghastly child, with stunted form and wicked face, hold forth on its unnatural sinfulness, and lament its being, so early, far away from Heaven—but think a little of its having been conceived, and born, and bred, in Hell! (47.619)

The argument is inspired by Lear's growing distrust, by the fourth act of the play, of all judging and faultfinding. "Plate sin with gold, / And the strong lance of justice hurtless breaks; / Arm it in rags, a pigmy's straw does pierce it. / None does offend, none, I say none" (IV.vi.165–168). If Shakespeare's dialogue is sententious and paradoxical, the novelist's discourse is moral and scientific. But note how the language of science glides into imprecations more typical of Lear and into themes of breeding and generation:

> Those who study the physical sciences, and bring them to bear on the health of Man, tell us that if the noxious particles that rise from vitiated air, were palpable to the sight, we should see them lowering in a dense black cloud above such haunts, and rolling slowly on to corrupt the better portions of a town. But if the moral pestilence that rises with them, and, in the eternal laws of outraged Nature, is inseparable from them, could be made discernible too, how terrible the revelation! . . . Then should we stand appalled to know, that where we generate disease to strike our children down and entail itself on unborn generations, there also we breed, by the same certain process, infancy that knows no innocence, youth without modesty or shame, maturity that is mature in nothing but in suffering and guilt, blasted old age that is a scandal on the form we bear. Unnatural humanity! (47.619–620)

The translation by Lear and by Gloucester of personal shock and suffering, the realization of their own ignorance and the capacity of evil in their children, into the perception of a need for some sort of distributive justice is one of the most difficult conclusions for Shakespeare's audience to grasp, expressed as it is only fitfully and variously in the many modes of performance. Yet Dickens managed to carry away from Macready's production of *King Lear* an argument that, while it is not fully persuasive with respect to Dombey, signaled a turning of his own perception of the world that characterizes all of his subsequent work and became the triumphant means of creating *Bleak House*. The events of his life, including disillusionment with America, were such as to take him in the direction of this social vision of England, but Shakespeare prepared him "for rousing some who never have looked out upon the world of human life around them, to a knowledge of their own relation to it, and for making them acquainted with a perversion of nature in their own contracted sympathies and estimates" (47.620). Neither writer neglected the demythologizing of nature that began as early as the sixteenth century: Shakespeare made Edmund's view of the universe sufficiently lively that many are taken in by him for a while; Dickens allowed Carker's taste and abilities to speak a little in his favor and gave approving notice on the whole to the arrival of the railway and the changes in Stagg's Gardens. These powerful writers cannot and will not oppose change, but at the same time they insist on continuity with the past by reasserting the bonds of family.[7]

Those who believe that *King Lear* is about the dangerous practice of dividing kingdoms, or the sacredness of kingship in Jacobean England, must miss altogether the relevance of the play to *Dombey and Son*. The play in a larger sense is about the surrender of authority by any peron accustomed to it, who thereupon depends implicitly on the gratitude of children and former dependents. In Lear's own words,

> 'tis our fast intent
> To shake all cares and business from our age,
> Conferring them on younger strengths, while we
> Unburthen'd crawl toward death.   (I.i.38–41)

It is fruitless to try to isolate the hero's tragic flaw in the first scene. His trouble is that he is old and that his authority, like that of most people, does not reach to the very end of his days. He has a temper, he has lost some power of judgment, but he has no more alternative than anyone else to the prospect of giving up everything he has. Nor can his children return anything to him, the dying person, except care and gratitude. So the testimony of love that he demands is a ritual both empty and full, according to its sincerity, because life itself is now emptying of everything but the consciousness of relations that comprise it. In a recent essay on *King Lear*, Thomas McFarland has argued well why it is important to see that the hero behaves "like a father and not like a king when he divides his kingdom." The principal effect of the subplot that Shakespeare introduced, of Gloucester and his sons, is to generalize on this theme: "the motifs of 'very verge' and 'extreme verge,' though emphasized by the aged fathers, actually pertain to all the characters and in truth to all human existence," and "it is Lear's definition as father that connects him with younger life and its attendant hope."[8] This understanding of the play helps immeasurably to explain its importance for the nineteenth-century novelist. Dombey is another father seemingly content with ritual obeisance but in need of something more than this from the young, as Dickens movingly demonstrates. At stake is nothing less than proof that his life has some value. He is not old, like Lear, but Dickens confronts him with death in the first number and again, with renewed force, in the death of Paul.

On the other hand, Dickens composes his tragedy around a much more conventionally flawed hero than Shakespeare's. Dombey is patently more sinning than sinned against, and in "The Thunderbolt" the nature of his unnaturalness is put in question, not his children's ingratitude. In this same climactic chapter, the only recognition that takes place is Florence's, as she rather than the parent is turned out of doors: "she saw him murdering that fond idea to which she had held in spite of him. She saw his cruelty, neglect, and hatred, dominant above it, and stamping it down. She saw that she had no father upon earth, and ran out, orphaned, from his house" (47.637). It is Florence's love that transcends this moment of truth, and her loyalty never wavers.

A striking difference between the novel and *King Lear* is this reversal of the relative weight given to father and daughter in the drama. Dickens did not fail this time, as in *The Old Curiosity Shop,* to give substance to his Lear, but the leading character of *Dombey and Son* may still be the daughter after all, as the title secretly intimates. For this construction of the story, he followed a critical tendency to shift the interest to Cordelia that was evident in Nahum Tate's adaptation of *King Lear* and still dominant in nineteenth-century readings of Shakespeare's text. Dickens's contemporary Victor Hugo may be cited as an extreme example of this position. "The father is the pretext for the daughter," Hugo wrote. "That admirable human creature, Lear, serves as a support to this ineffable divine creation, Cordelia. All that chaos of crimes, vices, manias, and miseries finds its justification in this shining vision of virtue."[9] Even A. C. Bradley, whose lectures brilliantly summarize the century's devotion to character in Shakespeare, testifies to the ascendency of Cordelia. Bradley carefully points out that she appears in only four scenes and "speaks—it is hard to believe it—scarcely more than a hundred lines," yet so successful is her characterization that "perhaps it is not too fanciful" to compare it with the opposite technique employed by Shakespeare for Hamlet. "No one hesitates to enlarge upon Hamlet, who speaks of himself so much; but to use many words about Cordelia seems to be a kind of impiety." This appreciation of the heroine, though more thoughtfully arrived at, is fairly close to Hugo's deification of her. Bradley tells of her "higher nature" than that of other Shakespearean heroines, and how her allegiance to truth becomes nothing less than "adorable in a nature so loving as Cordelia's."

But with this reverence or worship is combined in the reader's mind a passion of championship, of pity, even of protecting pity. She is so deeply wronged, and she appears, for all her strength, so defenceless. We think of her as unable to speak for herself. We think of her as quite young, and as slight and small. . . . Even her love for her father must have been mingled with pain and anxiety. She must early have learned to school and repress emotion. She never knew the bliss of young love: there is no trace of such love for the King of France. . . . We have to thank the poet for passing lightly over the circumstances of her death. We do not think of them. Her image comes before us calm and bright and still.[10]

Bradley's extrapolations from the text of Shakespeare obviously resemble what Dickens has done with Cordelia in imagining Florence Dombey, as well as the characters he would subsequently invent for Agnes Wickfield and Amy Dorrit.

Shakespeare might have been surprised at the pity expended on Cordelia's life before the action of the play and the anesthetizing of her cruel death. Despite the ideas of forgiveness and redemption entertained in the closing acts of *King Lear,* the playwright does not treat Cordelia as an angel or goddess of death. In the most cruel scene of all, Lear avows that if she could still live, it would "redeem all sorrows / That ever I have felt" (V.iii. 267–268). On one occasion, as Florence daydreams about her alienation from her father, Dickens is obviously faithful to this vision. She wonders, in typically Dickensian fashion, what would happen if she were dying and her father said to her, "Dear Florence, live for me, and we will love each other as we might have done, and be as happy as we might have been these many years!" She would embrace him with the words, "It is too late for anything but this; I never could be happier, dear father!" And then she would die (24.340). But Dickens goes much further than this reading of Shakespeare elsewhere in the novel. Florence watches over Dombey, "his unknown Good Genius always," as the plan for the novel demanded, but increasingly it becomes evident that she watches as a saving angel, contesting for him with that other power, "the remorseless monster, Death." Even as the railway rings in Dombey's ears its changes on the theme of death, "a face" accompanies him on his journey, which is the face of Florence and "a trouble to him" (20.277). Much later, after Dombey's fall from his horse, Florence watches over him in his sleep, in another chapter notable for the narrator's prophetic refrains—"Awake, unkind father! Awake, now, sullen man! The time is flitting by; the hour is coming with an angry tread. Awake!" By now the implication is unmistakable that Dombey must embrace Florence before he dies, and not when he wakes in the everyday sense of that word: "let him look for that slight figure when he wakes, and find it near him when the hour is come!" (43.583–584). In her final return to him in the dark house, after the fall of the House of Dombey, this reconciliation is achieved. If we ask why the reconciliation warrants such apocalyptic pronouncements, it is because Florence has been imbued with powers deriving from the deaths of her mother and little Paul. She can now prepare the hero for death, like Agnes pointing upward in Dickens's next novel.[11]

"What is the concept of love in *Dombey and Son?*" Hillis Miller has asked, and replied to his own question by pointing to "an authentic religious motif in the novel, the apprehension of a transcendent spirit, present in nature and reached through death, but apparently unattainable in this world." This love he reads primarily in "the sea of death" upon which the younger Paul is cast adrift, or "the authentic symbol of a nonhuman power whose chief characteristics are reconciliation and continuity."[12] The force of "authentic" in these formulations remains uncertain, because Miller attaches it to the symbol rather than to the force of love or death. Such metaphysical readings have been offered for *King Lear* in the same spirit, though they are not finally necessary for comprehending the tragedy in full and may even detract from the care that Shakespeare gave to the pre-Christian setting of the old story.[13] The rhetoric of *Dombey and Son* and the strategic placement of the deaths of Paul and his mother support Miller's answer to his question well enough; he might have added in evidence the remarkable demonic powers of Florence, which are the invention of a nineteenth-century mythography. It is the reconstruction of *King Lear* that gives us a glimpse of how these powers are supposed to operate. Freud, it may be remembered, was also one of those men of the nineteenth century who found Cordelia a more formidable figure than Lear. Like Dickens and Hugo, he saw something mainly maternal in this daughter, and from this quality he deduced her special powers over death. Though Freud of course did not believe in these powers, he went to extraordinary lengths to discover them: in recalling the final moments of *King Lear,* "one of the culminating points of tragedy in modern drama," he boldly reversed the original stage direction and asked his readers to imagine Cordelia bearing Lear's body in *her* arms, "like the Valkyrie" bearing heroes from the battlefield.

We might argue that what is represented here are the three inevitable relations that a man has with a woman—the woman who bears him, the woman who is his mate and the woman who destroys him; or that they are the three forms taken by the figure of the mother in the course of a man's life—the mother herself, the beloved one who is chosen after her pattern, and lastly the Mother Earth who receives him once more. But it is in vain that an old man yearns for the love of woman as he had it first from his mother; the third of the Fates alone, the silent Goddess of Death, will take him into her arms.[14]

Whether this scenario arises from a concept of love or of death, it has unquestionably been invented by male mythographers to serve male fears and defenses. Freud's own irony is peculiarly mixed, half deliberate and half wishful: it is in vain that one hopes for anything but death, he concludes, thereby dissociating himself from the palliative that he, and not Shakespeare, has imposed on the end of the play.

Among the great Victorian novelists, Dickens was seldom behind-hand in compressing "the three forms taken by the figure of the mother" into a single idealized heroine. Together with the roles that Freud enumerates, he included the even more versatile relation of "sister," popular with novelists since Richardson as a hedge against too apparent sexual expectations. In *Dombey and Son* he goes further than anywhere else in depicting the actual hostility of the male to the female eidolon he has created. He can manage this demonstration precisely because Florence is not the wife or mother of Dombey, but a putatively powerless daughter—and he can draw upon Lear's awakened hostility to Goneril and Regan. Because Dickens is critical of Dombey, with a more sustained criticism than that directed against any other male character in his fiction, his mythography has a depth to it that is quite astounding. From a feminist perspective, which this sustained criticism invites and Edith Dombey helps to enforce, the pride of Dombey is essentially his maleness, very much on the defensive against women. Simone de Beauvoir, fully alert to the apprehension of death and the compression of female roles, can usefully be cited on the nature of this pride, or the consciousness of Mr. Dombey as Dickens presents it:

what man cherishes and detests first of all in woman—loved one or mother— is the fixed image of his animal destiny; it is the life that is necessary to his existence but that condemns him to the finite and to death. From the day of his birth man begins to die: this is the truth incarnated in the

Mother. In procreation he speaks for the species against himself: he learns this in his wife's embrace; in excitement and pleasure, even before he has engendered, he forgets his unique ego. Although he endeavors to distinguish mother and wife, he gets from both a witness to one thing only: his mortal state. He wishes to venerate his mother and love his mistress; at the same time he rebels against them in disgust and fear.[15]

It may be objected that this fear of death, projected on mother and wife, does not explain Dombey's hostility to his daughter. But the evidence in the novel of Florence's association with death is overwhelming, and her innocence of sex and generation as a child make resistance to her simply wicked. Dickens is a feminist only to the extent that he holds Dombey up to scorn. Essentially, his procedure in the novel is to condemn his hero for not realizing a myth that he wishes to embrace, the myth of women who possess such powers without any threatening aspect. His special heroines are ambiguously "little mothers"—in the phrase that Chesterton borrowed from *Little Dorrit*.[16] He does not finally believe in the divinity of little mothers any more than Freud believes in goddesses, but he wishes to believe and exhorts his readers to join his attack against Dombey's unbelief and against Death. Shakespeare is a powerful authority for Dickens in this undertaking, but like Tate the novelist prefers his Cordelia to be a virgin, like Bradley he thinks of her as young and small and pitiable, and like Hugo he finds her loyalty to her father divine.

As Simone de Beauvoir wryly observes, "on the day she can reproduce, woman becomes impure."[17] Not surprisingly, Dombey's hostility is concentrated against Florence in the years of puberty and after. She is thirteen when Paul dies and almost seventeen when "the change from childhood to womanhood" is complete. At this important juncture— it is "The Thunderbolt" chapter once again—Dickens shows the father's hostility reflected in the daughter's consciousness. Not only does he fear her power, but perhaps rightly so, since she loves him now by thinking of him as dead, "as some dear one who had been, or who might have been." She ominously associates him with the memory of her mother and of little Paul, and no longer thinks of him as one of the living. "Whether it was that he was dead to her . . . she could not have told; but the father whom she loved began to be a vague and dreamy idea to her" (47.621). In the father's mind, at the end of this chapter, the daughter is associated with the sexually charged figure of

Edith. When Florence finds herself in the streets, however, she does not become a prostitute. Through Captain Cuttle she finds Walter Gay instead, who has returned to London the same day and whom she shortly thereafter marries. The coincidences are carefully thought out—we know that the novelist went back over his narrative to check Florence's age[18]—and the sexual significance of this turning lies not very far from the surface. Acceptance of his fate cannot be easy for Dombey, but for the outcome of his tragedy Dickens adopts something like the solution of Shakespeare's romances: the death implicit in procreation can be assuaged by focusing on the younger generation, as children become parents in their turn. When Florence eventually returns, she will be able to say, "Papa, love, I am a mother," and, "My little child was born at sea, Papa" (59.802). Then can he safely kiss her on the lips and pray out loud for forgiveness, and she can care for him as an old but live person.

Thus Dickens proffers a highly elaborated but basically simple myth of human—or at least male—existence, and no longer an introspective vision relieved by hilarity and multiple projection, as in *Chuzzlewit*. But it is important to acknowledge how heavily both the personal and the social claims of this myth depend on the exaggerated powers of the heroine, who is enlisted to save personal identity and to make tolerable the course of history. Readers have been right to see *Dombey* as the first of Dickens's novels about Victorian society as a whole. In this novel, according to Steven Marcus, "Dickens undertakes a comprehensive, unified presentation of social life by depicting how an abstract principle conditions all experience. That principle is change." Moreover, "there is no ambiguity about Dickens's attitude toward social change, nor any doubt about his being in favor of it."[19] The principle does not make Dickens a Marxist; it makes him, at least at this level of generality, a man of the nineteenth and twentieth centuries like nearly every other. Still, the acceptance of change is only half the story of *Dombey and Son*—which is about a daughter after all. The burden of Dombey's and the world's change falls heavily on Florence.[20] Without the strong counterpresence of the infinitely loving and patient heroine, it is as doubtful that Dickens would be comfortable with change as that Dombey would be comfortable with death. The novelist prepares the hero for the daughter's return in terms such as these: "He thought of her, as she had been that night when he and his bride came home. He thought of her as she had been, in all the home-events of the abandoned house. He thought, now, that of all around him, she alone had never changed. . . . she alone had turned the same mild gentle look upon him always." And when she does return, the narrator pronounces, "Unchanged still. Of all the world, unchanged" (59.796, 801). The abridgment of the syntax welds Dombey's recognition to Dickens's assertion. Only this unchanging female principle makes death and history acceptable.

Marcus observes that the novel is "almost obsessed" with change and time, and again his reading is very sensitive on this point. The obsessive involvement with the theme results in part from the Condition of England, the social problems that beset the eighteen-forties. More narrowly, it results from the condition of Dickens, the self-questioning of his identity between the writing of *Barnaby Rudge* and of *Dombey and Son*. The need for a constructive sense of personal identity is just as apparent in the Christmas books Dickens undertook during the writing of *Chuzzlewit* and completed after *Dombey*. The two most successful of those stories also engage with social issues, though Scrooge in *A Christmas Carol* and Trotty Veck in *The Chimes* dream of the course of events to which their present thoughts are committed, and the realities to which they awake, in chastened moods, are not so wretched after all. The device allows the protagonists to lead two lives, in effect, and to make a choice of identities. "Scrooge was better than his word," in a much loved line, "and to Tiny Tim, who did NOT die, he was a second father." Though these stories are deeply personal in origin, their messages about identity over time are public in the end. "I will live in the Past, the Present, and the Future!" as Scrooge decides in stave 5 of the *Carol;* or as Trotty Veck exclaims in the fourth quarter of *The Chimes*, another father-daughter story, "I know that our inheritance is held in store for us by Time. I know there is a sea of Time to rise one day, before which all who wrong or oppress us will be swept away like leaves. . . . I have learnt if from the creature dearest to my heart. I clasp her in my arms again."[21] The last of the Christmas books, though lacking the humor and satiric thrust of the first two, is biographically and psychologically the most revealing. Appropriately called *The Haunted Man,* the story is prototypic of psychoanalysis, for in it Dickens studiously argues that unpleasant memories cannot and should not be repressed indefinitely and must be dealt with in the present—advice that he puts into practice in his abortive autobiography and in *David Copperfield*.

In recovering from the mild depression and uncertainty of these years,

Dickens also recovered his audience. Of course everything is relative: many novelists then and now would be content enough with the initial sales of *Chuzzlewit*. Nevertheless *Dombey* pleased readers better, and Lord Jeffrey was delighted with Tiny Tim, whom he thought as charming as little Nell:

> And is not this better than caricaturing American knaveries, or lavishing your great gifts of fancy and observation on Pecksniffs, Dodgers, Baileys, and Moulds. Nor is this a mere crochet of mine, for nine-tenths of your readers, I am convinced, are of the same opinion; and accordingly, I prophesy that you will sell three times as many of this moral and pathetic Carol as of your grotesque and fantastical Chuzzlewits.[22]

By singling out the *Carol* from efforts that Dickens himself referred to as his *"Chuzzlewit* agonies," Jeffrey perceives a hopeful turning, the same that Forster would describe retrospectively as "the turning point" of the novelist's career. But Dickens cannot be reduced to the creature of his readers or of his friends: however much he valued both, he valued *Chuzzlewit* also and expected it to sustain his reputation "in the minds of thinking men." The personal message of *A Christmas Carol* was the caution against selfishness, again, and the need to live in "the Past, the Present, and the Future." In *Dombey* he committed himself wholeheartedly to such personal integration and its social responsibilities: he modeled the novel on the tragedy of Shakespeare that moved him most deeply, because tragedy is a means for taking us out of ourselves and enforcing recognition at the same time. This commitment he prepared for by uncertainty and delay—a moratorium that enabled reflection, rather than an involuntary trauma or a decisive turning point in his life.

Irony and comedy, and a little awkward romance, were Dickens's first literary recourse in this period: the free associations and chaotic borrowings of *Chuzzlewit* were anti-formative of the career for which *Dombey* was formative. The first of these novels manifestly extended the range of his humor; the second demonstrated a maturity that is not necessarily superior as art. To a great extent the control he exerted over *Dombey*, and indirectly over his own sense of his past, present, and future, depended on indulging a myth of a female "other"—or little mother—to support the hero against the ultimate epoch of life, which is death. In *Chuzzlewit* the heroine was a cipher, a presence that could only be deduced from the multiple affective lines of the plot or from the ghostly presence of Mary Hogarth in the author's life. But in *Dombey* she has become an article of faith, and though Dickens views his hero with implicit self-criticism, in respect to the powers of such heroines he is uncritical.

A career would become the subject of the next novel, *David Copperfield*. The wisdom of its heroine, Agnes Wickfield, would be deliberately cultivated by the novelist-hero, her powers over death seconded by powers over writing itself. The hero would only gradually allow himself to believe that she could be his partner in marriage—if he wished and wished, as in a fairy tale. The autobiographical novel thus served as a personal myth—if that is not a contradiction in terms—for Dickens. *Martin Chuzzlewit* affords the dodging and disarming sense of discovery of myths that are mocked; *Dombey and Son* and *David Copperfield* have the strengths and weaknesses of myths that are taken seriously.

VIII

A Novelist's Novelist

*T*he impress of *King Lear* upon Dickens's fiction can be traced well beyond the writing of *Dombey and Son*. It can be argued that *Little Dorrit* was to be his most deeply felt response to the play and, because of its fine ironic setting in the Marshalsea Prison, the greatest romantic interpretation of all—superior, let us say, to the opera that Verdi was never able to base directly on Shakespeare's *Lear* but adopted, instead, from the grotesque version of the story in Hugo's *Le Roi s'amuse*.[1] The project of *Little Dorrit* was to be less straightforward than that of *Dombey* and not finally tragic. Rather, Dickens would superimpose upon his great Lear figure, the Father of the Marshalsea and the father of Little Dorrit, his middle-aged hero and husband of Little Dorrit—a project so ambitious that it is scarcely more than hinted at by David Copperfield's replacement of the father in Agnes Wickfield's life.[2] In *Little Dorrit*, too, the Cordelia figure would come decisively into the foreground, in the title as well as the action of the novel. Dickens, in fact, cannot be said ever to have completed the study of *King Lear* inspired by Macready's production of 1838. His interest in pursuing the story was still strong in *A Tale of Two Cities*, in the relation of Lucy and Dr. Manette. A question worth pondering is why the novelist passed by, or occasionally made fun of, *Hamlet,* the play most widely regarded in the nineteenth century as Shakespeare's greatest, and responded so fully to *Lear,* the play that has dominated the canon and tried our consciences

104

in the second half of the twentieth century. It seems possible to conclude that Dickens was more concerned throughout his writings with the collapse of authority through approaching death, imagined from the point of view of the dying, than with a restoration of power consumed by mourning for the dead. He was, I believe, prematurely concerned with his own death.

In *David Copperfield* the novelist's personal history superintends, where it does not supplant altogether, his literary sources. This novel was to become, as Dickens wrote in the 1867 preface, the "favourite child" among his works. The substance of the first fourteen chapters was autobiographical, and the hero's chosen career, in the remainder of the novel, the same as that of his author. Where previous literature plays a part, it is a smaller part than in *Martin Chuzzlewit* and *Dombey and Son* and it is lesser literature: novels and fairy tales rather than epic and tragedy. Everything literary in *Copperfield* is quite as fine but less portentous—less meditated and less parodied—than in the previous two works. Because the matter of the novel was autobiographical, other literature was less called upon for its composition. Yet, as we have seen, Dickens's previous aping of *Paradise Lost* and prolonged contemplation of *King Lear* prepared him to write his own story. Beating up on selfishness and coming down on pride enabled him to come to grips with Charles the First at last.

Since the earliest memories of David Copperfield disturbingly feature the remarriage of his mother, this personal history would seem to offer an obvious opportunity for playing off *Hamlet*. And indeed there are allusions to *Hamlet* in the novel, but all of a very trivial sort. Thus a semblance of "the Ghost in Hamlet" appears in the first scene,[3] but only in the person of Mr. Chillip, the doctor attending Copperfield's birth. In the next important scene, a Claudius appears in the person of Mr. Murdstone, who introduces himself by declaring David to be "a more highly privileged little fellow than a monarch" (2.15). Something is made, in fact, by Murdstone and his friends of his rivalry for intimacy with the pretty woman who is David's mother, but this rivalry is not very significantly based on Shakespeare. Its basis is life and, as Sylvia Manning has pointed out, the timing of David's supersedure corresponds to the ordinary supersedure of one sibling by another in a family of small children, and not necessarily to the special circumstances of the boy Dickens.[4] Another allusion to *Hamlet* in the novel is prompted by the black velvet dress and hat of one Mrs. Henry Spiker. Dickens plays with the idea of this person as Hamlet's aunt—she had "the family failing of indulging in soliloquy," for example—but this sort of humor (25.316–320) implies that *Hamlet* itself is rather a joke, such as it becomes in Wopsle's performance of the play in *Great Expectations*.[5] The same cannot be said of the traces of *King Lear* in *Copperfield*, because the loyalty of Agnes Wickfield to her mistaken and increasingly helpless father replicates that of Cordelia, an image of faithfulness that Dickens takes very seriously. Even this relation, however, is now overtaken by a novelistic commonplace, in which a heroine's unswerving loyalty to her father is the best promise of her loyalty to a husband. An experienced novel reader can identify Agnes as the true heroine just from her thoughtful waiting upon her father, and especially when "her bright calm face lighted up with pleasure as she went to meet him" (16.196). No doubt wise young men with disciplined hearts regularly observe the behavior of young women toward their fathers in real life, and choose accordingly. The wisdom of David Copperfield is much belated in this respect, and insofar as it reflects the history of Charles Dickens, both belated and wishful.

Because Dickens only partially disguises himself and his career, the kind of literature he explicitly invokes in *Copperfield* consists of novels written by his forbears, which are virtually his hero's only legacy.

> My father had left in a little room up-stairs, to which I had access (for it adjoined my own) a small collection of books which nobody else in our house ever troubled. From that blessed little room, Roderick Random, Peregrine Pickle, Humphrey Clinker, Tom Jones, the Vicar of Wakefield, Don Quixote, Gil Blas, and Robinson Crusoe, came out, a glorious host, to keep me company. They kept alive my fancy, and my hope of something beyond that place and time,—they, and the Arabian Nights, and the Tales of the Genii,—and did me no harm; for whatever harm was in some of them was not there for me; *I* knew nothing of it. (4.48)

The ghost of this child's father is apparently these few books, which are not rebuked for heating the hero's imagination, as in histories written in the tradition of Cervantes but dearly embraced as so many gifts to life. They have no bearing at all on the youth's undisciplined heart, and the mature narrator goes out of his way to imply that, in general, fiction cannot morally corrupt a child. That these precedents do bear on the materials and strategies of *Copperfield* as a novel has long been accepted by students of Dickens. Forster commented that the method of *Copperfield* was "common to the masters in his art," and by this he meant the practice of disguised autobiography—not so much the evocation of the novelist's memories of his own feelings and behavior, however, as his free use of persons of his acquaintance, evidenced especially by Dickens's use of his father as a model for Wilkins Micawber.[6] Others have claimed more for the technique or episodic development of *Copperfield* as deriving from the eighteenth-century novel. Yarmouth, it has been suggested (since Dickens had only recently become acquainted with Yarmouth), may have been chosen as a setting because it was the location of Crusoe's first shipwreck as it was of Steerforth's[7]— and indeed there are scattered allusions to Defoe's novel in *Copperfield*, but of no greater significance than the allusions to *Hamlet*. Surely the foremost conclusion to be drawn about these novelistic sources, also, is that Dickens's experience of life rather than literature preponderates.

Copperfield's tribute to the novelists who entertained him as a boy, and whose stories he retold for the appreciation of Steerforth at school, reflects the wholeheartedness with which Dickens now regarded *himself* as a novelist—a proposition that would scarcely need underlining except for the difficulties he had experienced with writing in the years after his journey to America. In Jerome H. Buckley's summary, the life of the writer celebrated in *David Copperfield* entails "the achievement of an inner discipline, the sense of self-knowledge in the control of his chosen medium, the quiet assertion of a slowly realized and always gentle but ultimately well-assured identity, the unexpressed conviction that a man, within limits, may become the hero of his own story."[8] As much might be said, after discounting a little the moral uplift characteristic of much Victorian fiction, for Dickens personally at the time of writing his autobiographical novel. A relatively short interval passed between the completion of *Dombey and Son* and the commencement of *Copperfield*, the first number of which was published in May 1849. After the new year, as he planned the work, his eighth child and sixth son was born. The name first chosen for this child was Oliver Goldsmith, whose biography Forster had just completed and whose *Vicar of Wakefield* Dickens had used to good purpose in *Pickwick*. But the name of the child was now changed to Henry Fielding Dickens—according to Forster, "in a kind of homage to the style of work he was now so bent on beginning." Harrison Ainsworth, a friend and still another novelist, was godfather to the child.[9] Meanwhile, a contemporary novelist more formidable than Ainsworth had just established himself, with the publication of *Vanity Fair* in 1847–48. William Makepeace Thackeray was a year older than Dickens; his autobiographical novel, *The History of Pendennis,* had already begun to appear in November 1848. Whatever decisiveness this rivalry, or the appearance of Charlotte Brontë's *Jane Eyre* in 1847, added to Dickens's sense of his own career, the period of uncertainty between his unprecedented early success and the enthusiastic reception of *Dombey* was at an end. He could positively celebrate his profession as a writer and accommodate his memories to it. The boyhood trauma of which he chose to write in his new novel was pointedly not traumatic at the time of writing. It could not possibly threaten Dickens's present identity or the calm of Copperfield, which was not all due to Agnes.

To appreciate that *David Copperfield* was written from the assured perspective of a relatively stable sense of identity, one can compare the letter to Lord Morpeth, just two years earlier, inquiring about commissionerships or inspectorships and mentioning his interest in becoming a police magistrate, with a letter of June 1848 in which Dickens summarized for a Scottish acquaintance his present state of life:

> My oldest daughter . . . has one sister and five brothers representing a little flight of stairs of which the bottom step is one year old. They are all well, all good, and all happy. I am not rich, for the great expences of my position have been mine alone from the first, and the Lion's share of its great profits has been gorged by the booksellers. But I have changed all that, within these three years or so,—have worked back half of all my copyrights which had gone from me before I knew their worth—and have got, by some few thousand pounds (I could count the thousands on one hand) ahead of the world. Dombey has been the greatest success I have ever achieved. Although Literature as a profession has no distinct status in England, I am bound to say that what I experience of its recognition, all through Society, in my own person, is honorable, ample, and independent. I find that to make no exacting assertion of its claims, on the one hand—and steadily to take my stand by it, on the other, as a worthy calling, and my sole fortune—is to do right, and to take sufficient rank. Go where I will, in out of the way places and odd corners of the country, I always find something of personal affection in people whom I have never seen, mixed up with my public reputation. This is the best part of it, and it makes me very happy.[10]

The whole statement is remarkable for its balance, not to speak of the ease of writing of such matters to a relative stranger. The combinations of progressive heights of children and profitable books, of the possession of copyrights without notable querulousness about those he still lacks, of literature as a "profession" and as a "calling," of acquired "fortune" and attendant "rank," and finally of "personal affection" with "public reputation" contrast utterly with the uneasy grappling with fame and personal affront that characterized his response to his American journey a few years back. From this relatively serene sense of his own fatherhood and social relations Dickens launched, early in 1849, the autobiographical fiction of his childhood and fictional autobiography of a novelist— to borrow William C. Spengeman's terms for the successive phases of *David Copperfield*.[11] Not only did Dickens begin *Copperfield* and incorporate sentences from his autobiographical fragment securely within it, but he inaugurated at this time his new periodical *Household Words*, which was to become, along with its sequel *All the Year Round*, the vehicle for some of the best fiction of the age as well as an impressive range of journalism.

The novelist David Copperfield apparently shares—not to say cultivates—this equanimity about writing. So lightly does the narrator of his own life touch upon his career that as readers we are a little taken aback and have to remind ourselves that this is a novel about a novelist. We have noted that David was a lively and observant child, who first made an impression by retelling the stories of Smollett and others at school. Then in the fifteenth number of *Copperfield*, we just hear him mention that he "wrote a good deal now, and was beginning in a small way to be known as a writer," before he skates away on a story of Dora's struggle in writing up the household accounts (44.551). In case we have missed the bare hint of his career, so casually dropped in the narrative, Mrs. Steerforth a couple of chapters later compliments him on his growing fame—though without indicating what he is famous for:

> "And are you doing well? I hear little in the quiet life I lead, but I understand you are beginning to be famous."
> "I have been very fortunate," I said, "and find my name connected with some praise."
> "You have no mother?"—in a softened voice.
> "No."

"It is a pity," she returned. "She would have been proud of you. Good night!" (46.575)

The subject of the hero's fame and its unspoken relation to writing quickly yields to different themes: Mrs. Steerforth's hungry attachment to her son, a reflection on Mrs. Copperfield's premature death, and indirectly perhaps Elizabeth Dickens's or Catherine Dickens's failure to appreciate sufficiently the fame of Dickens. David Copperfield, we can understand, is going to be both cautious and modest in telling us what it is like to be a famous novelist. In the upshot, he hardly tells us at all.

The narrator's primary move, with respect to what he has to say about his career, has already been made by his addressing not novel writing but the mastery of shorthand—an initial test in wresting a career from the world that Dickens too had passed. The deliberate strategy of the narrator is to pose as a man no different from any other except in application to the task at hand. By choosing to moralize about learning shorthand, obviously, Copperfield can elevate hard work over talent before the question of novel writing even arises.

> I have been very fortunate in wordly matters; many men have worked much harder, and not succeeded half so well; but I never could have done what I have done, without the habits of punctuality, order, and diligence, without the determination to concentrate myself on one object at a time, no matter how quickly its successor should come upon its heels, which I then formed. Heaven knows I write this, in no spirit of self-laudation. The man who reviews his own life, as I do mine, in going on here, from page to page, had need to have been a good man indeed, if he would be spared the sharp consciousness of many talents neglected, many opportunities wasted, many erratic and perverted feelings constantly at war within his breast, and defeating him. . . . Some happy talent, and some fortunate opportunity, may form the two sides of the ladder on which some men mount, but the rounds of that ladder must be made of stuff to stand wear and tear; and there is no substitute for thorough-going, ardent, and sincere earnestness. Never to put one hand to anything, on which I could throw my whole self; never to affect depreciation of my work, whatever it was; I find, now, to have been my golden rules. (42.517–518)

Conclusions arrived at "now"—that is, retrospectively—must apply to writing novels as well as shorthand, but we have no confirmation that

Copperfield becomes a novelist for several more chapters. These struggles are behind him before he puts pen to any novel, and "sharp consciousness of many talents neglected, many opportunities wasted, many erratic and perverted feelings," is precisely what will not be mentioned again in connection with his writing.

The attitudes posed here are no doubt admirable. Indeed, this passage from Dickens's autobiographical novel can serve as a primary text on the meaning of earnestness for the Victorians. Not too surprisingly, *Copperfield* insists on the virtue of hard work while it neglects to account for what it is like to be a novelist.[12] The rule "never to affect depreciation of my work" is almost certainly a hit at Thackeray, yet Thackeray in the rival novel *Pendennis* tells us more of the world of novelists and journalists than Dickens does, and this despite his own inhibitions in the matter.[13] In *Copperfield* only the arrival, the becoming of a famous novelist, is modestly taken note of, and Philip Collins rightly complains that "Dickens does too little to make David's turning to authorship seem probable, let alone inevitable."[14] Dickens was obviously aware that he was giving the reader little idea of his experience, because he subsequently has Copperfield deny that such is his purpose. The first denial accompanies another general statement about work and fame, notable for the sincerity of its complacency:

> I labored hard at my book, without allowing it to interfere with the punctual discharge of my newspaper duties; and it came out and was very successful. I was not stunned by the praise which sounded in my ears, notwithstanding that I was keenly alive to it, and thought better of my performance, I have little doubt, than anybody else did. It has always been in my observation of human nature, that a man who has any good reason to believe in himself never flourishes himself before the faces of other people in order that they may believe in him. For this reason, I retained my modesty in very self-respect; and the more praise I got, the more I tried to deserve.

Such Victorian language about the discharging of duties inevitably suggests anality today, and conceivably the work ethic owed something to the toilet training of the age. Copperfield most obviously associates work that is appreciated with a sense of identity, the identity of one who "believe[s] in himself" and appears properly before "the faces of other people." Respect and self-respect, praise and deserving come to-

111

gether, whereas they had threatened to come apart in the American adventure and in the hilarity and humiliations discharged in the two previous novels. This achievement of an identity is essentially the subject of *David Copperfield* and, having written thus of work and fame, the narrator declares, "It is not my purpose, in this record, though in all other essentials it is my written memory, to pursue the history of my own fictions. They express themselves, and I leave them to themselves. When I refer to them, incidentally, it is only as a part of my progress" (48.588–589). His progress? Toward death, of course, but for the present toward that which he is in himself and which even his books cannot share with him. And Copperfield will repeat the point a second time, after his adherence to Agnes Wickfield: "I do not enter on the aspirations, the delights, anxieties, and triumphs of my art. That I truly devoted myself to it with my strongest earnestness, and bestowed upon it every energy of my soul, I have already said" (61.723).

Besides such bows to earnestness, Dickens conducts one other generalized move to give primacy to Copperfield's identity as a novelist. This move can be discerned in the specular role accorded to Agnes. Now Agnes is undoubtedly Copperfield's angel, and I would hope that no one can any longer doubt that her association with the light from church windows and her continually pointing upward signify her connection with death, but she is just as surely the hero's private auditor, who replaces Steerforth as chief listener in life as well as angel, and to the very end she is his muse. Dora Copperfield cannot interest herself much in her husband's work; Agnes Copperfield's very silence is eloquent of approval, and she most certainly does not nod asleep when he writes late. Even before our "blind, blind, blind" hero (35.430 and 60.716) realizes that he can marry such a wife—and it cannot be easy to realize this of an angel or a muse—he discovers her usefulness to him as a writer. After his return from Switzerland, where he has gone to mourn the deaths of Dora, Steerforth, and Ham, and to be reminded of Agnes in the calm valleys, he acknowledges that "however loud the general voice might be in giving me encouragement, and however fervent the emotions and endeavours to which it roused me, I heard her lightest word of praise as I heard nothing else." Thus the unpredictable acclaim of mass readers of print, or of audiences of strangers who may seem almost repellent in their sudden assumption of intimacy with the author, can be assuaged and comfortably reduced before this fit audience of one. This realization, it seems, is what drives Copperfield *to* his second, and highly idealized, marriage, for in this chapter he will finally break through to the knowledge of her love. "When I read to Agnes what I wrote; when I saw her listening face; moved her to smiles or tears; and heard her cordial voice so earnest on the shadowy events of that imaginative world in which I lived; I thought what a fate mine might have been—but only thought so, as I had thought after I was married to Dora, what I could have wished my wife to be" (62.733–734).

A few pages later they are in each others' arms at last, and at *the* last—the last of his novel and proleptically of his novelist's life—they are still together:

> And now, as I close my task, subduing my desire to linger yet, these faces fade away. But, one face, shining on me like a Heavenly light by which I see all other objects, is above them and beyond them all. And that remains.
>
> I turn my head, and see it, in its beautiful serenity, beside me. My lamp burns low, and I have written far into the night; but the dear presence, without which I were nothing, bears me company.
>
> O Agnes, O my soul, so may thy face be by me when I close my life indeed; so may I, when realities are melting from me like the shadows which I now dismiss, still find thee near me, pointing upward!   (64.751)

Though Copperfield's account of his progress ends fittingly with this prevision of his end, the vision is also of the act of writing. J. Hillis Miller rightly stressed that a presence "without which I were nothing" was emblematic of a nineteenth-century tendency to substitute persons for God.[15] I invoked the same passage to illustrate the presence of the angel of death and to call attention to the prominence of the face in the tableau: for a face, as Erikson has suggested, is above all the face of the mother and signifies trust.[16] Barry Westburg has since called Agnes "the priestess of the childhood shrines."[17] But assuredly she is also the Muse, "a Heavenly light by which I see all other objects," as well as the intimate audience for "these faces" and "the shadows" that people his fiction. It is literally the writing lamp that burns low, figuratively the lamp of life; and the situation is that of one who has "written far into the night," with this specular creature bearing him company.

113

Agnes Wickfield has the important function of mediating in the novel between the childhood suffering of the hero and his career, on which his identity is centered even though it is scarcely described. She is the highly unreal character who also makes it possible for *David Copperfield* to be such an original work, unmediated by previous works of literature. With reference to the autobiographical intent of the novel, she is the muse who enables Dickens to resolve the experience of the blacking warehouse, to dedicate his suffering as a child to future endeavors as a novelist. This much becomes evident from her role at several junctures in the action, but especially in the delicate epistles she remits to the hero in Switzerland.[18] Significantly, the letters are not given directly in the novel but indirectly, as Copperfield assimilates her writing to his writing:

> She gave me no advice; she urged no duty on me; she only told me, in her own fervent manner, what her trust in me was. She knew (she said) how such a nature as mine would turn affliction to good. She knew how trial and emotion would exalt and strengthen it. She was sure that in my every purpose I should gain a firmer and a higher tendency, through the grief I had undergone. She, who so gloried in my fame, and so looked forward to its augmentation, well knew that I would labor on. She knew that in me, sorrow could not be weakness, but must be strength. As the endurance of my childish days had done its part to make me what I was, so greater calamities would nerve me on, to be yet better than I was; and so, as they had taught me, would I teach others. She commended me to God, who had taken my innocent darling to His rest; and in her sisterly affection cherished me always, and was always at my side go where I would; proud of what I had done, but infinitely prouder yet of what I was reserved to do. (58.698)

Such is the narrator's version of what he read when he "read the writing of Agnes." Ingeniously, he has either borrowed her wisdom of life or attributed his own conclusions to her. Though the message is framed as consolation for the loss of Dora, it touches at its deepest his childhood suffering. It is not even clear that Agnes, the character in the novel, ever knew of Murdstone and Grinby's or what her friend Trotwood (as she calls David) suffered there. She is therefore a true daughter of memory, whether of Copperfield's memory or of Dickens's. The thought attributed to Agnes, that "endurance of my childish days had done its part to make me what I was," more nearly echoes Dickens's reflection on his days at Warren's Blacking—"I know how all these things have worked together to make me what I am"[19]—than anything she has overheard in the novel. Just so, Agnes commends the hero to God in her letter, but begins by affirming her trust in the man and concludes on the note of pride. The indirect style modestly allows that whatever pride he has emanates from her. A strong sense of personal identity—conferred by Agnes—anticipates greater achievements to come: "proud of what I had done, but infinitely prouder yet of what I was reserved to do." The syntax of this parting thrust displays the ambiguity in authorship of the whole letter. Though "proud" presumably modifies Agnes, she has been elided at this point: the nearest pronouns to which "proud" and "prouder yet" can refer are "I" and "me" in the previous clause. The overarching design of the novel itself—the rather sparse logic attaching the autobiographical fiction of the first fourteen chapters to the fictional autobiography of the novelist in the rest of the book—is here attributed to Agnes, though it surely originates elsewhere. What suffering has taught Copperfield and Dickens, they will contrive their best to teach others as novelists.

It is sometimes objected that readers of a novel ought somehow to refuse such critical intervention with their willing suspensions of disbelief: that is, if the narrator claims that he is recounting what another character wrote in a letter, then he did not write it himself; if the narrator claims that he is David Copperfield, then he is not Charles Dickens. But in practice, as we know, suspensions of disbelief may be willing but never quite single-minded or uninterrupted. If the narrator wished to pretend strictly to have nothing to do with the letter, then he might have couched it in direct discourse. And if Dickens wished to remove himself further from Agnes's views of Copperfield's career, he need not have slipped in the moral drawn from the autobiographical fragment. Dickens need not have undertaken to write an autobiographical fiction or a fictional autobiography, or both in combination, in the first place. Readers on their part may know nothing about Dickens, just as they may never have heard of *Le Tartuffe* or *Paradise Lost* or *King Lear,* and read with a different level of awareness accordingly. But once awareness or detection intervenes, the suspension of disbelief itself becomes suspended—irregular, suspicious, and inquiring.

Dickens made sure that alert readers of *David Copperfield,* without any special knowledge, could realize that certain games were being played. Like other great novelists and even at his most serene—as he seems to have been or become in writing *Copperfield*—Dickens could not refrain from providing an ironic context or counterpart for each positive representation he desired to make (so that if Copperfield works hard, for example, a character named Micawber waits for something to turn up). More particularly, in this novel about the "progress" of a writer, every writer but the hero—or his muse—writes wildly or hopelessly. The very refusal of the narrator to tell of his professional writing bespeaks confidence; the confusion and redundancy of nearly every other producer of writing whom he describes—Mr. Micawber, Dr. Strong, and the curiously named Mr. Dick—tell another story. If these other experiences with writing were merely recorded to set off Copperfield's success, that would be one thing—and not disruptive of any reader's credulity. But in fact they seem to comment a little mischievously on Dickens's enterprise in writing this novel and, by extension, any other novel.

Hillis Miller called attention to the "transcendence through language" practiced by Mr. Micawber in the novel. Micawber, of course, would almost rather write a letter than speak, and when he speaks, voluminously, he sometimes provides himself in advance with written memoranda. His rhetoric is grandiloquently excessive and compensates for the financial straits in which he constantly finds himself. He uses language, as Miller and others have suggested, to overcome realities. "Perhaps, indeed, there is a secret identity between the linguistic enterprise of Micawber and that of Dickens himself, as it is transposed in the attempt by David Copperfield to tell all that he remembers about himself and about his experience."[20] If there is such an identity with Micawber, it would seem to be nearly opposite to the confirming relation with Agnes, whose tending of memories is hieratic but not to be thought of as exaggerated. Micawber, after all, achieves transcendence only from a certain point of view; his actions—or rather words, words, words—are from a material point of view entirely futile and, being endlessly so, are far from constituting a progress. So it is with that other master of words, the lexicographer Dr. Strong. He is innocent and considerate, but his Dictionary will never be completed or read by anyone. At the end of the novel we read that Strong is still laboring "somewhere about the letter D," and it is fair to take the hint that "D" may also stand for Dickens, the novelist having wryly admitted in this fashion the ultimate unlikelihood of transcending the self by writing.[21]

Stanley Tick was the first to argue persuasively that Mr. Dick was "an image of the author himself," and not merely one of the series of characters who assist Copperfield on his way.[22] The name itself, "Mr. Dick," is the giveaway. The history of the name, which has been known for some time from the manuscript of *Copperfield* and is retraced in the textual notes of the Clarendon edition, reveals that Dickens was mischievously poking fun at himself. As well as being quite mad, Mr. Dick is of course a writer, working away on his famous Memorial. The said memorial is both a petition, an appeal to the Lord Chancellor or someone in authority to save him from his obsession about his identity—his identification, no less, with King Charles the First—and an autobiographical fiction that accommodates this obsession. Mr. Dick has the charming method of publishing portions of this unfinished, never to be finished, manuscript by sending it aloft as a kite—a method likely to reach about as many readers as Dr. Strong's Dictionary. His real name, which is Richard Babley, must never be mentioned because he is sensitive, like Dickens, to the way his family has abused him. Dickens's own manuscript, of *Copperfield*, shows that Mr. Dick was conceived as a Mr. Robert, and that his obsession with the head of Charles the First began as nothing more original than something about a bull in a china shop. The author revised the name and the obsession and made them refer, by a scarcely secret code, to his own project. In doing so he struck humorously at his own complacency as well as the inherent complacency of all celebrations of the self.

Mr. Dick cannot make progress with or out of his Memorial because he cannot get King Charles out of his head; Charles was beheaded in 1649, exactly two hundred years before the writing of the fifth number of *Copperfield*. As if these associations with Dickens at the time of writing were not enough, the character has a few sporting connections with Copperfield, of which the author himself may not have been fully aware. At first sight Mr. Dick's head (not King Charles's) reminds the narrator "of one of Mr. Creakle's boys' heads after a beating" (13.165). The narrator first sees Mr. Dick peering from his window in Betsey Trotwood's home in Dover; later, in a visit to his own home in Blunderstone, he similarly observes a "poor lunatic gentleman" in the window of his old room—"and I wondered whether his rambling thoughts ever went upon any of the fancies that used to occupy mine" (22.272–273). Eventually Mr. Dick—who already gives sage advice to Betsey Trotwood—will prove himself useful in the reconciliation of Dr. Strong and his young wife and, equally improbably and pleasantly, in the bringing to book of Uriah Heep. But Dickens also pursues the parallel to his hero's progress in respect to writing: even Dick must apply himself and make his writing count for something.

The occasion is the supposed bankruptcy of Aunt Betsey, who has charitably supported both Dick and Copperfield until now. "If I could exert myself," Dick expresses the general feeling—"if I could beat a drum—or blow anything." The hero's friend Traddles has the notion that Dick, since he is such an eager writer, might earn something by law copying, if only his mind can be kept from thoughts of King Charles. The result is an economical and usually overlooked instance of Dickens's meaningful good fun:

> On the table by the window in Buckingham Street, we set out the work Traddles procured for him—which was to make, I forget how many copies of a legal document about some right of way—and on another table we spread the last unfinished original of the great Memorial. Our instructions to Mr. Dick were that he should copy exactly what he had before him, without the least departure from the original; and that when he felt it necessary to make the slightest allusion to King Charles the First, he should fly to the Memorial. We exhorted him to be resolute in this, and left my aunt to observe him. My aunt reported to us, afterwards, that, at first, he was like a man playing the kettle-drums, and constantly divided his attentions between the two; but that, finding this confuse and fatigue him, and having his copy there, plainly before his eyes, he soon sat at it in an orderly business-like manner, and postponed the Memorial to a more convenient time. (36.451)

The disciplining of Mr. Dick, by giving free play to his obsession, assimilates his activity to the hard work, the "determination to concentrate myself on one object at a time, no matter how quickly its successor should come upon its heels," advocated elsewhere for all workers by Copperfield. The latter is never tempted to write about *his* obsession, if he has one, though in order to excel at novel writing he obviously cannot stop at law copying—he will have to live one way or another with the notoriety of being Charles the First. The nearer model for Dick to follow is Traddles, the school friend of Copperfield so unlike Steerforth that he begins his career with humble copying and ends as a judge.

The sorts of alternative lives of writing I have been tracing, though they may be subversive, are further evidence of the originality of *David Copperfield*. There is finally no secret about them, but rather a partial withholding, as in a guessing game. The game played with the reader in regard to Mr. Dick is deliberate on Dickens's part, as the revisions of his draft of the novel demonstrate. Other connections are so odd as to seem outrageously teasing—or else unconscious on Dickens's part. The year in history associated with Mr. Dick's Memorial relates also to Dr. Strong's Dictionary, since one of the schoolboys at Canterbury conjectures out of the blue that the Dictionary "might be done in one thousand six hundred and forty-nine years, counting from the Doctor's last, or sixty-second birthday" (16.203). The Dictionary and the Memorial already have something in common as instances of obsessive and futile writing; here they are joined by the same code number, 1649. Why the doctor's sixty-second birthday? This was about John Dickens's age at the time Dickens was writing, but that reflection glances back to older interpretations of Mr. Dick and Dr. Strong as father figures: substitutes for Copperfield's deceased father or, like Mr. Micawber, for Dickens's own father.

A minor respect in which *Copperfield* is not quite so original, but dependent on literature of the past, becomes useful in showing how such figures are *both* fathers of a sort and distant projections of the novelist. The key figure here is Mr. Wickfield—not the hero's father indeed but the heroine's, and the dim shadow of Lear once again (though not as dim as Dr. Strong). We happen to know, from the record preserved by Forster, that Dickens did not initiate the novel solely with the purpose of introducing himself as Copperfield. So persistent was his need to interpret *King Lear,* or the momentum of his own story of Lear and Cordelia in *Dombey and Son,* that there lodged in the plan for *Copperfield* a distinct role for the heroine's father that connects this gentleman to Lear and to Dickens—and was accompanied by a glance at Pecksniff! Forster's account of what he called "the many outward signs of fancy and fertility that accompanied the outset of all [Dickens's] more important books" retrieves just this one illustration from the undertaking of the novel. The idea, which Dickens tried out on his friend, had expressly to do with a character always inquiring about others' motives:

What should you think of this for a notion of character? "Yes, that is very true; but now, *What's his motive?*" I fancy I could make something like it into a kind of amusing and more innocent Pecksniff. "Well, now, yes—no doubt that was a fine thing to do! But now, stop a moment, let us see—*What's his motive?*"²³

From the fifth number of *Copperfield* it is clear that the character Dickens had in mind became Wickfield, but the first reference to motives is this, for which he apologizes even as he enters: "I was engaged for the moment, but you'll excuse my being busy. You know my motive. I have but one in life" (15.188). Missing from the query to Forster, or else added to the conception before writing this number, is the crucial designation of Wickfield's motive, to which he is committed as single-mindedly and persistently as he is to doubting the motives of others. The exclusive motive of his life, it appears, like Triboulet's in *Le Roi s'amuse* or Rigoletto's in the opera, is a pathetic devotion to a daughter, the angelic heroine of the action to follow. However dim a reincarnation the bourgeois and alcoholic Mr. Wickfield may be, his conception suggests that Dickens partly began this most confident of novels by thinking himself into the Lear character again—and self-critically, as he had in *Dombey*. Whereas Dombey neglects and comes to hate a loving daughter, Wickfield allows his fondness to overwhelm his capacity for dealing with the world. This time the criticism is leveled at overindulgence in obsessive love, a behavioral exaggeration in fiction of a mental indulgence of its author, possibly his thoughts of Mary Hogarth. But in keeping with his other meditations on memory and mental life in this period, and most notably *The Haunted Man,* Dickens seeks to examine the indulgence objectively. Wickfield will conclude that it is because he has loved exclusively his daughter, and mourned exclusively the loss of her mother, that "weak indulgence has ruined" him. "Indulgence in remembrance, and indulgence in forgetfulness. My natural grief for my child's mother turned to disease; my natural love for my child turned to disease" (39.493). The criticism in the novel of Wickfield's fixation on his daughter thus serves as a kind of check, though in miniature, to the earlier criticism of Dombey's fierce hatred and to the possible implication that fulsome love might have succeeded where hatred had failed. The psychology is a bit fantastical, again, but it bears the authority of Agnes herself:

"Oh, Trotwood!" cried Agnes, putting her hands before her face, as her tears started on it. "I almost feel as if I had been papa's enemy, instead of his loving child. For I know how he has altered, in his devotion to me. I know how he has narrowed the circle of his sympathies and duties, in the concentration of his whole mind upon me. I know what a multitude of thoughts he has shut out for my sake, and how his anxious thoughts of me have shadowed his life, and weakened his strength and energy, by turning them always upon one idea. If I could ever set this right! If I could ever work out his restoration, as I have so innocently been the cause of his decline!" (25.316)

The novel proffers a rather conventional solution of the dilemma: the father must die and the hero take his place. Wickfield suffers from a debilitating sublimation of his love, though in *Copperfield* it takes the libidinously charged voice of Uriah Heep to bring this out: "Agnes Wickfield is, I am safe to say, the divinest of her sex. May I speak out, among friends? To be her father is a proud distinction, but to be her usband—" (39.492). As for the other side to Wickfield's obsession, his questioning of everyone else's motives, that much more patently resembles a need of one who writes novels. The writer within and of this novel, *Copperfield*, is almost too blatantly linked to Wick*field* by name as well as by substitution in the action.[24] In the passage just cited, in which Heep stakes his claim, the hero stands by Wickfield—constrains the father in his arms, in fact—and urges him to be calm in the light of *his* friendship with his daughter. It is one of those passages, not always credited by the critics, in which Dickens clearly intends the reader to understand Copperfield's interest in Agnes even when the character himself is blind to it. At the same time, Dickens's commitment to the older figure, a man old enough to be a heroine's father, persists in minor ways within and without the novel.

Forster tells us that *Copperfield* virtually wrote itself after Dickens got started, and that "his principal hesitation occurred in connection with the child-wife Dora, who had become a great favourite as he went on; and it was only after her fate had been decided, in the early autumn of 1850, but before she breathed her last, that a third daughter was born to him, to whom he gave his dying little heroine's name."[25] But obviously this real Dora Annie, who survived less than a year, was named for Annie Strong as well as Dora Copperfield. In the novel, Mrs. Strong is another sort of child-wife, being only about one third the age of her husband Dr. Strong. She is the contemporary of Agnes Wickfield but married to a man older than Agnes's father. If David Copperfield, who

121

marries one child-wife, is the acknowledged stand-in for Charles Dickens, then Strong, who marries the other child-wife, may curiously and wistfully represent the novelist also. Strong is most closely associated in the novel with Wickfield, and the latter remotely—terribly, foolishly, vaguely—associated with Pecksniff, in Dickens's first conception of his character. The link with Dickens, however tenuous, would seem to be confirmed by the teasing humor of the Dictionary, the letter D, and the figure 1649 associating Strong with Mr. Dick.

IX

Women Passing By

*O*ne result of concentrating too exclusively on the story of Copperfield's childhood, reinforced as it is by the autobiographical fragment,
is to miss the interest in women as sexual beings that is expressed in
the novel. Not that the women have gone unnoticed: Dora Copperfield,
in particular, has had her champions. Forster himself declared Dora's
affection "more attractive than the too unfailing wisdom and self-
sacrificing goodness of the angel-wife, Agnes."[1] Q. D. Leavis has since
dissected the Victorian sentiments that made men like Forster and
Dickens prefer, or pretend to prefer, childlike women, but she praises
David Copperfield nonetheless for treating "Love as a reality, not a Victorian convention."[2] Here I shall refer only briefly to Copperfield's first
marriage in order to say a little more of the novel's fallen women.

To a surprising extent this autobiographical novel is concerned not
only with success as a writer, or with childhood and parenting, but
with women as possible sexual partners. To borrow a curious classifi-
cation of the second sex by Mr. Micawber, one could say that the novel
explores "the tripartite character of woman, wife, and mother" (49.599).
Since in ordinary parlance wives and mothers are subsets of the class
comprising women, Micawber's skewed taxonomy calls attention to
woman as woman; he may signify any number of male characterizations
of woman but most likely a sexual characterization. He writes so of
Mrs. Micawber, and the Micawbers are, after all, the one married and

123

breeding couple that the novel supports until the end, when David and Agnes Copperfield come on. Not to make too fine a point of Micawber's language, *Copperfield* in a number of quiet ways stresses "woman." At the extremes one can cite the feminization of the hero himself, noted thirty-five years ago by Sylvère Monod,[3] or the comic plight of Traddles and Sophy surrounded by the latter's many sisters: "The society of girls is a very delightful thing, Copperfield. It's not professional, but it's very delightful" (59.706). Nearer the center of the novel are the examination of "undisciplined" marriage based on sexual attraction and also the seduction of women outside marriage. In the second instance, it is almost as if the fortunate falls of *Chuzzlewit* and the tragic fall of *Dombey* were displaced by *Copperfield*'s interest in fallen women: if the fall of an ambitious man can be conveniently displaced as temptation in childhood, as in the Oedipus complex, then a fall can be displaced onto women who are bought or seduced by men.

Both Copperfield and Thackeray's Pendennis pay visits to English productions of August von Kotzebue's *The Stranger*. In Dickens's novel the allusion to Kotzebue is as brief as it is witty: "I went to see 'The Stranger' as a Doctors' Commons sort of play, and was so dreadfully cut up, that I hardly knew myself in my own glass when I got home" (26.330). It is also a sly hit at Thackeray's novel, which had made so much of the actress who starred in the same play: by the writing of this, the ninth number of *Copperfield*, the hero of *Pendennis* had been to see the play over and over again and fallen passionately in love with the Fotheringay, the actress who played—or rather modeled—the role of Mrs. Haller. Why should two such promising young men, well before they became famous writers, go to see *The Stranger*? What Kotzebue's "Doctors' Commons sort of play" allowed them to glimpse or imagine was a beautiful woman who had married at sixteen, who had coupled and uncoupled with her husband, had an affair with another man, and returned as a lovely penitent—after examples of charity on both sides—to her husband and children. The foreign play, in short, invited a young man to contemplate rather rosily what men and women can do together whether married or unmarried. Very early in *Copperfield*—so early, in fact, that it is the first conversation the narrator records of his own memory—the child who will one day be famous crossexamines his nurse about the rules of marriage:

"You mustn't marry more than one person at a time, may you, Peggotty?"

"Certainly not," says Peggotty, with the promptest decision.

"But if you marry a person, and the person dies, why then you may marry another person, mayn't you, Peggotty?"

"You MAY," says Peggotty, "if you choose, my dear. That's a matter of opinion." (2.14–15)

Thus in his earliest remembered conversation (which is both funnier and more touching as a whole than the excerpt given here), the hero wins Peggotty's reluctant consent to the second marriage that will bring the novel to a close sixty chapters on, while she no doubt inwardly is already refusing consent to her namesake's second marriage to Murdstone. Second marriages are very much the scene in the novel from beginning to end: the beauty and thrill of Mrs. Haller's example in *The Stranger* point to the further possibility of coupling outside marriage.

If we are to look for an autobiographical significance of the two possible violations of monogamy, present and future, they have to be pure fantasy on Dickens's part. Still, the main action of *David Copperfield* might be described as the replacement of one wife by another, and that action stands independently of the seduction of Emily by Steerforth or any other sexual matter. Dickens bestowed much affection and memory of young love on his hero's courtship of Dora Spenlow. Five years after writing the novel he identified Dora—for one correspondent—with Maria Beadnell, his own first love. There is no need to question this identification, which most students of Dickens have accepted, except that the correspondent was Maria herself, since married to Louis Winter. Dickens opened Mrs. Winter's letter, he wrote, "with the touch of my young friend David Copperfield when he was in love," as if he could use the authority of a novel to reawaken fantasy in his life and replace his second love with his first. Five days later he was writing to the same correspondent as follows:

I fancy—though you may not have thought in the old time how manfully I loved you—that you may have seen in one of my books a faithful reflection of the passion I had for you, and may have thought that it was something to have been loved so well, and may have seen in little bits of "Dora" touches of your old self sometimes and a grace here and there that may be revived in your little girls, years hence, for the bewilderment

of some other young lover—though he will never be as terribly in earnest as I and David Copperfield were. People used to say to me how pretty all that was, and how fanciful it was, and how elevated it was above the little foolish loves of very young men and women. But they little thought what reason I had to know it was true and nothing more nor less.

By 1855 Dickens seems to have forgotten that Copperfield himself recognized the foolishness of his young love. A week later, in a third letter, he was advising his old love how they might meet privately.[4]

It simply does not make sense, however, to identify Dora exclusively with Maria: Dora Spenlow, yes, but not Dora Copperfield, whose situation can only bear resemblance to that of Catherine Dickens. Again, hindsight about the writing of the novel can be misleading, since Dickens's marriage did not break up until 1858, but some of the inspiration for Dora must have been shared by Catherine. One cannot do better than cite Philip Collins on this point. "Dora dies," Collins believes,

> partly because this sort of novel demands it, but also in answer to a need in Dickens's emotional life. The tone of his letters to Maria in 1855, and the intensity of his anticipations about their reunion do not suggest that he felt disillusioned about her, rather that he still felt disappointed that she had not married him. It seems probable, indeed, that Dora, particularly after the marriage, takes on some of the qualities of the woman Dickens had married and was later to eject from his life. Her pettish manner and her being treated like a child remind one of the tone of Dickens's letters to Catherine during their courtship, and though Dora's domestic incompetence and intellectual unfitness to be a helpmeet to a rising literary man can certainly not be attributed in full to Catherine, it was one of Dickens's complaints that her "weak hand . . . could never help or serve my name in the least."

Collins goes on to ask how unhappy Dickens might have been with his marriage in 1849–50, to reject Georgina Hogarth as a model for Agnes, and to point out the closer resemblance of Agnes to Mary Hogarth. "Dickens, no doubt, had no conscious wish for Catherine to die as Dora had done," he concludes: "but David effectually kills Dora, as Murdstone had killed Clara, by domination, and David's expressions of sorrow have never been found very convincing. . . . One regrets that Catherine's views on *David Copperfield*, like John Dickens's, have not been recorded."[5]

Collins is certainly closer to the mark than those students of Dickens who have too readily accepted, from the evidence of the novelist's letters, that the inspiration of Copperfield's first marriage was primarily the early love for Maria Beadnell. Yet there is little external evidence of marital discontent at the time of writing the novel, and even Maria had not yet made her reappearance in Dickens's life.[6] The marriage in reality seems to have been stable enough and its reflection in *Copperfield* light-hearted. The ebullience of the chapters describing David's life with Dora is perhaps chargeable to a genuine humor of relief—relief, that is, from some simmering discontent with his marriage. Relief then drains off into fantasy of release, tinged with blame and mourning. For Barbara Hardy, this experience is not depicted seriously or straightforwardly enough in the novel: "Dickens is really only approaching, and then retreating from the idea of showing the disenchanted life."[7] But other critics, notably George H. Ford and Robin Gilmour, have been moved by a sadness and loneliness that are difficult to sort out, or point to in so many words, in Copperfield's story.[8] Monroe Engel tallies the number of losses from death alone in *Copperfield* and concludes that a Steerforth philosophy of "life as a race to be won is a preposterous affront" to so much evidence of unhappiness. This observation, however, takes in Copperfield as well when Engel adds that "any notion of success is an affront, given the pathetic insufficiency of prudence or wisdom to slow or change the current of man's life into death."[9] If these critics, with their differing points of view, have sensitively read an undercurrent of mourning in this generally cheerful work, the source of the undercurrent in Dickens's life at the time was probably his marriage: mourning in the double sense of self-pity and grief for the imagined loss of Catherine entailed by the fantasy of release. The loneliness of the author and hero of *Copperfield* was apparent at times to the author, as a question he put to Forster in late 1854 or early 1855 attests: "Why is it, that as with poor David, a sense comes always crushing on me now, when I fall into low spirits, as of one happiness I have missed in life, and one friend and companion I have never made?" Forster cites the letter in his chapter on the breakup of Dickens's marriage, a chapter discreetly entitled "What Happened at this Time."[10]

When this much is said and done, the undercurrent of mourning cannot be said to drown the book. If anything, it floats the theme of success onward to a happy ending. It almost makes success worthwhile, by beaching it high above the floodtide after loss. Barkis and a number of others go out with the tide, and Copperfield comes home on it. Energy is not lost to mourning, as in *Hamlet*. Instead, much energy in *Copperfield* is expended in positioning the hero with respect to the women in his life. Mothers and stepmothers have to be moved out; surrogate mothers, moved in. The heart has to be disciplined, and this aim is achieved, more strenuously, by moving Dora out. Finally, in the most difficult maneuver of all, the hero has to mate with his angel, the writer with his muse. David and Agnes have to be brought face to face in such a way that, without presumption and without her telling him, he can realize her love. All this positioning in respect to women, especially the two wives, represents most of the work in plotting the novel; the men in this personal history, even Steerforth, fall more readily in and out of place. Novelist and novelist-hero conduct the business smoothly: the partial exception, or residual tension, in management occurs mainly with little Emily. With Rosa Dartle and the prostitute Martha, Emily is the focus of a small constellation of fallen women whose fate is also controlled by the two novelists. Being neither wives nor mothers, they come closest to what Micawber singles out as "woman" and they suffer what the title of the chapter relating Emily's seduction refers to as "A greater Loss" than death.

For two years before the commencement of the novel, Dickens had been engaged with Angela Burdett Coutts in the establishment of a shelter, or "Home," for ex-prostitutes at Shepherd's Bush.[11] This was not, as some writers on Dickens have implied, a daring innovation but rather a modest version of a kind of charity common in London since the eighteenth century. Dickens was acting as almoner for Coutts, an extremely wealthy woman who was providing for the education of his eldest son at the time. His involvement was businesslike, imaginative, and—as Victorian philanthropy went—kindly. The work did bring him into contact with women who had been prostitutes, but the only direct transfer to *David Copperfield* of the novelist's experience would seem to be Martha Endell, who is instrumental in locating the lost Emily. In the words of Mr. Peggotty (words that filter most of what we learn of Emily at the end), Martha "walked among 'em with my child," stole her from among the unreformed prostitutes of London, "and brought her safe out, in the dead of the night, from that black pit of ruin!" (51.623). By contrast with Emily, in fact, the good bad girl Martha is quite a real person, a version of what Dickens and his associates hoped to accomplish at Shepherd's Bush. Like some few of the reformed women from the home, Martha is destined to reach Australia and to marry there. Martha, whom Mr. Peggotty once regarded as "dirt underneath my Em'ly's feet," earns his respect (46.577).

The relatively forthright treatment of Martha Endell in the novel contrasts sharply with the narrator's treatment of her friend. Copperfield actually offers her his arm as they hurry to meet Emily, who seems to have become someone monstrous as the result of Steerforth's seduction. Emily cannot even be looked upon by the hero after her fall, let alone touched, and the strength of this avoidance can be measured by its multiple directions. On the one hand, Ham and Copperfield concur that it might be "too painful" for Emily to see them; on the other, Emily herself, escaping from Littimer at night near Naples, imagines she is on the beach at Yarmouth, "calling out to us," in Mr. Peggotty's account, "to turn away our faces, for she was a coming by" (51.620). Copperfield on his part does not speak even to Mr. Peggotty when he encounters him at night in London, searching for Emily in the streets: "I never speak to him at such an hour. I know too well, as his grave figure passes onward, what he seeks, and what he dreads" (43.536). Such avoidance is incongrous with Dickens's involvement at Shepherd's Bush, as it is with Copperfield's treatment of Martha, however melodramatic. Martha was a decent girl who became a prostitute and then decided to reform, but Emily is a contradiction of motives from beginning to end.[12] Her remorse begins well before she elopes with Steerforth and grips her so consistently that it is impossible to believe she could have run away. It is she, not Martha, who suffers the proverbial fate worse than death, and for whom it might "have been better . . . to have had the waters close above her head that morning in my sight," when she and the narrator were children (3.31). Unlike Martha, she refuses decent proposals of marriage in Australia—an affront to the best hopes of Shepherd's Bush. Little Emily, one judges, is a projection of Copperfield's guilt and desire and is doomed from the start. Among his women, she is the one in whom he has glimpsed sexual desire, chiefly because she is aroused by his account of Steerforth. When he first meets her, they are both children; when they meet again, only he is a child, and "when she drew nearer, and I saw . . . her whole self prettier and gayer, a curious feeling came over me that made me pretend not to know her, and pass by as if I were looking at something a long way off" (10.121). When it comes to positioning himself toward this woman, the narrator is most nearly relentless. The image is always that of a woman passing by and the male trying not to look.

The story of Emily's fall today seems something of a power play. Dickens engaged in power plays at Shepherd's Bush, too, but there he could not invent personalities and had to work with the material at hand, sometimes stubborn material. Even to locate a promising candidate for the home was difficult, and to keep her, should she not comply with the rules, was not desirable. There was the case of one Julia Mozley, who "might be secretly holding communication with some person, over or through the garden fence, in consequence of her regularly absenting herself from the long room, for the last ten evenings or so, immediately after tea, and remaining absent, a quarter of an hour or twenty minutes." Dickens carefully weighed the "circumstances" that told against Mozley and her manner when he questioned her. The gardener had twice accosted a man outside, but "you will understand that the gardener did not see her, and that the man did not communicate, or try to communicate, with anybody inside, while he was there. We agreed that if we could, beyond all doubt, connect her with the man, that would be sufficient reason for immediately dismissing her; but there is no such proof at all." Dickens's own impression is that Mozley "is in the restless state which precedes the determination to go away." His "reason for desiring to know accurately what she is about, is, that we may be beforehand with her, and, if we have any reason to believe she is going, that we may—for the general example—discharge her."[13] The move contemplated here is the ultimate Victorian weapon of exclusion—the same weapon, it might be argued, that helped to create, or at least to define, the "fallen woman" of this society in the first place. Three days later Dickens wrote that Julia Mozley's "manner of replying, in the presence of the rest, was so very sullen and insolent that I fear some noice of it must be taken on Tuesday," though in accordance with the policy of the home he says nothing of it at this time.[14] There cannot be any doubt about who must win this little struggle, since however pleasing and thoughtful the arrangements the women enjoy, there can be no Home without its purposive authority.

As in the novel, there could also be pathos in the home, pathos created by the exercise of authority and exclusion. The case of Isabella

Gordon, a spirited woman who "danced upstairs . . . holding her skirts like a lady at a ball," Dickens and his associates investigated "with the utmost care." "We were all of opinion that the authority of the place *must* be upheld . . . We therefore had her down again some time afterwards, and, to her utter bewilderment and amazement and that of the whole house, dismissed her." To this casting out at gate Dickens was witness, since he and another member of the committee remained to be sure Gordon did no more mischief before she left:

> Her going away, was a most pitiable sight. They all cried bitterly (Mrs. Morson and Mrs. Macartney [the matrons] included) . . . The girl herself, now that it had really come to this, cried, and hung down her head, and when she got out at the door, stopped and leaned against the house for a minute or two before she went to the gate—in a most miserable and wretched state. As it was impossible to relent, with any hope of doing good, we could not do so. We passed her in the lane, afterwards, going slowly away, and wiping her face with her shawl. A more forlorn and hopeless thing altogether, I never saw.[15]

The evidence of such letters suggests that Dickens, like most of us, was fonder of narrating lapses than triumphs of virtue, but that he was nonetheless moved. His description of Isabella Gordon's departure evokes both Victorian sternness and traditional Christian attitudes toward such a fall.

In Victorian novels the symbolic relations of fallen women are often with other women. A favorite cautionary device is to juxtapose a prostitute, excluded from society, with another woman still within its bounds, perhaps the heroine herself. Dickens thus juxtaposed Alice Marwood with Edith Dombey or Martha and the still innocent Emily. But the links among women in *David Copperfield* are not solely cautionary. Copperfield cannot bear to see or be seen by the fallen Emily, yet when he boards the emigrants' ship at Gravesend with Peggotty, he "thought" he saw "a figure like Emily's; it first attracted my attention, by another figure parting from it with a kiss; and as it glided calmly through the disorder, reminding me of—Agnes!" (57.694). When a character glides calmly in this novel, the reader knows well enough that it *is* Agnes, the same Agnes who became intimate with the hero's child-wife in her last illness. Both relations are confirmed later, when Agnes "spoke to me of Emily, whom she had visited, in secret, many times; spoke to me

tenderly of Dora's grave" (60.718). Thus Agnes would seem immune
to the baleful sight of a fallen woman and positively wants to know
these earlier friends of her Trotwood, quite possibly to gain by the
acquaintance. The ministration of that parting kiss is not only from
angelic purity to fallen sexuality but usefully the other way around as
well.[16] Agnes contacts thereby a sexuality that the hero dares not look
upon, so much does he desire it. These partially hidden relations among
women are fancied by Dickens on behalf of his young man Copperfield.
The same writer not long before imagined a relation between pro-
spective candidates for the home and Burdett Coutts, their patroness
and his. In a leaflet for distribution, describing the project at Shepherd's
Bush, he wrote:

> There is a lady in this town, who, from the windows of her house, has
> seen such as you going past at night, and has felt her heart bleed at the
> sight. She is what is called a great lady; but she has looked after you with
> compassion, as being of her own sex and nature; and the thought of such
> fallen women has troubled her in her bed. She has resolved to open, at
> her own expense, a place of refuge very near London, for a small number
> of females, who, without such help, are lost forever: and to make of it A
> HOME for them.[17]

The prostitutes pass by in the night, but the philanthropist too is
"woman." She is not at all a sex object, like Emily in the novel, but in
the age-old fashion for men she too represents sexuality—"her own sex
and nature"—as she lies troubled in her bed.

Relations among women do not exhaust the possibilities inherent in
fallen women, however, and sexuality is not the only ground of identification with them. Fallen women may also be contemplated or created
for reasons of personal history, like the history that underlies the childhood chapters of *David Copperfield*. Dickens urged the benefactress of
the home to visit a prison, so that she might fully realize the before
and after of their effort to reclaim homeless women,[18] and surely behind
this invitation lies the value he himself places on such a comparison.
Each candidate for reform has a past, a past that is both the cause of
what she is today and the reason she would change. For this model of
the self, the past is disjunctive: there was a fall from innocence and her
reformation will constitute still another break with the past. But her
reform cannot, even ideally, be a return to innocence, since the fall

must be remembered as well as forgotten. The model is very clear and pertinent for Dickens. A rule for the matrons and visitors to Shepherd's Bush is that the inmates' "past lives should never be referred to, at the Home,"[19] yet he also urges that they not forget the past, for "no woman at the Home who is not quite satisfied that her past life was vicious and miserable, will ever keep out of it when she is free again."[20] This combination of concealment and remembrance is very like that which Dickens proposed for himself in his autobiographical fragment and his novel.

The leaflet by Dickens advertising the home begins by addressing any woman who "has lived miserably" and ends by appealing to earlier memories:

> If any remembrance ever comes into your mind of any time when you were innocent and very different, think of [the home] then. If you should be softened by a moment's recollection of any tenderness or affection you have ever felt, or that has ever been shown to you, or of any kind word that has ever been spoken to you, think of it then. If ever your poor heart is moved to feel, truly, what you might have been, and what you are, oh think of it then, and consider what you may be yet![21]

Memory, of both misery and tenderness, is what the early chapters of *Copperfield* are all about. From the writing of *A Christmas Carol* on, Dickens had been urging the case for "what you might have been, and what you are . . . [and] what you may be yet" with respect to male figures, from Scrooge to the personification of himself as novelist; and once the five Christmas books were behind him, he continued to address the subject in his Christmas stories for *Household Words* and *All the Year Round*.[22] Dickens insisted especially on the value of *un*pleasant memories in securing a present sense of identity. *The Haunted Man* was the story of one who thinks he would like to forget his memories of sorrow and wrong but learns that he must remember. As with young Copperfield, so with Redlaw and his double: "A stranger came into my father's place when I was but a child, and I was easily an alien from my mother's heart. My parents, at the best, were of that sort whose care soon ends."[23] The tendency of such fictions, typical of fairy tales and prior to psychoanalysis, is to posit a fall that takes place in childhood: but this fall could also be displaced sideways upon women whose pasts so much more obviously needed managing in the present, and whose concealed shame and remembrance had something in common with the situation of Dickens, involved in his partial revelation to Forster, his autobiographical fiction, and his fictional autobiography.

A fallen woman is a mythical figure of a self that is discontinuous; and a reformed prostitute, an image of the necessity of concealing the past while privately remembering. These are my grounds for suggesting that Dickens could partially identify with such figures, real and imagined. Though he only briefly supervised the lives of former prostitutes, he is one of our prominent creators of fallen women in fiction. He may sometimes have imagined a cabal of women, a secret interconnectedness as of the speculative Burdett Coutts troubled in her bed by those in the street, or the gliding Agnes embracing the woman on whom Copperfield ("blind, blind, blind" to more than one) cannot look; but he also seized these homely and professional opportunitites to shape authoritatively persons like himself but more simply conceived. In this period Dickens was fortunate and happy, and found "something of personal affection in people . . . mixed up with my public reputation."[24] That he and his public had shameful pasts, or because of the demand of the times for rising in the world felt as if they had shameful pasts, may partially explain their persistent interest in fallen women. Little Emily invites such interest in one of her letters home: "Oh, take comfort in thinking that I am so bad. Oh, for mercy's sake, tell uncle that I never loved him half so dear as now. Oh . . . try to think as if I died when I was little, and was buried somewhere" (31.386). Male identification with a fallen woman, obviously, can only be intermittent at best. That this identification is possible, however, is apparent from the invitation "to think of me as if I died when I was little," which recalls little surrogate heroes like Dick in *Oliver Twist* or the infant half-brother who is buried in *Copperfield*. At the same time, a woman must remain other and apart if one is to "take comfort in thinking" that she is bad—a practice that requires heroes to stay out of trouble and explains the need for Steerforths.

This survey of women who pass by in the street and the woman who passes before Copperfield's averted eyes would not be complete without some notice of Annie Strong, a character supposed to be bad but truly very good. As we have already seen, certain clues—the Dictionary, the letter D, the figure 1649—link Annie's husband to Dickens, and while writing *Copperfield,* at about the time it became necessary to kill off

Dora, the writer named his newborn child Dora Annie. Within the novel, Annie is a rather more dangerous child-wife than Dora, a less certainly reliable daughter than Agnes. All that quizzical suspense about her possible interest in Jack Maldon cannot fail to leave its impression. Though she is not, like Rosa Dartle and Martha Endell, related to Emily and Yarmouth, the prospect of her sexual availability takes her in the direction of an unfallen fallen woman. Her beauty is significantly "mistrusted" by young Copperfield as well as by Wickfield, who is afraid her company may taint his Agnes (19.240). Yet Annie Strong has a privileged position in the novel—and not just as a young person who gives her name to the novelist's daughter. Hers is the voice that states the moral that Copperfield finds himself repeating over and over with regard to his own first marriage: "there can be no disparity in marriage like unsuitability of mind and purpose" (45.564).

Students of *David Copperfield* have taken due note of the moral[25] without worrying very much why it should travel such an oblique route to the hero's consciousness. Its triply negative formulation—"no disparity in marriage like unsuitability of mind and purpose"—makes the comparison hard to refute. As in all comparisons of the form "nothing like *x*," the rhetorical emphasis falls on the second term, here "unsuitability of mind and purpose." This phrase alludes to the marriage Annie Strong refrained from making with Jack Maldon. She has resisted the advances of Maldon before and after her marriage to Strong, and by extension her example would seem to rebuke the interest of the hero in his own Dora: by repeating the saying Copperfield circumspectly admits to himself that he married only for sex. But what of the "disparity in marriage" dismissed in the first term of the comparison under the negative universal? The logic sweeps this term aside—there are no bad oranges like a bad apple either, and any disparity will serve the purpose. Yet in point of fact the disparity muted here is a much more staring one than the barely hinted differences in temperament between Annie and Jack: it is the obvious disparity in age between Annie and the man she did marry. To resist the rhetoric of the saying in this way, and to unpack the triple negative, is to find a defense of parity or suitability in the Strongs' marriage. The valorization of their obvious disparity helps explain why the saying might lodge in Copperfield's mind and emerge as the moral of his own story. Annie Strong is a desirable woman whose availability becomes a matter for discussion; she is proof that an attractive young woman—at least in a novel—can pair successfully with a man old enough to be her grandfather; and that same man has vague self-depreciating associations with Dickens. In this extravagant, not to say tortured, demonstration the novelist toyed with a flattering sexual interpretation of Cordelia-like loyalty to a husband. In order to indulge this demonstration at all, it would seem that he had to forget his critical representation of Lear-like obsession in Wickfield's behavior to his daughter. Despite his severe treatment of Wickfield, however, he fell into fantasizing a little about Strong.

In *Le Roi s'amuse* Hugo chose to turn King Lear into the court jester whose daughter Blanche sleeps with François I. For Hugo's capacious romantic imagination Cordelia could *be* a fallen woman, and this despite his strenuous admiration for the divine girl, as she appeared to him, of Shakespeare's play. His Blanche could become the ill-fated mistress of the king and still be a thoroughly idealized heroine: the sexual fall merely adds to the range of possibilities for men that she can represent. Dickens, even in his most romantic version of the story of Lear and Cordelia, keeps his heroine pure for marriage, which in *Little Dorrit* partakes of something like a divine comedy. Agnes's purity, in *David Copperfield*, is so evident that the hero finds it hard to believe that he is worthy of her or that anyone might bed her. But Dickens makes room in the novel for brave Annie Strong and for another idealized figure, Emily, who may not be loved by the hero but is passionately and unremittingly loved by Mr. Peggotty. The purity of *his* love confers with a fallen woman face to face, and the love of the older man for a young woman exults in fierce sublimation. Mr. Peggotty, who all along has regarded the orphaned Emily as his daughter, pursues her after her fall with a determination that Dickens suggests is virtually the highest love on earth. The sexual relation with Emily that is denied to Copperfield and granted to Steerforth is thus permanently sublimated by this self-appointed, self-sacrificing parent: "All night long, her arms has been about my neck," Mr. Peggotty can inform the hero at last; "and her head has laid heer; and we knows full well, as we can put our trust in one another, ever more" (51.623).

We have seen that *King Lear* still had its impress on this novel that is mainly about Dickens's childhood and his assured identity as a novelist, as Dickens. If *David Copperfield* was the favorite child among his novels, the public reading he prepared from it in 1868, two years before

his death, was also a favorite with him. In the performance, his acting of Mr. Peggotty's part reminded at least one newspaper critic of Lear.[26] We have also seen that Freud believed, a little Micawber-like in his tripartite division, that Cordelia was mother, wife, and death, and that Lear was a man like every other. By preferring Mother Earth or the Goddess of Death as the third type of woman, he avoided the more commonplace daughter favored by Dickens and Shakespeare. The mother is the one essential figure in Freud's scheme, and it is as if in death Oedipal longings were warranted at last—while by referring so insistently to childhood, his theory could play down the temptations of women passing by. Dickens, like so many other novelists, generally disposes of mothers or is careful to ridicule them. One of the virtues of Agnes Wickfield, clearly, is that she has disposed of her mother very early: " 'Mama has been dead ever since I was born,' she said, in her quiet way" (16.196). That is very promising for a person so young, in her first conversation with the hero. Dickens, of course, had Shakespeare to guide him and may have recalled from *Pericles* the words of Marina,

> My mother was the daughter of a king,
> Who died the minute I was born
> (V.i.157–158)

or from *The Winter's Tale* the words of Perdita,

> Dear queen, that ended when I but began,
> Give me that hand of yours to kiss
> (V.iii.45–46)

though their mothers are surprisingly still alive.

All of these stories—Freud's, Dickens's, Shakespeare's—are more or less graceful evasions of "woman" and the death that men fear from the act of generation, which they imagine women do not fear. If the tension of Copperfield's relation to Emily—the scene, for example, in which he stands idly by while Rosa Dartle administers a tongue-lashing to her unsurpassed for cruelty in any of the novels—at times seems unresolved or perplexed, or the whole treatment of sexuality in the novel at once dire and hopeful, it may be useful to think that Dickens was writing *David Copperfield* at about the same age as Shakespeare when writing his so-called problem comedies, with their vexed attitude toward sexuality and dramatized resistance to marriage, family, and death.

Still, the novel reads so smoothly as the "life" of the novelist that the problems it addresses along the way can easily be overlooked. It is time to turn to the means by which *Copperfield* achieves its impression of easy humor, its fairy-tale confabulation and fulfillment. Helpless as a child and passive as an adult—except in his devotion to work—the hero owes his eventual good fortune to an aggressive plot, and this passive-aggressive design of the novel as a whole can be enjoyed in the humor as well—not least in the happy invention of Wilkins Micawber.

X

Perfection of English Mirth

$\mathcal{T}$he kind of literature that may finally bulk largest in the pages of *David Copperfield* is of the sort commonly devoted to childhood in the nineteenth century and collectively denominated fairy tales. It is no accident that this novel occupies the center of Harry Stone's study of the fairy-tale content of Dickens's fiction. The motifs that Stone takes up, and which *Copperfield* shares with literature expressly for children, are by no means confined to the early chapters: a general superintendance of a fairy godmother, Betsey Trotwood; abandonment by the child's own parents and sufferance under stepparents; the transformation of the hero into an animal who bites and his later meeting with a woman guarded by a small dog; the frightening journey, which is not really picaresque and features a man who cries "Oh, my liver," and "goroo"; the quasi-supernatural presence of Uriah Heep and coincidental appearances of Martha Endell; the fierce sexual intensity of Rosa Dartle and fairy sexuality of little Emily; and of course the marvelously happy ending. "In real life," as Stone observes of the last point, "there are no Agneses."[1] It is some kind of a tribute to Dickens that the other contemporary student of his work who devotes equivalent space to this novel, Sylvère Monod, can report that "the reader's first impression of *David Copperfield* is one of profound truthfulness."[2] We may simply have to settle for Barbara Hardy's conclusion that Dickens, like Charlotte Brontë, worked "very close to life in some respects, and very far away from it in others."[3]

Some of the fairy-tale content of *Copperfield* was anticipated by what Forster generalizes as the "method" of Dickens's masters in the novelist's art. Smollett and Fielding did not write picaresque fiction in its original Spanish mode but adopted its incidental and episodic structure to stories with the contented happy endings of comedy. There was plenty of fairty-tale content in the novels of Dickens's forebears, even as there was in the novels of Richardson and Austen. When, fifty years ago, T. A. Jackson tried to characterize the influence of Defoe on *Copperfield*, he suggested that "such plot as there is must, on this method, seem to be fortuitous and extraneous, since the main theme is the arrival of the hero at his self-appointed end—in this case prosperity and happiness with his second wife."[4] About twenty years ago, touching on another possible influence, *Jane Eyre*, E. D. H. Johnson wrote that "Jane and David undergo similar ordeals entailing loss of innocence through revolt against injustice and banishment from their homes."[5] Dickens was not the first or even the last great novelist to work into his designs the kinds of incident, displacement, and wish fulfillment found in fairy tales, and the bow to his predecessors within the novel may indicate his awareness of the fact. They are, with the exception of Cervantes and Le Sage, English novelists whom he celebrates. His Copperfield, for the most part passive and correct, like other nineteenth-century heroes, is constrained by middle-class manners—though insofar as his adventures become discreetly aggressive, he might be said to veer back to a true picaresque line.[6]

The plot in this autobiographical work exemplifies what Hardy calls "a very neat graph of progress."[7] The plan to base the novel on his own life obviated the kind of effort required for Dickens to fashion himself objectively as Mr. Dombey or even subjectively as the dying little Paul; at the same time, *David Copperfield* does not exhibit the rather wild projection of the author characteristic of *Martin Chuzzlewit*. Not to play down the achievement in any way, there was less for Dickens to do—and fewer leaps and bounds for his unconscious projections to do for him—in *Copperfield*. The result was a novel much more accessible for most readers, over the years, than either of the prevous two. Instead of multiplying on his author this time, the hero prudently adapts as necessary to each successive epoch of his life. As we know, Dickens spent some time searching out a name for his hero, and when he was done, Forster had to point out to him that in "David Copperfield" he had reversed the two initial letters of his own name. In two surviving memoranda, "Charles" itself appears as a name for the hero.[8] The name so carefully sought by the novelist then proceeds to change, in the course of the novel, with each significant set of characters the hero encounters. Monod observes that Murdstone alone firmly addresses him as "David."[9] His mother calls him "Davy" and Peggotty "Master Davy," dialect versions of which are employed by the Yarmouth characters, Mr. Peggotty and Ham. His aunt, who prefers to think of him as the girl-child Betsey Trotwood Copperfield, calls him "Trot" for short. His school chums address him as "Copperfield," except for Steerforth, who has the privilege of calling him "Daisy." Uriah Heep deliberately stumbles over "Mister" so that he can go on using the juvenile "Master Copperfield." Dora, his first wife, can manage "Doady"; and Agnes, his second, permanently settles for "Trotwood." Little Emily dares not name him at all. So carefully christened by Charles Dickens, David Copperfield accepts all his names with equanimity except for Heep's "Master—I should say Mister," which irritates him no end. These names speak his history: the novelist who all the while gives each and every one of the characters names in writing of them passively acquiesces, apparently, in the destiny they shape for him. Paradoxically, the hero of many names emerges with more substantial identity than either of the two Martin Chuzzlewits, nor does he suffer a tragedy like that of either of the two Paul Dombeys. The sum of his names is evidently greater than its parts.

The novel's one outstanding displacement confirms the hero's general passivity. Uriah Heep is a Doppelgänger, like Rigaud in *Little Dorrit* and Orlick in *Great Expectations,* in whom the aggressive and sexual demands of the hero are strangely absorbed and whose criminal doings, as eventually exposed, clear the hero of blame.[10] Heep is the one character who is obviously misnamed in the novel, and who—with a reversal apparently unconscious on Dickens's part, like that of the reversal of his own initials in the naming of Copperfield—should by rights be named David. For in the Bible it is Uriah the Hittite who has legitimate claims to his wife Bathsheba and King David who lusts after the woman he ought not to have.[11] In the novel, of course, Agnes is not forbidden because she is another man's wife but because she is, in the hero's eyes, "so much too loving and too good for any one." Agnes is attached to her father to begin with, and Heep slyly points out the sex appeal of such goodness. His plan is generally to blackmail her into submission by shaping himself as a threat to Wickfield: "she's so much attached to her father, Master Copperfield (oh what a lovely thing it is in a daughter!), that I think she may come, on his account, to be kind to me." Their echoing language—Heep's spoken words, "so much attached," immediately enter Copperfield's thoughts as "so much too loving"—and the way in which Heep constantly confides in him, much to the hero's disgust, mark the former as a true Doppelgänger, whose main function in *David Copperfield* is to embody sexual longing and to take the offensive against the father who stands in its way. To express his meaning, Dickens appeals to symbolism and dreaming:

> I believe I had a delirious idea of seizing the red-hot poker out of the fire, and running him through with it. It went from me with a shock, like a ball fired from a rifle: but the image of Agnes, outraged by so much as a thought of this red-headed animal's, remained in my mind when I looked at him, sitting all awry as if his mean soul gripped his body, and made me giddy. He seemed to swell and grow before my eyes; the room seemed full of the echoes of his voice; and the strange feeling (to which, perhaps, no one is quite a stranger) that all this had occurred before, at some indefinite time, and that I knew what he was going to say next, took possession of me. (25.326–327)

In the next chapter Copperfield meets Dora Spenlow, falls into immediate "Captivity"—or protective custody, in effect—and so is out of harm's way for a while. The other episode in which Heep and Copperfield come this close ("*I* knew what *he* was going to say next"; "his mean soul gripped *his* body, and made *me* giddy"; my "red-hot poker" and that "red-headed animal's") is that in which Heep tries to intervene in the marriage of Annie and Dr. Strong. By the time he is finally brought to book by spirits friendly to the hero, it is unmistakable that Heep is a creature of "odious passions" and not just an upstart after Mr. Wickfield's money (52.641). At the same time, the whole conception of Uriah Heep as the "umble" hypocrite shadows darkly Copperfield's rise in the world through earnestness and hard work. The Doppelgänger is in revolt against the deference demanded of the young and ambitious in all societies, but with particular severity in Victorian England.

Privilege and freedom of movement—and their corruption—are

memorably represented in the novel by Steerforth, who is nearly uniformly addressed by that name—"Steerforth"—so suggestive of his role. Copperfield has a schoolboy crush on him that he never altogether surrenders, and if Dickens was trying to express the attraction of a certain higher-class type and to sound a warning about misplaced confidence, he did so without portraying him as demonic. Agnes worries that Steerforth may become a "bad Angel" as well as a "dangerous friend" to Copperfield (25.313), but in truth he is a subtly drawn character who acts in the novel on quite a different level of representation than that of the demonic Heep.[12] Heep would not exist without Copperfield; Steerforth performs in the world as the hero would like to yet is a separate person, beloved by Copperfield. He does not merely writhe with longing the way Heep does: he satisfies himself, with that minimal degree of guilt commensurate with his class and particular upbringing.[13] Steerforth's dashing about contrasts with the hero's passivity, as Heep's creeping about undermines it. He cuts a swathe at school and at Yarmouth that Copperfield would like to cut. He half offers a discarded Rosa Dartle to his friend and goes about seducing Emily—the woman most sexually attractive to Copperfield, if he could bear to look at her. Steerforth's behavior is all wrong, but the hero cannot help admiring it in part. In another curious twist of a biblical text—of the New Testament this time—Steerforth becomes the gentlemanly equivalent of the lilies of the field.[14] He on his part admits to, but is not moved by, a certain admiration for the innocent Daisy: "we'll drink the daisies of the field, in compliment to you; and the lilies of the valley that toil not, neither do they spin, in compliment to me— the more shame for me!" (20.252).

Steerforth and Copperfield are not equals, and the hero cannot help loving the superior being. Dickens both criticizes and accepts this relation, and makes his hero "not afraid to write":

> I never had loved Steerforth better than when the ties that bound me to him were broken. In the keen distress of the discovery of his unworthiness, I thought more of all that was brilliant in him, I softened more towards all that was good in him, I did more justice to the qualities that might have made him a man of a noble nature and a great name, than ever I had done in the height of my devotion to him. Deeply as I felt my own unconscious part in his pollution of an honest home, I believe that if I

had been brought face to face with him, I could not have uttered one reproach. I should have loved him so well still . . .

The hero just mentions his own "unconscious part" in the seduction of Emily, and it is difficult to gauge how far forgiveness masks the swift justice that he and Dickens have in store for his friend. "Yes, Steerforth, long removed from the scenes of this poor history! My sorrow may bear involuntary witness against you at the Judgment Throne; but my angry thoughts or my reproaches never will, I know!" (32.388). After this seemingly heartfelt apostrophe, "involuntary" testimony, and assurances from Copperfield that he is not angry, one already wonders what will become of Steerforth. The hero's attitude is much like that of Redlaw in *The Haunted Man*, and Dickens more than once expressed himself so on his own account: he did not "write resentfully or angrily" about the blacking warehouse, but neither did he want the part his parents played to be forgotten.[15]

The courage and stamina of the child, in *David Copperfield*, reappear as a fundamental optimism and capacity for work in the man as he grows up. Though this basically decent person is no self-lacerating or even self-critical hero, it is evident that the narrator of his own life intends to expose his ignorance at the time of Steerforth's flaws and Agnes's love, and even to admit that during his first marriage he caused Dora some pain. What is less certainly admirable is an aggressive turn of events in the novel that Dickens closely coordinates with the hero's passivity. The brilliantly evoked, humorously exaggerated helplessness of childhood continues as a fairy tale of a somewhat different magnitude, in which, though he is no longer a child, the young man attains what he wishes and those who stand in his way are bowled over—not by his own actions but by the course of events unrolled by Dickens. In fact, when the narrator acknowledges "that life was more like a great fairy story, which I was just about to begin to read," he is already past childhood and looking about for himself, after leaving Dr. Strong's school in Canterbury (19.233). These words apply to his subsequent history, and in the manuscript of *Copperfield* Dickens added a second clause about the fairy story—"and of which the hero was David from the very first page"[16]—that compounded its egotism and answered the famous opening of the novel—"Whether I shall turn out to be the hero of my own life, or whether that station will be held by anybody else, these pages must show"—as if there could subsequently be no doubt of the identity of the hero or the turn of events. Presumably the extra clause was struck out because it contravened the modesty of the opening, but even so the note of self-depreciating irony in "a great fairy story" is soon lost in *Copperfield*. Instead of the humorous perspective of the early chapters—some of it at the child's expense—the novelist-hero and real novelist tend to join forces. Copperfield remains passive and law-abiding; Dickens goes about eliminating characters who stand in his hero's path and rewarding "thorough-going, ardent, and sincere earnestness."

There are exceptions to the tendencies of both portions of the novel, before and after "I make another Beginning" (chapter 15), but by and large a more arbitrary form of egocentricity supplants what we feel is only natural in a child, and those who have crossed or inconvenienced the hero, Steerforth not excepted, feel the wrath of the master novelist behind Copperfield. The much admired "Tempest" (chapter 55), in which both Ham and Steerforth meet their deaths, is merely the best evidence of novelistic aggression. The word painting in that chapter stirs up a storm uncharacteristic of the calm of *David Copperfield* as a whole—because Dickens is up to one of his murders again, as if Jonas Chuzzlewit or Sikes were still at large. Despite the hero's depression and confusion and premonitions during the storm, we always know exactly where he is, and the narrative establishes his alibi. In vain he tries to stop Ham from risking his life to save Steerforth: "I held him back with both arms; and implored the men with whom I had been speaking, not to listen to him, not to do murder, not to let him stir from off that sand!" The alibi keeps building along with the storm; the ship goes down. First they recover Ham's body: "they drew him to my very feet—insensible—dead . . . and, no one preventing me now, I remained near him." Then he is led up the beach to Steerforth: "I saw him lying with his head upon his arm, as I had often seen him lie at school" (55.680–681). The storm and the chapter are over.

For a novel that Forster, along with many other readers, admires for its "free and cheery style" and "uniform pleasantness of tone,"[17] *Copperfield* tells of a good number of deaths, all of which satisfy some wrong to the hero or facilitate his eventual happiness. Ham and Steerforth win the most dramatic and symbolic deaths, and of course they have both competed with Copperfield for the love of Emily. Steerforth, with his head upon his arm, has additionally represented the love that a hero must not have for a man. Even Barkis is a rival, of sorts, for the attentions of Peggotty, though his death—characterized as "A Loss" (chapter 30)—serves mainly to foreshadow the fall that is worse than death— "A greater Loss" (chapter 31)—of Emily herself: the fall, that is, of one who should have been content to love her childhood sweetheart, whether Ham or Master Davy. Two fathers of desirable women, Spenlow and Wickfield, die or vanish almost magically before they can oppose the hero's desires or inconvenience him as fathers-in-law. Even his mother, Clara Copperfield, has opposed his interest at the outset by remarrying and bearing another child, and she promptly dies as a consequence. Notoriously his child-bride, Dora Copperfield, dies commending him to Agnes, while the unfriendly Jip expires, in Phiz's drawing, between Doady's feet and the famous Pagoda. Whereas the evil personages of the fairy tale—Murdstone and Heep and Littimer—live on in situations fraught with irony about the world in which they operate, mistaken and loving persons who get in the hero's way are swept to their deaths. Though Ross H. Dabney has suggested that Dickens must have been uneasy about what he was doing in *Copperfield* if he could make Dora even want to die and be out of her husband's way,[18] the deaths in the novel are all narrated so surely that readers seldom notice the accumulated aggression behind them. That Dickens could get away with so much willed mortality, in a successful novel about personal success, argues how comfortably passive-aggressive designs suit the fantasy lives of the bourgeoisie.

David Copperfield is an extremely well-told story. Though Dickens's later novels often dominate academic criticism today, this is for reasons intrinsic to those novels and to modern times, and not usually an implied criticism of *Copperfield*—which indeed still has its champions.[19] Yet its "neat graph of progress," as Hardy implies, is a little too neat and the brilliance of its telling a little dulled by our awareness of what it leaves unsaid. The regret of Angus Wilson that the novel is "so bounded by middle-class horizons" and "the epitome of Victorian bourgeois morality"[20] is like a cruel mirror glancing back a hundred years upon the satisfaction that John Forster took in the same text. For Forster, who placed the turning point of Dickens's career slightly earlier, underscoring the financial security attained with *Dombey and Son,* the making of *Copperfield* was clearly the epitome of Dickens's moral and artistic achievement. The humor and moderation of the book appealed to Forster, and even its narrative ordering—more straightforward than usual for Dickens. Though he judged that autobiography "in imaginative literature has too often led to the indulgence of mental analysis, metaphysics, and sentiment, all in excess," he believed that Dickens "was carried safely over these allurements by a healthy judgment and sleepless creative fancy."[21] The premium placed on moderation, health, and safety by this praise is evident. Only the fancy of the writer is sleepless—a supposition entirely consistent with a passive-aggressive construction of the novel as a whole.

For Forster, this creative fancy never disrupts the orderly narrative of the growth of David Copperfield to manhood:

> That the incidents arise easily, and to the very end connect themselves naturally and unobtrusively with the characters of which they are a part, is to be said perhaps more truly of this than of any other of Dickens's novels. There is a profusion of distinct and distinguishable people, a prodigal wealth of detail; but unity of drift or purpose is apparent always, and the tone is uniformly right. By the course of the events we learn the value of self-denial and patience, quiet endurance of unavoidable ills, strenuous effort against ills remediable; and everything in the fortunes of the actors warns us, to strengthen our generous emotions and to guard the purities of home.

There could hardly be a more delicate statement of official morality and aesthetics than this Victorian celebration of purpose amid profusion. Forster completely forgets that the fiction was constructed and the fortunes of the actors made, even though he has just recounted how Dickens consulted him on the death of Dora. From such fictions "we learn the value of self-denial and patience," and Forster's admiration of the novel thereby endorses the same remorseless wish fulfillment as the writing of it. He particularly admires, and informs us that Dickens admired, "the Peggotty group," in which the goodness and heroism of the humblest classes are displayed. This reflection leads inevitably to a recall of the denouement in that action:

> the storm and shipwreck at the close of *Copperfield*, when the body of the seducer is flung upon the shore amid the ruins of the home he has wasted and by the side of the man whose heart he has broken, the one as un-

conscious of what he had failed to reach as the other of what he has perished to save, is a description that may compare with the most impressive in the language.[22]

Here as elsewhere, Forster goes on to testify to Dickens's emotion and exhaustion from the writing of such scenes. The beauty of the tragic scene for him, and perhaps for most readers, is that Ham and Steerforth cannot and do not experience any recognition whatever. The irony to which he expertly calls attention thus conspires in another silence, related to that which allows the aggressive strain of the plot to go unnoticed. Only David Copperfield, who was present but constrained from action, can savor the coincidence of the deaths and convey the justice of it to his readers. The hero's passivity is no less obvious here, in the aftermath of the terrible storm, than it is in the scene in which he stands by while Micawber and Traddles deal with Uriah Heep. But he possesses knowledge that the other actors lack, and the justice of it pleases.

Forster was calling attention to the very real success of *David Copperfield*. The effects he admires are not without value, and he stresses far more the humor of the book than its guarding of the purities of home. "It is," he says, "the perfection of English mirth," and there are many who are disposed to agree with him. Even if *Chuzzlewit* is the funniest book in the language, the mirth of *Copperfield* may be perfect as Forster defines perfection. Such mirth combines "the ludicrous in any object or incident" with "its most enchanting sentiment," though both conditions remain somewhat vague and entangled with Mr. Micawber's contribution to the novel. Even Micawber, apparently, cannot raise *Copperfield* to rank among the funniest of Dickens's novels, yet his characterization seems to guide what the critic has to say about the superlative quality of this one:

> Mr. Micawber's presence must not prevent my saying that it does not take the lead of the other novels in humorous creation; but in the use of humour to bring out prominently the ludicrous in any object or incident without excluding or weakening its most enchanting sentiment, it stands decidedly first. It is the perfection of English mirth. We are apt to resent the exhibition of too much goodness, but it is here so qualified by oddity as to become not merely palatable but attractive; and even pathos is heightened by what in other hands would only make it comical. That there are also faults in the book is certain . . .

150

Truly it is harder to understand this, the highest praise Forster accords to Dickens, than his bow to the domestic virtues or his contention that there can hardly be "a reader, man or lad," who does not identify with the hero.[23] The perfection of English mirth is framed by apologies— Micawber is not the funniest of Dickens's creations, and the book has its faults. But the phrase itself also confers an apology, because perfection finally means compromise. The critic leads into the praise by celebrating the "ludicrous" not without "sentiment" and leads out of it by celebrating "goodness" not without "oddity." Though he does not spell out the meaning of these terms, a compromise is apparent that renders English mirth harmless. Some of the forces compromised, I suggest, are the combined passive and aggressive longings that Dickens so successfully imitated from fairy tales and employed for his own fictional confession of progress. Hobbesian or Freudian spirits will argue in any case that mirth is not possible without aggression; Forster in effect claims that aggression and suffering are intolerable without mirth. To live comfortably with such affective forces is English, and that which is not English is extreme.

This highest praise for Dickens's humor hesitates over Mr. Micawber, and yet that gentleman is undoubtedly the "object" Forster has most in mind[24] and is possibly the most famous caricature by Dickens *of* passive aggression. The compromise represented by Micawber encompasses nearly abject obeisance to fate and defiance of fate at the same time. The behavior of the man is routinely passive, his expression everlastingly hopeful. We have to credit more than words alone in this man of words, for he sees the world in such ineluctable colors of despair that hope itself is heroic. In a key episode of the novel, overwhelmed by a particular difficulty after his employment by Heep, Micawber proposes to meet Copperfield outside the King's Bench Prison in London. Merely to make this appointment requires an epistle of impressive dimensions: "in stating that I shall be (D.V.) on the outside of the south wall of that place of incarceration on civil process, the day after to-morrow, at seven in the evening, precisely," the penultimate paragraph of the letter winds down, "my object in this epistolary communication is accomplished." Such wielding of the passive voice in Micawber's communications can be thought of as passive-aggressive heroism of a high literary order. His selection of the prison as a meeting place speaks eloquently of the Micawber world view, since his fondness

151

for the place is compounded of helplessness and resistance. The debtors' prison is a veritable fortification of irresponsibility against the world. Copperfield and Traddles find their friend there before the appointed hour, "standing with his arms folded, over against the wall, looking at the spikes at the top, with a sentimental expression, as if they were the interlacing of boughs of trees that had shaded him in his youth."

"And this," said Mr. Micawber, nodding his head sorrowfully, "is the Bench! Where, for the first time in many revolving years, the overwhelming pressure of pecuniary liabilities was not proclaimed, from day to day, by importunate voices declining to vacate the passage; where there was no knocker on the door for any creditor to appeal to; where personal service of process was not required, and detainers were merely lodged at the gate! Gentlemen," said Mr. Micawber, "when the shadow of that iron-work on the summit of the brick structure has been reflected on the gravel of the Parade, I have seen my children thread the mazes of the intricate pattern, avoiding the dark marks. I have been familiar with every stone in the place. If I betray weakness, you will know how to excuse me." (49.599, 602)

It has to be stressed that Micawber has no other reason for meeting his friends in this place than to bolster his spirits. His state of mind is especially precarious on this occasion; his friends cannot tell what the matter is. Only after they travel together to Highgate, where Mr. Dick and Betsey Trotwood also prepare to comfort him, does the emotional state of Micawber make itself clear. He is angry: the anger he has been holding in has put him in this state of mind.

The anger is against Heep. But where else in his writing has Dickens given anger such a chapter-long build up and conveyed it, with all the comedic exaggeration, so dramatically? Surely not, for example, in the anger expressed by old Martin Chuzzlewit and beat in with his cane on the back of Pecksniff. The whole point of the scene with Micawber is the suppression of anger and its expression. Copperfield and the others assure him that he is among friends and may speak freely. Micawber himself points out that unrepressed anger strains friendship, demolishes politeness, attacks the limits of everyday discourse: "it is principally because I *am* among friends that my state of mind is what it is." Once he has begun to reveal his thoughts, he exclaims, "The struggle is over!" The struggle has been to repress and not to express, in the name of that passivity which is civilized behavior itself, even justifiably hostile feelings. It is all very enjoyable to hear the anger pour forth at last, spattering the liquid of Mr. Micawber's usual style:

> "I'll put my hand in no man's hand," said Mr. Micawber, gasping, puffing, and sobbing, to that degree that he was like a man fighting with cold water, "until I have—blown to fragments—the—a—detestable—serpent—HEEP! I'll partake of no one's hospitality, until I have—a—moved Mount Vesuvius—to eruption—on—a—the abandoned rascal—HEEP! Refreshment—a—underneath this roof—particularly punch—would—a—choak me—unless—I had—previously—choaked the eyes—out of the head—a—of—interminable cheat, and liar—HEEP! I—a—I'll know nobody—and—a—say nothing—and—a—live nowhere—until I have crushed—to—a—undiscoverable atoms—the—transcendent and immortal hypocrite and perjurer—HEEP!" (49.606–607)

Of course there is very serious aggression, as well, in Micawber's way of life. His philosophy that something will turn up is a dangerous travesty of nineteenth-century political economy, which seems to allow freedom but dictates the earnestness of individual economic drives. The only largess permitted by that economy, in theory, exists within the family, where it flows mainly from parents to children. The inactivity of Micawber is an affront to this duty, both in the world at large and at home. There is a definite backlash to Mrs. Micawber's constant refrain, "I shall never desert Mr. Micawber," in that he has effectively deserted her and their children. But for all that Micawber is rather a benign figure. Garrett Stewart is probably wrong to classify him in the same "naughty company" with Pecksniff of *Martin Chuzzlewit* and Chadband of *Bleak House,* whose aggressions are so much more obvious.[25] It is because Micawber's aggression is so repressed and entwined with despair—not merely disguised—that Forster can place him near the center of this novel's perfection. Micawber comes into being in *David Copperfield* only when the hero has come as far as Murdstone and Grinby's warehouse, as "the stranger" known to Murdstone who will make room for young Copperfield at the top of his house (11.134). Resemblances between his manner and that of John Dickens were noticed before Forster wrote his *Life* and were defended by him as authentic and appreciative of Dickens's father—Forster contrasted the depiction of Leigh Hunt as Harold Skimpole in *Bleak House.*[26] In the novel Copperfield makes a very sober point of noting that Micawber never asked *him* for money, never harmed him in the way he could so easily harm Traddles and others: "I was probably indebted to some compassionate recollection he retained of me as his boy-lodger, for never having been asked by him for money. I certainly should not have had the moral courage to refuse it; and I have no doubt he knew that (to his credit be it written), quite as well as I did" (36.458). Thus the narrator compliments both the father figure and himself, in a sort of moral stand-off. In the novel Micawber also acts morally, for once, against Uriah Heep, as a father ought or might against a son's wicked other self. Stewart explores ways in which "Micawber is the great rival author in *David Copperfield,* a commanding stylist against whose prose David must define his own expressive tendencies," and calls attention to the digression on style in which the narrator goes out of his way to criticize Micawber's prose in the very act of his opposing Heep.[27] Still, the older man is fighting the younger man's battle in that scene in which the villain suddenly goes limp and ceases to be a threat to anyone. Heep collapses verbally as well: "Copperfield, I have always hated you," is one weak parting shot, and "Micawber, you old bully, I'll pay *you!*" is the other (52.650–651). If hero and father figure are rivals in anything more than writing, it may be in the suppression of anger so successful that Copperfield displays almost none after the biting of Murdstone's hand and Micawber displays his only against HEEP.

As in the inventions of Mr. Wickfield and Dr. Strong, the provenance of Mr. Micawber seems somewhat divided between fathering and indirect association with Dickens. The coalescence of two generations of the writer's family has been suggested as a possible instigation of both the autobiographical fragment and the novel, and from two directions. Albert Hutter argues that when Dickens wrote the fragment, his eldest child, Charley, was between ten and twelve years old, or the same age at which the writer found himself in Warren's as a boy.[28] The Mackenzies make a similar point in regard to the instigation of *Copperfield* and carry it to the older generation as well, to suggest an association between the writer and his father: "he was almost at the age at which his father had collapsed under his debts, broken up his home, and entered the Marshalsea, and the Twelfth Night party [of 1849] was to celebrate Charley's twelfth birthday—the age at which Dickens had been sent to the blacking factory."[29] Over the long course of the novel, however, Dickens carefully works free of Micawber as a possible father figure and even deposits something of his own past in that character's future.

Though Copperfield thanklessly holds up the older man as an example of ludicrous "piling up of words" (52.645), he cannot be said to confuse the issue of which of them is the novelist. Only four years earlier, remember, Dickens still idly wished that he might become a police magistrate.[30] Micawber, at the end of *Copperfield,* he sends down under to become, in the words of a local paper, "our distinguished fellow-colonist and townsman, WILKINS MICAWBER, ESQUIRE, Port Middle-bay District Magistrate."

XI

Young Man Copperfield

Strictly speaking, the "great fairy story" of Copperfield's life commences only after he meets Agnes Wickfield, Mr. Wickfield, and Uriah Heep in chapter 15, attends a new school, and makes "another Beginning." I have deliberately put off until last consideration of the early experiences of the hero because the perspective of memory places them last. Memory looks backward; earliest experiences are farthest away in time; and from this perspective childhood comes after adulthood. Dickens did not begin a life of writing by writing *David Copperfield*. He wrote this version of his childhood when he was thirty-seven and pretty well had to accept that he was the hero of his own life.

We do not know when Dickens discovered or decided that his experience in the blacking warehouse was traumatic. A reasonable assumption is that he did not recognize it as such before the writing of his autobiographical fragment and of *Copperfield*. I have pointed out that some of the language of the fragment came to him earlier in New York, when he was suffering from blows to his adult ego. To imagine that his recollection and estimate of a childood experience was continuous from the time of occurrence goes against all that we know of ourselves and what psychoanalysts tell us of the analytic situation, which in this case can be thought of as the time of writing; and though we remain ignorant of the course of Dickens's memory, we are told that Copperfield's memory, at least, was intermittent. At the time of his second beginning in life, that soon-to-be-famous writer thought little about his childhood and recent past. The experience at Murdstone and Grinby's warehouse could not have seemed traumatic then, because the "misty ideas" and "visionary considerations" of youth intervened:

> Misty ideas of being a young man at my own disposal, of the importance attaching to a young man at his own disposal, of the wonderful things to be seen and done by that magnificent animal, and the wonderful effects he could not fail to make upon society, lured me away. So powerful were these visionary considerations in my boyish mind, that I seem, according to my present way of thinking, to have left school without natural regret. The separation has not made the impression on me that other separations have. I try in vain to recall how I felt about it, and what its circumstances were; but it is not momentous in my recollection. I suppose the opening prospect confused me. I know that my juvenile experiences went for little or nothing then; and that life was more like a great fairy story, which I was just about to begin to read, than anything else. (19.233)

Thus in musing over a particular lacuna in his memory, Copperfield realizes that his juvenile experiences meant little to him at the time. He did not look backward but forward. Only latterly has he felt that early hardship shaped his character, therefore, and this belated response was undoubtedly true for Dickens as well: only during early middle life, when he had time to question his identity, did he formulate the autobiography that the early chapters of the novel enclose. Like Copperfield, he would sit down to write his story but not without indirectly acknowledging, through Copperfield, that youth—"that magnificent animal"—had little time for suffering. After taking the world by storm, after traveling to America, after writing *Chuzzlewit* and *Dombey* and reflecting on memory itself in the Christmas books, Dickens thought back on his childhood and singled out the episode of the blacking warehouse. With this investment in his childhood experience he thus confirmed in advance the theories of Steven Marcus and Edmund Wilson, and in this way of thinking in general he anticipated Freud.

In other words, however we interpret the narrative of the blacking warehouse and its revision in the novel, we have to address the question of why Dickens composed the narrative—both why he recalled the episode and why an experience of childhood suited his purposes. Since he has not told us why, in so many words, some reasoned presumptions have to be made. The first, which I have stressed all along, is that he had resolved the uncertainties about his identity that he experienced after completing *Barnaby Rudge* and that came to a crisis during the journey to America. Though the crisis was mild enough according to the evidence of his daily life, it was amplified and worked out through the writing of *Martin Chuzzlewit, Dombey and Son,* and the Christmas books. Second, if we can believe John Forster, he was stimulated by his friend's curiosity to write something about his experience, which had generated enough distress between the child and his parents to cause them to pretend it had never happened. Third, precisely because Dickens now felt secure and certain of his vocation, he could take satisfaction in contemplating such wrongs and misfortunes that he had overcome—as a hero overcomes his enemies. The more bitterly he could taste the memory of wrongs, the more credit, at this distance, he could extract from them. He virtually spelled out this motive in the meditations of Redlaw, in *The Haunted Man.* Fourth, he determined to exploit this contemplation of the past in a more ambitious fiction, the autobiographical novel. His motive here was mainly opportunistic, the motive of a professional writer: he had his plot and characters and was ready to begin. But Dickens's elaboration of his memories and his situation of *the* traumatic event in childhood are too much like a fairy tale, on the one hand, and the Oedipus complex, on the other, for us to discount the possibility of a broad cultural motive behind the direction the story took. This motive can be thought of as the need to justify a rise in the world, so desired by the sons of the nineteenth century. Rather than the spur of ambition in the child, the incident can be seen as the justification of ambition in the adult. Both the imputation of general passivity and the displacement of conflict to childhood worked well for men of that era, whether they were novelists of genius, founders of psychoanalysis, or far more commonplace individuals. We may begin to see how this is so by reconsidering *David Copperfield* and the Oedipus complex as well, from a point of view as culturally neutral as possible.

Fairy tales themselves have a way of situating in childhood incidents that are both traumatic and somehow good for people to experience, if only at second hand. The epoch that Dickens believed to be crucial in his own life, disguised as the Murdstone and Grinby's episode in the novel, is only a part of this story. Some general characteristics of fairy tales adopted in the early chapters of *Copperfield* include the splitting of parents into more than one representation, the helplessness and

158

relative passivity of a child-hero, and the courage and stamina of the child—notwithstanding his or her weakness in the face of the adult world. Stepparents abound in fairy tales because real parents appear to a child in opposite guises, as providers of care and governors of behavior. Not suprisingly, they are fictively multiplied into "good" and "bad" parents, as well as into parents who seem one thing and act another. In *Copperfield* the child's actual father appears only by repute, as a man rather gently susceptible to women and a bestower of books. His mother appears as a beautiful child-wife,[1] all too susceptible to men. The one parent is out of the way before the action commences and the other soon after, and they are replaced by the cruel and rigorous Murdstones (who naturally turn up later in charge of Dora or bending other brides to their will). But the child's Aunt Betsey and nurse Peggotty are kindly grotesque parents, showing love beneath rough exteriors, and the Micawbers are kindly helpless parents—rather like children themselves—who have an agreeable way of treating a boy as their equal. Many children, in real life, experience the pleasure of encountering such foster parents—persons with whom they may be only slightly acquainted but who treat them respectfully, without the contradictions so apparent in actual parents.

Children *are* nearly helpless to begin with, and for a good number of years after birth. This is one of the crucial facts of human experience, which Dickens realizes with profound memory of his own childhood and great good humor in the early chapters of his novel. (The inclusion of these memories makes the novel seem much more modern than Thackeray's *Pendennis*, which begins with the hero's coming of age and his first courtship.) It is the relative vulnerability of the child, a reflection forced upon us by Dickens, that speaks to the idea that we are all in some sense helpless before the circumstances of modern life. An advantage of the fairy-tale approach to this idea is that the helplessness of a small person can be exaggerated and thereby discharged in tears or laughter. Perhaps the most extravagant (and purely make-believe) instance of helplessness in *Copperfield* is the episode in which the waiter, in the inn at Yarmouth, consumes David's ale and his dinner for him as casually as if that were the function of waiters everywhere. Childhood confers such rapidly changing awareness that mental as well as physical differences from adults are readily apparent, and comprehension in the child normally outstrips the capacity to respond to adults. So in the coach journey to London that follows the waiter episode, David is mercilessly squeezed between adult passengers whose mistaken merriment further prevents him from eating supper, through sheer embarrassment; or David half understands and half does not understand, as we gather from his recall of the conversation and his repeating it to his mother, the sexual meaning of the talk among Murdstone and his men friends, in the course of which the stepfather-to-be concedes the boy's sharpness by referring to him in code as the cutler "Brooks of Sheffield" (2.20). The sheer rapaciousness of the adult world—according to this account of it—the narrator conveys as a kind of joke upon himself when a child; his recall of the past repeatedly features moments in which bewilderment and insight converge, and thus constitute growth and learning in the ways of the world. The narrative, finally, is replete with a sense of the child's overcoming helplessness and fighting back. The novel as a whole will celebrate the survival and success of Copperfield, but even early on the reader can relish the sinking of a hero's teeth into Murdstone's murderous hand, or the secret credit in the sign of shame that he is required to wear at Creakle's school: *"Take care of him. He bites"* (5.67). The sign is a portent as well as a stigma. "Take care" can mean either beware or cherish, and it comes to mean both.

It is no wonder that many readers have found these early chapters of *David Copperfield* the best in the book. Dickens did here what few other writers could do; his recall of what it is like to be a child is extraordinary; and this portion of the book has seemed authentic. William Spengeman, for example, argues that the autobiographical fiction of the early chapters is somehow more genuine than the fictional autobiography of the later chapters.[2] To some degree, obviously, this judgment depends on the hindsight shared with readers since the publication of Forster's *Life*. Because Dickens incorporated the substance and even whole paragraphs of his autobiographical fragment here, the validity of the first part of the novel seems confirmed. "I know enough of the world now," the chapter on Murdstone and Grinby's begins, "to have almost lost the capacity of being much surprised by anything; but it is matter of some surprise to me, even now, that I can have been so easily thrown away at such an age." That fresh concession about the way of the world shows that Dickens could already see the experience in perspective, but he let his hero continue, actively paraphrasing and quoting from the fragment. "A child of excellent abilities, and with strong powers of observation, quick, eager, delicate, and soon hurt bodily or mentally, it seems wonderful to me that nobody should have made any sign in my behalf." He either had the language of the fragment by heart or it lay on the desk before him as he made Copperfield write:

> No words can express the secret agony of my soul as I sunk into this companionship; compared these henceforth every-day associates with those of my happier childhood—not to say with Steerforth, Traddles, and the rest of those boys; and felt my hopes of growing up to be a learned and distinguished man, crushed in my bosom. The deep remembrance of the sense I had, of being utterly without hope now; of the shame I felt in my position; of the misery it was to my young heart to believe that day by day what I had learned, and thought, and delighted in, and raised my fancy and emulation up by, would pass away from me, little by little, never to be brought back any more; cannot be written.

The following paragraphs, from later in the chapter, Dickens also borrowed nearly word for word from the fragment:

> I know I do not exaggerate, unconsciously or unintentionally, the scantiness of my resources or the difficulties of my life. I know that if a shilling were given me by Mr. Quinion at any time, I spent it in a dinner or a tea. I know that I worked, from morning until night, with common men and boys, a shabby child. I know that I lounged about the streets, insufficiently and unsatisfactorily fed. I know that, but for the mercy of God, I might easily have been, for any care that was taken of me, a little robber or a little vagabond.
>
> Yet I held some station at Murdstone and Grinby's too. Besides that Mr. Quinion did what a careless man so occupied, and dealing with a thing so anomalous, could, to treat me as one upon a different footing from the rest, I never said, to man or boy, how it was that I came to be there, or gave the least indication of being sorry that I was there. That I suffered in secret, and that I suffered exquisitely, no one ever knew but I. How much I suffered, it is, as I have said already, utterly beyond my power to tell. But I kept my own counsel, and I did my work. I knew from the first, that, if I could not do my work as well as any of the rest, I could not hold myself above slight and contempt. I soon became at least as expeditious and as skilful as either of the other boys. Though perfectly familiar with them, my conduct and manner were different enough from theirs to place a space between us. They and the men generally spoke of me as "the little gent," or "the young Suffolker." A certain man named Gregory, who was foreman of the packers, and another named Tipp, who was the carman, and wore a red jacket, used to address me sometimes as

"David:" but I think it was mostly when we were very confidential, and when I had made some efforts to entertain them, over our work, with some results of the old readings; which were fast perishing out of my remembrance. Mealy Potatoes uprose once, and rebelled against my being so distinguished; but Mick Walker settled him in no time. (11.132–133, 139)

And there are other borrowings as well.

Two questions arise about the truthfulness of this part of the novel, neither of which can be satisfactorily answered. First, is it really more true to life, seemingly validated as it is by the fragment, than the principal fiction of the later part of the novel, in which Copperfield is supposed to be a famous novelist like Dickens? Second, is the special proof of its validity, the presence of the autobiographical fragment within the pages of the novel, to be regarded as altogether trustworthy? To reply to the second of these questions with still another, should we believe that the autobiographical fragment itself is the truth and nothing but the truth? We have some corroborating testimony in Forster's account of how he first came to hear of the episode and little reason to doubt that Dickens, as a boy, experienced something very like what he recalled. But mainly we know that he wrote of the episode in middle life, in words that seemed faithful to his memory at the time; and we have more and more come to feel that whether stories are told and how they are told are more significant questions for interpretation than what the stories are finally "about." Two such thoughtful and different students of Dickens as Albert Hutter and Robert Patten have argued recently that the fragment itself, if we are to appreciate its significance, ought to be regarded as a fiction.[3] Even the "editing" of the fragment that took place as it entered the novel suggests something of the instability of the original. For example, in the last paragraph given above from the novel, Dickens omitted after "beyond my power to tell" this sentence from the fragment: "No man's imagination can overstep the reality."[4] Did he leave out the sentence because its rhetoric was redundant, because it was untrue on the face of it, or because it jarred with his present sense of fiction and reality? Mr. Quinion in the novel supplies the place of "my relative at the counting-house" of Warren's Blacking. In the previous paragraph, did Dickens's substitution of "if a shilling were given me by Mr. Quinion at any time" for "if a shilling or so were given me by anyone" in the fragment[5] perhaps *restore* an element of truthfulness to the memory? By vaguely crediting anyone's occasional generosity, in his first version of the episode, Dickens deprived his relative of credit. Perhaps his family was not so cool to his plight as he pretended. But the reasons for all such differences in the two narratives are matters of speculation.

To the first question, whether the childhood of the hero is more true to life than his adult years, the answer is equally uncertain. The narrative of childhood is the rarer achievement, but the facts do not correspond any more closely to the life of Dickens. There are just as grave lies, so to speak, in the first fourteen chapters of *David Copperfield* as in the remaining fifty. Dickens's parents were very much alive when he undertook to write both his autobiographical fragment and his autobiographical novel. In the novel, Copperfield is not only a posthumous child, as he states right away, but he loses his mother shortly thereafter, through her marriage to Murdstone and her death in bearing a second child. Dickens provided his hero two stepfathers, the one immediate and sadistic and the other tangential and irresponsible. He gestured perfunctorily at a wicked stepmother in Jane Murdstone and provided lavishly for two surrogate mothers, in the pleasing convention of rough-seeming fairy godmothers. These out-and-out embellishments on his own life enable some remote wish fulfillment to take place immediately. The nurse Peggotty is called Peggotty because her first name, Clara, is the same as that of Copperfield's mother; Peggotty also gets married when the hero is still a child, but only through Davy as an intermediary and for convenience in caring for him. His Aunt Betsey, who will later adopt him as she has already adopted Mr. Dick, disapproves of the hero's actual mother all along and proposes an alternative identity for him as a tough-minded girl like herself, named Betsey Trotwood Copperfield. These powerful allies and surrogate mothers, who are unparalleled in Dickens's life, outlive by many years Copperfield's parents and outweigh his stepfathers and possible fathers-in-law. Three widowed mothers in the novel—Mrs. Steerforth, Mrs. Heep, and Mrs. Markleham—will show how fortunate Copperfield is in Dickens's choice of Peggotty and Aunt Betsey. Instinctively the hero will seek in marriage two women with weak fathers, the first a childish replica of his own childish mother and the second with all the nurturing love of his godmothers but calm and beautiful, with nearly occult powers for writing and encountering death, and abundantly able to resupply what Erikson calls "basic trust." All this emphatic mothering, the sum total of which is remarkable, is a fiction heaped by Dickens upon *his* surrogate Copperfield both early and late in the novel. This fiction alone is large enough to dwarf the "facts" of Dickens's childhood as thinly disguised in chapter 11.

What is more remarkable is that Dickens should feel sure that an account of early days and of trauma would be useful in coming to terms with a lifetime. The narrative that the author led Forster to lead us to believe[6] was inspired by memories of a specific incident in childhood suddenly comprises the entire life, from birth to death, of the very person who is writing it. The writing follows, as Hillis Miller notes in one essay, "exactly the structure of human temporality" and persists, as the same critic observes in his book on Dickens, until "David has that relation to Agnes which a devout Christian has to God."[7] Miraculously, *The Personal History, Adventures, Experience, & Observation of David Copperfield the Younger, of Blunderstone Rookery (Which He never meant to be Published on any Account)*—as the title appeared on the cover of the monthly parts—began with birth and concluded with death. That is quite a stretch in either direction from the days in Murdstone and Grinby's or in Warren's.

> Whether I shall turn out to be the hero of my own life, or whether that station will be held by anybody else, these pages must show. To begin my life with the beginning of my life, I record that I was born (as I have been informed and believe) on a Friday, at twelve o'clock at night. It was remarked that the clock began to strike, and I began to cry, simultaneously.

With the stroke of the clock and no fractional time of day, this secular life begins, and the narrator covers for the unremembered time of infancy with light mockery of the birth of heroes. Even before we read that he is a posthumous child, we find that he was born with a caul, a charm aginst drowning that initially allows Copperfield and his readers to laugh at the need of others to believe in luck but, at the same time, introduces the possibility of death and hints that the hero will not drown with Ham and Steerforth.[8] Copperfield's is a life dedicated to work and influenced mainly by women. That he should immediately be concerned in the narrative with death and his father's grave nearby— even before his story can arrive at the point of conscious memories of childhood—could not be altogether surprising to readers of Dickens from *Oliver Twist* onward. Erikson, in fact, throws some indirect light on this phenomenon here and elsewhere in Dickens's writings when he attributes similar feelings to Martin Luther: "Premonitions of death occur throughout Luther's career," he contends, "but I think it would be too simple to ascribe them to a mere fear of death. A young genius has an implicit life plan to complete; caught by death befo his time, he would be only a pathetic human fragment."[9] Erikson's perhaps too generous defense of genius may help explain the infant half-brother of Copperfield who, buried with his mother at the end of the second number of the novel, "was myself" (9.115), as well as the hero's need throughout his personal history for new beginnings, surrogate mothers, and above all Agnes.

Autobiography in the form of a fairy tale is bound to progress and regress in the same narrative. Fairy tales, as a kind of literature enjoying a vogue in the nineteenth century, insist on telling over and over again the trials of childhood. After the extensive use Dickens made of *Paradise Lost* and *King Lear*—however facetious or partial—in his previous two novels, his use of fairy-tale material in *David Copperfield* might be thought of as regressive even from a literary point of view; for better or worse, it was certainly regressive in personal terms for a man approaching middle age. "But must we call it regression," Erikson asks, "if a man thus seeks again the earliest encounters of his trustful past in his efforts to reach a hoped-for and eternal future?" Like Dickens's autobiographical enterprise in *Copperfield*, Erikson's biography of genius seeks to take in the life from beginning to end, even though its ostensible subject is the young man Luther. In the novel we have the birth of the novelist at the beginning and Agnes pointing upward at the close; in the biography of the religious leader we have a reconstruction of childhood that will explain his rediscovery of eternal life for others as well as himself. "I have implied that the original faith which Luther tried to restore," writes Erikson, "goes back to the basic trust of early infancy."[10]

It may be objected that Dickens was writing a novel by and about a famous novelist, himself, while Erikson has written a study of the formative years of a genius of very different fame, not himself. He is an analyst working at many removes from the memories that comprised the life to construct a biography that still purports to be fact. The way to bring these two very different modes of biography together is to point out that the second is also largely fictional. The admission of fiction does not make either mode dishonest. Dickens alters, suppresses, and above all invents his life, but always within the bounds of trying to make sense of it to himself and his readers. He puts in an excess of mothers, for example, but the resulting life must add up to something, and has added up to something, for readers worldwide. Erikson acknowledges again and again that almost nothing is known of Luther's youth, almost nothing about the man before his strong challenge to an accepted religion. He fills this vacuum in the historical record with extensive analysis, under the aegis of Freud and within the bounds of his own knowledge and readers' acceptance, of a young man's relation to his father and what is possible in that relation. Erikson is frank about this construction and seems to assert the necessity of a fiction not only to biography but to the subject of biography. To the objections of a psychiatrist of a different school,

> we would reply that most certainly we would ascribe to Luther an Oedipus complex, and not a trivial one at that. We would not wish to see any boy—much less an imaginative and forceful one—face the struggles of his youth and manhood without having experienced as a child the love and the hate which are encompassed in this complex: love for the maternal person who awakens his senses and his sensuality with her ministrations, and deep and angry rivalry with the male possessor of this maternal person. We would also wish him with their help to succeed, in his boyhood, in turning resolutely away from the protection of women to assume the fearless initiative of men.

Thus Erikson provides his subject with an Oedipus complex because he needs one, and because "only a boy with a precocious, sensitive, and intense conscience would *care* about pleasing his father as much as Martin did."[11] Similarly Dickens, recalling his childhood or inventing where necessary, provided himself with conflicts that, he acknowledged, "have worked together to make me what I am" and provided Copperfield with "the endurance of my childish days" that, according to Agnes's letter, "had done its part to make me what I was."

Erikson's notion of what is essential to childish days is steeped in cultural assumptions about the "ministrations" of women and the "initiative" of men. These assumptions are both its strength and its weakness. They establish a coherent idea of Luther's career, but they are more deeply rooted in the nineteenth century than in the sixteenth.

Dickens was no less constrained by convictions about hard work and good women, codes he described and inscribed for the use of the culture. Not surprisingly, the two biographers share many beliefs: especially when Erikson writes critically of the culture, he almost seems to take up his pen where Dickens left off. The measure of Luther's sensitivity or of his father's viciousness, now lost in time,

> pales before the general problem of man's exploitability in childhood, which makes him a victim not only of overt cruelty, but also of all kinds of covert emotional relief, of devious vengefulness, or sensual self-indulgence, and of sly righteousness—all on the part of those on whom he is physically and morally dependent. Someday, maybe, there will exist a well-informed, well-considered, and yet fervent public conviction that the most deadly of all possible sins is the mutilation of a child's spirit; for such mutilation undercuts the life principle of trust, without which every human act, may it feel ever so good and seem ever so right, is prone to perversion by destructive forms of conscientiousness.

Erikson speculates a good deal about the beatings Luther received as a child, presumably from both parents but especially from the father. Again he generalizes in such a way that the facts hardly matter:

> It takes a particular view of man's place on this earth, and of the place of childhood within man's total scheme, to invent devices for terrifying children into submission, either by magic, or by mental and corporeal terror. . . . Special concepts of property (including the idea that a man can ruin his own property if he wishes) underlie the idea that it is entirely up to the discretion of an individual father when he should raise the morality of his children by beating their bodies. . . . The device of beating children down—by superior force, by contrived logic, or by vicious sweetness—makes it unnecessary for the adult to become adult. . . . The child, forced out of fear to pretend that he is better when seen than when unseen, is left to anticipate the day when he will have the brute power to make others more moral than he ever intends to be himself.[12]

Dickens moves in his own fashion toward similar conclusions. Though there is no Dotheboys Hall in *David Copperfield,* readers have come to value the early chapters of the novel for what they imply in general about such an institution. We have no evidence that Dickens as a child was beaten by a father in the least like Murdstone, or experienced in person the systematic torture of a schoolmaster like Creakle—"an incapable brute, who had no more right to be possessed of the great trust he held, than to be Lord High Admiral, or Commander-in-chief: in either of which capacities, it is probable that he would have done infinitely less mischief" (7.77). These are fictions enlisted more for their generalizing value than for their personal significance either to Dickens or to Copperfield, and for quite similar purposes Erikson elaborates the early life of Martin Luther.

Copperfield is about a rise in life and not a fall. The previous two novels, in which Dickens questioned his personal identity much more sharply, invoked the greatest literary models of falling. *Chuzzlewit* hilariously, but also seriously, deployed an epic enactment, from Milton's *Paradise Lost,* of the myth of the fortunate fall. *Dombey* followed heroically in the path of Shakespeare's *King Lear,* to mount an attack on pride and become the novelist's principal study of a tragic fall. *Copperfield* is about a rise, and is a novel more emulated than emulating other literature. Undoubtedly, with its hero so ingeniously and repeatedly positioning himself in relation to mothers, the novel is at least partially what we would call Oedipal in design. But remember that Dickens is beforehand in this regard. Freud read *David Copperfield* well before he invented psychoanalysis or even concentrated on childhood. He named it his favorite, praised the novel for many of the same qualities that Forster saw in it. Like Forster, he thought the later novels less pleasing and less true. He made a gift of *Copperfield* to Martha Bernays and wrote her that it was most nearly free of mannerisms among those he had read: "the characters are individualized; they are sinful without being abominable."[13] At this time Freud was twenty-seven, ten years younger than Dickens had been when writing the novel. He never, so far as we know, linked the early chapters to his own rediscovery of childhood and formulation of the Oedipus complex when he was forty. But of course the novel as a whole tells of ambition, in the guise of a great fairy story about a young man's rise in the world. Now that we are more able to see Freud in historical perspective, it should be evident how intimately psychoanalysis is bound up with the very kinds of narrative for which it has proved useful as a tool of investigation.[14]

The point is not that Dickens and Freud had similar thoughts or personalities, but that the discovery of psychoanalysis is historically much closer to the era of the nineteenth-century novel than to our own era, and that reflection on this fact is overdue.[15] The interest of psychoanalysis in the penetration of secrets, the conditions of repression and scandal, the claim to restore a continuity of self, the coming to terms with ambition opposed by the traditional culture, are some of the ground shared with the institution of the novel. It is tempting to compare the process of self-examination by Dickens that culminated in *David Copperfield* with the origins of psychoanalysis, because Freud attributed his discoveries to his own self-analysis in early middle life. The principal result of this introspective experiment was *The Interpretation of Dreams,* and Freud may be said to have later encouraged his followers to believe that the movement had a personal basis. The counterargument to this myth, which is something like the myth of the blacking warehouse in Dickens studies, is the impressive study of the scientific background of psychoanalysis by Frank J. Sulloway.[16] We have gathered now from many sources how ambition served Freud, just as it has served other scientists and discoverers. The early fame of Dickens obviously did not satisfy *his* ambition as a writer, and he was still carefully trying to control and account for it in *Copperfield.* It is noteworthy that both men first confided their memories of childhood in writing to male friends, John Forster and Wilhelm Fliess, and at about the same age. Here is Freud's famous discovery, as reported privately to Fliess:

A single idea of general value dawned on me. I have found, in my own case too, [the phenomenon of] being in love with my mother and jealous of my father, and I now consider it a universal event in early childhood, even if not so early as in children who have been made hysterical. (Similar to the invention of parentage [family romance] in paranoia—heroes, founders of religion.) If this is so, we can understand the gripping power of *Oedipus Rex,* in spite of all the objections that reason raises against the presupposition of fate . . . the Greek legend seizes upon a compulsion which everyone recognizes because he senses its existence within himself. Everyone in the audience was once a budding Oedipus in fantasy and each recoils in horror from the dream fulfillment here transplanted into reality, with the full quantity of repression which separates his infantile state from his present one.[17]

As in the case of Dickens, there is a substantial literary component to the self-discovery, here and elsewhere in the writings of Freud: the next paragraph of the letter explores the analogy to Hamlet. And as with most such speculations on personal identity, the writer assumes that "everyone" is either male or an adjunct to the male.

Copperfield is a piece of the culture of the nineteenth century from which the Oedipus complex emerged. It is not hard to see how this is so. Even if a case for infantile sexuality is not quite articulated in the novel, aggression—scarcely concealed beneath a wary passivity and extending as far as death-dealing in the plot—is essential to the rise of the hero. The killing in the novel, in fact, is about equally proportioned among mothers, fathers-in-law to be, and rivals of the hero; the two childlike women, Clara and Dora, are not spared. The psychoanalyst D. W. Winnicott puts the general case well, without recourse to a full Oedipal plot or infantile sexuality, by arguing that "growing up means taking the parent's place. *It really does.* In the unconscious fantasy, growing up is inherently an aggressive act."[18] This perception has more to do with the relative size of parents and children, before the latter are grown up, than it has to do with sexuality. In Dickens's novel it has also to do, by analogy, with the soon-to-be-adult hero's perception of his own death and the need for his angel Agnes. The degree of aggression, like the sexual component of the Oedipus complex, need not be thought of as limited to the nineteenth or twentieth centuries of the modern era, but the reasons that Freud discovers the Oedipus complex, wields it, and uses it to explain human identity or behavior are to be found in texts like *Copperfield* that are predicated on a rise in the world—and not just the rise of a uniquely situated or dangerously ambitious man, nor even the rise of a nefarious hypocrite like Heep, but the rise of tame young men like Copperfield.

Examine again Erikson's mild protest: "We would not wish to see any boy—much less an imaginative and forceful one—face the struggles of his youth and manhood without having experienced the love and hate which are encompassed in this complex." Is not this the story that Dickens has written about himself as Copperfield? It is primarily in the nineteenth and twentieth centuries that *any* boy—never mind the imaginative and forceful novelist—must in theory be prepared "to assume the fearless initiative of men": that is, to pursue a career different from his father's, to enter the market place with his labor, to try his hardest to do well. The necessary ambition is not a matter of personal choice (Copperfield never decides to become a novelist, as we have seen), but the kind of maximizing of personal effort—of selfishness, if

170

you will—that is essential to the body politic and especially to the assumptions of modern economics. When Dickens has Copperfield preach the necessity of work, he deliberately downplays his own extraordinary talent and insists upon the ordinary talent and necessary ambition of any boy. The ambition of all, the energy available to progress for society as a whole, cannot be construed as tragic. And yet—and yet—it is still ambition and demands a more prominent role in life than that enjoyed by our fathers before us. The Oedipus complex assumes and assuages ambition not believed necessary before the nineteenth century for any but exceptional boys. Now all boys are exceptional, and all must identify, as Forster suggests, with the hero who is Copperfield.

The famous complex, as Dickens's novel helps to make clear, is more like a myth of the fortunate fall transposed to childhood than it is like the tragedy of Oedipus; it is a dream of murder and sex from which one turns "resolutely away" after being tempted, in Erikson's terms, and not a fate to be endured, as Freud's language sometimes suggests. There is no use experiencing an Oedipus complex unless one can leave it behind, and in *Copperfield* Dickens helps to codify the very assumptions about early life that bring psychoanalysis into being. The tale of childhood that *Copperfield* tells—the weaning of the child from his mother and the biting of the hand that wards him—frees the man for labor and the punctual discharge of duties. It breeds the "stuff to stand wear and tear" and prepares for "thorough-going, ardent, and sincere earnestness" (42.518). Take care of that young man: he bites. The rise of the hero is prepared but also justified by a fall and recovery in childhood.

To show that the Oedipus complex, instead of an etiology, ought to be regarded in the light of an apologetics is well beyond the scope of this book. Yet the main point is clear: both Dickens and Freud made the move to narrate childhood experience when they were entering middle age and were deeply occupied with careers. I have argued that there is enough evidence in the case of Dickens, at least, that the process culminating in a story of childhood began with an adult's awareness of his vulnerability as an adult. The novelist scrambled, as we say of jet fighters, to find and destroy the enemy—who was himself—in *Martin Chuzzlewit,* and once in control of the skies, he concentrated self-criticism in the tragic mode of *Dombey and Son.* Only then was he prepared to present himself in the guise of ambitious novelist and to recall a

171

traumatic childhood in *David Copperfield*. I think it fair to say that Freud's *Interpretation of Dreams* records another scramble, another mastery and justification of the life. From our perspective today these exercises of the will begin to look like cultural appropriations of the self, justifications of essential ambition. No longer can we suppose that fixed patterns of childhood conflict were discovered merely by coincidence at the end of the nineteenth century. Human nature, especially in its social relations, does not remain constant, and almost certainly the Oedipus complex shares in the same assumptions as the "Personal History" of young Copperfield.

XII

Expectations

$\mathcal{J}$f *David Copperfield* is less indebted to any single previous literary text than either *Martin Chuzzlewit* or *Dombey and Son,* this originality seems to have made it foremost among the novels of Dickens to which other writers have responded in turn. It may be that Copperfield's first marriage and Dr. Strong's marriage lie behind Lydgate's and Casaubon's marriages, respectively, in George Eliot's *Middlemarch.*[1] Almost certainly the marriage to Dora inspired the first marriage of Prince Andrew in Tolstoy's *War and Peace.*[2] Copperfield's personal history thus seems to have some bearing on the work of two great novelists of character, creators of a kind of literature for which Dickens himself is not especially renowned. The book had also an extraordinary influence on Kafka, though one might think that of all of Dickens's novels this would have the least interest for a modernist.[3] While writing *David Copperfield* Dickens received a letter of appreciation from his Russian translator, Irinarch Ivanovich Vvedensky, averring the English novelist's "wide celebrity in Russia": thereafter, according to Forster, whenever his friend experienced difficulties of any sort with his readers at home, he was fond of saying that he was packing up for the move to Siberia.[4]

Of the uses made of *Copperfield* by other novelists, none is more revelatory than that by Dostoevsky in *The Devils.* It has long been accepted that Dickens's Steerforth partly inspired the character Stavrogin,[5] yet the latter has a much more central role in *The Devils* than

Steerforth has in *Copperfield*. Almost everything that the Russian novelist takes over from the story of Copperfield's mainly domestic progress is pressed into a satire and allegory of the times: so much so that the result is like a rebuke of the apparent ease, wish fulfillment, and complacency of *Copperfield*, and like a raw exposure of some of the latent aggression we have noticed. Dickens stresses the wasted potential of Steerforth, "the qualities that might have made him a man of a noble nature and a great name" (32.388), and forecloses this potential with the seduction and betrayal of Emily. Dostoevsky magnifies both the potential and its ruin in the actions of Stavrogin. In this satire, Stavrogin has the messianic potential of saving Russia but is at the same time so depraved—and bored, like Steerforth—that he debauches not one seaside orphan but every woman he encounters, including, in the excised chapter of *The Devils,* a girl of twelve—all in fact but the crippled and retarded woman whom he instead insults by marrying and never touching. Like Steerforth, he has his good side; and like Steerforth, this good side extends about as far as the possession of a bad conscience and no farther—which possession Dostoevsky exaggerates to match an apocalyptic vision of Russia and then abruptly reduces to suicide.

It is easy to feel that the mirroring of *Copperfield* in *The Devils* goes beyond the replication of Steerforth alone. The absurdity of Micawber, and especially the mixture of fondness and ridicule with which he is described, reappears in the treatment of Stepan Verkhovensky, the long-winded voice of liberal Russia that nonetheless sounds a first faint note of hope from his conversion at the end.[6] Again, the scale of Dickens's creation is domestic, that of Dostoevsky's national and apocalyptic: Micawber waits for something to turn up to feed his family; Verkhovensky waits in vain for history to save Russia. The most worrying aspect of *The Devils* as a reflection of *Copperfield* can be posed as a question: what has become of the hero himself in the Russian novel? The strange answer, if one were to pursue the question, would have to be the young man who worships the Steerforth character: that is, the nihilist Peter Verkhovensky, who adores Stavrogin and scorns his own garrulous father. Such parodic treatment of an earlier novel is justified by satire; the hidden aggression conducted by the plot on behalf of David Copperfield becomes meaningless aggression conducted by a secret revolutionary group on behalf of Peter Verkhovensky against any person, man or woman, who has slighted him. The indirection of Dickens's autobiographical novel provided Dostoevsky with an irony that he could deploy with devastating effect in his political novel.

The Devils, which was written in the years immediately after Dickens's death in 1870, in no way alters the perfection of English mirth—merely reinvents it as Russian satire. If there is room for doubt that this is exactly what Dostoevsky "did" with *David Copperfield,* there can be no doubt that Dickens himself exploited, criticized, and etched deeper the lines of his autobiographical novel when he came to write *Great Expectations.* He hit upon the idea for that novel just ten years later; it is his only other novel narrated entirely in the first person; and except for the need to boost circulation of his weekly *All the Year Round,* it would have been another novel in twenty monthly parts. He wrote to Forster of the first installments of *Great Expectations*:

> The book will be written in the first person throughout, and during these first three weekly numbers you will find the hero to be a boy-child, like David. Then he will be an apprentice. You will not have to complain of the want of humour as in the *Tale of Two Cities.* I have made the opening, I hope, in its general effect exceedingly droll. I have put a child and a good-natured foolish man, in relations that seem to me very funny. Of course I have got in the pivot on which the story will turn too—and which indeed, as you remember, was the grotesque tragic-comic conception [of Pip and Magwitch] that first encouraged me. To be quite sure I had fallen into no unconscious repetitions, I read *David Copperfield* again the other day, and was affected by it to a degree you would hardly believe.[7]

While taking precautions against "unconscious repetitions," Dickens managed to write a novel that resembled his earlier story of boy and man in some respects and implicitly criticized it in others. Even the shift from straightforward celebration of "earnestness" to the suspenseful critique of hollow "expectations" cannot disguise the autobiographical thrust of this second effort. The title *Great Expectations* was not an invented phrase but one already current for the expectation of an inheritance, a theme seemingly remote from the life of its self-made author; yet under this banner the more general case of ambition to rise in the world could be attacked freely, and Dickens uses the novel to reexamine the implications, as he now saw them, of a progress like that of his earlier hero. Though Pip is not a novelist like Copperfield, today's readers may feel that he is even closer to a "portrait of the author."[8] The reason *Great Expectations* seems more genuine to us is that it is more self-critical, and this is our sense of what autobiography ought to be.

Dickens still argues that the meaning of his hero's life turns on a childhood experience. The term "pivot" that he uses in writing to Forster apparently refers quite specifically to the violent turning upside-down of Pip in the hands of Magwitch in the first chapter. The mystery of their relation—the convict and the boy with expectations—encompasses the entire novel. But the traumatic moment from which the narrator's recall of his own past begins is, from the perspective of Dickens's life, unmistakably a convenient fiction this time. An echo of the autobiographical fragment can be heard in the early chapters of *Great Expectations* also, but with an important difference from the suffering endured by Dickens and Copperfield. The blacking warehouse becomes for this purpose the blacksmith's forge of Pip's apprenticeship. In the fragment, Dickens made clear that one of the excruciating aspects of his experience as a boy was that he could be seen from the street through the window of Warren's Blacking: "people used to stop and look in. . . . I saw my father coming in at the door one day when we were very busy, and I wondered how he could bear it."[9] In the novel, Pip dreads merely the thought of Estella looking in:

> What I wanted, who can say? How can *I* say, when I never knew? What I dreaded was, that in some unlucky hour I, being at my grimiest and commonest, should lift up my eyes and see Estella looking in at one of the wooden windows of the forge. I was haunted by the fear that she would, sooner or later, find me out, with a black face and hands, doing the coarsest part of my work, and would exult over me and despise me. Often after dark . . . I would look towards those panels of black night in the wall which the wooden windows then were, and would fancy that I saw her just drawing her face away, and would believe that she had come at last.[10]

The traumatic opening of the novel we judge to be a fiction because it is so unlike anything in Dickens's or most boys' experience. This experience at the forge, which recalls the autobiographical fragment, comes to us already judged as fear, prefaced with questions and disclaimers, and dismissed as pure fancy. "What I wanted, who can say? How can *I* say, when I never knew?" These questions hover over the memory of trauma, and the implied answer is that Pip's fears were needless. Estella never comes to look upon the hero's shame.

The passage has to do, of course, with Pip's relation to a kind of heroine who is new, and important, in Dickens's late fiction. Yet his chapter begins, "It is a most miserable thing to feel ashamed of home," and Estella and Miss Havisham are introduced as two who instill shame and must never see the forge "on any account" (14.100). Throughout the novel their supposed perspective comments ironically on Pip's own snobbery and feelings about what is shameful, and their names suggest how he is torn, between the pull of "stella" and the crush of "sham." They have the symbolic functions of building and destroying expectations, and this externalization effectively attacks the "traumatic" imaginings of the apprentice blacksmith. Of Estella, later in the novel Pip will say, "Truly it was impossible to dissociate her presence from all those wretched hankerings after money and gentility that had disturbed my boyhood—from all those ill-regulated aspirations that made me ashamed of home and Joe"; and he will recall the dread of imagining her "to look in at the wooden window of the forge and flit away" (29.223). Thus Dickens indirectly criticizes his own feelings as a boy in the window of Warren's Blacking. Those feelings, which were recollected in his thirties as suffering imposed upon him, he now treats as if they might be partly imagined or produced by his own "wretched hankerings after money and gentility." Dickens was now approaching fifty years of age, and one can read his *Great Expectations* with less imputation of autobiography than his *David Copperfield*. But the critical thrust of the later novel *against* ambition divorced from origins is unmistakable, and in defense of an autobiographical reading, there is the curious evidence of a visit to a blacking warehouse that seems to place the old dread in perspective:

> "Have you seen anything of London, yet?"
> "Why, yes, Sir," said Joe, "me and Wopsle went off straight to look at the Blacking Ware'us. But we didn't find that it come up to its likeness in the red bills at the shops doors: which I meantersay," added Joe, in an explanatory manner, "as it is there drawd too architectooralooral."
> I really believe Joe would have prolonged this word (mightily expressive to my mind of some architecture that I know) into a perfect Chorus, but for his attention being providentially attracted by his hat, which was toppling. . . .   (27.210)

Providentially or not, the entertaining hat distracts Pip and the reader from too close inquiry into what architecture is meant. Does Joe send it spinning around the room because he knows he is treading dangerous ground?

The "exceedingly droll" effect that Dickens promised by bringing Pip and Joe together in the opening chapters substitutes for some of the women in David Copperfield's life. Joe has all the gentle maternal instincts toward the boy; he comforts him, feeds him, and protects him as best he can from tickler, the instrument of Mrs. Joe's government. His idea in marrying Mrs. Joe was to keep her from suffering as his mother had suffered and—a little like Copperfield's Peggotty—to provide a home for Pip. Mrs. Joe has the masculine edge of Peggotty and Aunt Betsey without their kindness, and about as much feeling as the Murdstones. Indeed she is the punishing stepfather, without a name other than "Mrs. Joe" to indicate her gender. The droll relation of the three—Pip, his sister, and her husband—sets up a kind of parody of fairy-tale beginnings. Even Magwitch, by name and disposition, seems potentially maternal—a mother who "would have been proud of you," as Mrs. Steerforth once said to Copperfield.

The one obvious parallel of the women in *Great Expectations* to those in *Copperfield* is that of Biddy to Agnes. Biddy is quiet and superior and a teacher, and Pip says to her, "I shall always tell you everything." They go on walks together and she becomes associated with beautiful weather rather than church windows, as befits her difference in class from Agnes. Pip tells her of his love for Estella, as his predecessor spoke of his love for Dora. But all in all he treats this childhood friend with a thoughtlessness that Copperfield was never quite capable of admitting.

> "Biddy," said I, when we were walking homeward, "I wish you could put me right."
>
> "I wish I could!" said Biddy.
>
> "If I could only get myself to fall in love with you—you don't mind my speaking so openly to such an old acquaintance?"
>
> "Oh dear, not at all!" said Biddy. "Don't mind me."
>
> "If I could only get myself to do it, *that* would be the thing for me."
>
> "But you never will, you see," said Biddy.   (17.123)

The reader can only wince for Pip, while admiring him for telling this tale against himself. The relationship of Copperfield to Agnes is being told over again, but critically, as if Dickens could now read his earlier novel with fresh eyes and understand that even Agnes might have ideas of her own. The critical thrust of this particular action is driven home at the end of *Great Expectations*, when Pip vainly supposes he can marry Biddy only to find that she is already married to Joe.

In the offing, lusting after Biddy as Heep lusted after Agnes, is Orlick: "I was very hot indeed upon Old Orlick's daring to admire her; as hot as if it were an outrage on myself" (17.124). Later, when Pip seeks Estella at Satis House, Orlick turns up there also. As Julian Moynahan has shown, Orlick and Drummle—who pursues Estella more closely— are doubles for Pip.[11] Again, however, the reenactment of a role from the earlier novel takes a more serious turn and casts a deeper shadow. Whereas Uriah Heep diets on lust and fraud, Orlick goes in for murder, and this Doppelgänger is brought into closer relation to the hero. "I was at first disposed to believe that *I* must have had some hand in the attack upon my sister," we read, and "it was horrible to think that I had provided the weapon"—the convict's leg iron (16.113–114). Conversely, in the scene at the limekiln, Orlick is more outspoken than Heep. "It was you as did for your shrew sister," he contends; "it warn't Old Orlick as did it; it was you" (53.404). Orlick and Drummle, in fact, have fewer motives for their behavior independent of the hero than Heep does. The action of *Great Expectations* is more dreamlike than that of *Copperfield,* and the hero is more implicated in the aggressive motions of the plot. But even on the surface of the narrative Pip is open to criticism, including self-criticism, in a way that Copperfield is not. Forster can still take pleasure in the later novel, even though the time of the perfection of English mirth has passed: "the scene in which Pip, and Pip's chum Herbert, make up their accounts and schedule their debts and obligations, is original and delightful as Micawber himself."[12] But one of the superior virtues of David Copperfield as a hero was not falling into habits like those of Micawber; he kept steady, took himself more seriously than Pip does, and had a far higher estimate of his own worth.

The broadest and deepest difference between the two novels can be measured by the stain of criminality that permeates *Great Expectations*. Orlick and Drummle, of course, are not the main criminals: the convict Magwitch and, behind him, the unmitigated Compeyson loom up from the marshes in the opening of the novel and struggle for the last time in the Thames near the close. Dickens uses the evil of Compeyson to show Pip's secret benefactor as ambiguously good or evil; but in contrast

to *David Copperfield,* the rise of the hero in the world, with his pretensions to money and gentility, is orchestrated by a criminal agent whose
subsequent revelation has the force of a tragic peripeteia. In the earlier
novel, as distorting mirrors of the hero's ambition, there were only Heep
and the harmless Mr. Micawber, Mr. Dick, and Dr. Strong. Pip, in his
rise, is set up for a very bad fall indeed, though the novel never drops
him all the way back to the forge or the marshes—and it was lucky
that Biddy did marry Joe, perhaps, since the hero is better suited in the
end for a small business, where "we . . . worked for our profits, and did
very well" (58.456). The personal moral of the novel opposes overweening ambition and severing of ties; the larger implications for society
of its exposure of criminality have been much debated. There is hunger
in *Great Expectations* as there had been in *Copperfield,* but more dog
eating dog and allusions to portable property in its law offices. As a
satire it does have the breadth and depth—though not a comparable
style or approach—of Dostoevsky's *The Devils.* The portent of its criminality is more like that of Balzac's *Splendeurs et misères des courtisanes,*
in which the archcriminal Vautrin sponsors the career of Lucien de
Rubempré (though I know of no record that Dickens read Balzac's
novel).

The criminality uncovered in *Great Expectations* and the more nearly
explicit burden of guilt borne by the hero make it seem more modern
than *Copperfield.* The shame that Dickens associated with the blacking
warehouse he overcame more or less straightforwardly with the story
of success in the first novel; in the second, in a routine that also may
be thought of as a model for psychoanalysis, he exchanged shame for
guilt. Such is the usefulness of the idea of guilt in our lives, as compensation for present ambition, that we are likely to make it universal,
as in the imputation of an Oedipus complex to all, girls as well as boys.
"Luther," according to Erikson, "all his life felt like some sort of criminal"—Erikson does not systematically review the evidence for this
feeling; he more or less takes it for granted.[13] Dickens, in the novel
Great Expectations, supplies a great deal of evidence of the hero's guilt,
and he shows how the behavior of the adults surrounding Pip induces
guilt. There is more such excellent psychology in that novel, and it is
also one of the mythmaking books of modern times, though one that
sets out to demolish the myth of expectations.

It is scarcely surprising that Dickens invented another adventure of
mythic proportions in *Great Expectations.* He had done so, with com-

parable doses of bafflement and uncertainty for his readers, in *Martin Chuzzlewit* and *Dombey and Son,* to say nothing of *Bleak House* and *Little Dorrit*. Each of the novels we have looked at closely, however, also served as a fable of his own identity. Each begins with a thought of death immediately superimposed upon a birth—a murder in the first family of man, the fatal lying-in of Mrs. Dombey, a glimpse of the elder David Copperfield's grave. Not the least astonishing thing about Dickens's narratives of personal identity is the cheerfulness with which they get under way. "To five little stone lozenges, each about a foot and a half long," says Pip, he is indebted for the knowledge of his brothers, and his belief "that they had all been born on their backs with their hands in their trousers-pockets, and had never taken them out in this state of existence." Though Copperfield had only one dead little brother, Pip has five. The posture he imagines them to rest in implies some malingering; or else five little surrogates guessed what they were in for and jammed their hands in their pockets on purpose. A little of Mrs. Gamp's impertinence plays about this narrator's self-critical beginning. But Gamp has surely been around ever since the Chuzzlewit madness struck. She also lurks behind the "meandering" business with the caul that interrupts *Copperfield*'s highly controlled narrative even as it gets started.

From the point of view of readers of Dickens, the self-discoveries and recoveries of the novelist count for nothing except his books. He may have projected his ambition unconvincingly in young Martin, tragically in the older Dombey, and serenely in David Copperfield—not to say sharply in Pip. But what matters for readers of Dickens—those who learn from Dickens—are his verbal representations. In *Chuzzlewit* Dickens ascribes to Tom Pinch, after the latter's fall from grace, "a shadowy misgiving that the altered relations between himself and Pecksniff, were somehow to involve an altered knowledge on his part of other people, and were to give him an insight into much of which he had had no previous suspicion" (37.580). If Pinch is seen as a stand-in for the author, this is tantamount to saying that after one Dickens has seen through another Dickens, he would have no difficulty in seeing through other people. He certainly made good in the novels, again and again, this typically prescient opinion of himself. Some "altered knowledge" is what we all desire for ourselves but are usually forced to borrow from someone like Dickens or Freud.

Notes

I. Charles Dickens

1. Edmund Wilson, *The Wound and the Bow* (1929; rpt. New York: Oxford University Press, 1959), p. 6.
2. John Forster, *The Life of Charles Dickens*, 2 vols. (London: Everyman, 1927), I, 19. On the problems of dating the autobiographical fragment, see Nina Burgis, ed., *David Copperfield* (Oxford: Clarendon , 1981), pp. xv–xxii; and Philip Collins, "Dickens's Autobiographical Fragment and *David Copperfield*," *Cahiers victoriennes et edouardiennes*, 20 (October 1984), 87–96.
3. Forster, *Life of Dickens*, I, 20–24.
4. Ibid., I, 32.
5. See Albert D. Hutter, "Nation and Generation in *A Tale of Two Cities*," *PMLA*, 93 (1978), 448–462; and Dianne F. Sadoff, *Monsters of Affection: Dickens, Eliot, and Bronte on Fatherhood* (Baltimore: Johns Hopkins University Press, 1982), pp. 22–38.
6. Wilson, *The Wound and the Bow*, p. 14.
7. Steven Marcus, "Who Is Fagin?" in *Dickens: From Pickwick to Dombey* (London: Chatto and Windus, 1965), pp. 369–378.
8. Albert D. Hutter, "Reconstructive Autobiography: The Experience at Warren's Blacking," *Dickens Studies Annual*, 6 (1977), 12.
9. Cf. Robert Newsom, "The Hero's Shame," *Dickens Studies Annual*, 11 (1983), 1–24.
10. Forster, *Life of Dickens*, I, 25.
11. Edgar Johnson, *Charles Dickens: His Tragedy and Triumph*, 2 vols. (London: Gollancz, 1953), I, 45–46.
12. Forster, *Life of Dickens*, I, 290–291.
13. Johnson, *Charles Dickens*, I, 234–253; Robert L. Patten, *Charles Dickens and His Publishers* (Oxford: Clarendon, 1978), pp. 28–156.
14. Forster, *Life of Dickens*, I, 171–173.
15. Erik H. Erikson, *Identity: Youth and Crisis* (New York: Norton, 1968), pp. 155–158; see also *Childhood and Society*, 2nd ed. (New York: Norton, 1963), pp. 262–263.

16. Erik H. Erikson, *Young Man Luther: A Study in Psychoanalysis and History* (1958: rpt. New York: Norton, 1962), p. 43; also pp. 99–104.
17. Forster, *Life of Dickens,* I, 167, 171.
18. To Messrs Bradbury and Evans, 3 November 1845, *The Letters of Charles Dickens,* ed. Madeline House, Graham Storey, et. al. (Oxford: Clarendon, 1965–), IV, 423–424.
19. To Lord Morpeth, 20 June 1846, *Letters of Dickens,* IV, 566–567.
20. Marcus, *Dickens,* pp. 269–292.
21. Jerome Meckier, "Dickens Discovers America, Dickens Discovers Dickens: The First Visit Reconsidered," *Modern Language Review,* 79, pt. 2 (1984), 266–277.
22. B. L. Packer, *Emerson's Fall: A New Interpretation of the Major Essays* (New York: Continuum, 1982), p. 167.
23. J. Hillis Miller, *Charles Dickens: The World of His Novels* (Cambridge: Harvard University Press, 1958), p. x.
24. See my "Waverley, Pickwick, and Don Quixote," *Nineteenth-Century Fiction,* 22 (1967), 19–30, and *Reflections on the Hero as Quixote* (Princeton: Princeton University Press, 1981).
25. James R. Kincaid, *Dickens and the Rhetoric of Laughter* (Oxford: Clarendon, 1971), p. 156.
26. Charles Dickens, *Martin Chuzzlewit,* ed. Margaret Cardwell (Oxford: Clarendon, 1982), ch. 52, pp. 809–810. Further citations are from this edition and will be given by chapter and page in parentheses.
27. The "livin skelinton" was a popular exhibit of 1825, and similar historical being can be presumed for other features in this show. See Richard D. Altick, *The Shows of London* (Cambridge: Harvard University Press, 1978), pp. 261–263, and for dwarfs, pp. 42–44.

II. *Our English Tartuffe*

1. *Introductory Lectures on Psycho-Analysis* (1916–17), in *The Standard Edition of the Complete Psychological Works of Sigmund Freud,* ed. and trans. James Strachey et al., 24 vols. (London: Hogarth, 1953–1974), XVI, 280–281, 436–437.
2. Freud, *Standard Edition,* XVI, 281.
3. Molière, *Oeuvres complètes,* ed. Maurice Rat, 2 vols. (Paris: Gallimard, 1956), II, 235, 246.
4. Forster, *Life of Dickens,* I, 294.
5. To H. K. Browne, [June 1844], *Letters of Dickens,* IV, 141.
6. Cf. Stuart Curran, "The Lost Paradises of *Martin Chuzzlewit,*" *Nineteenth-Century Fiction,* 25 (1970), 51.
7. G. K. Chesterton, *Charles Dickens* (1906; rpt. New York: Schocken, 1965), pp. 148–149. Cf. Dickens, to C. C. Felton, 31 December 1842, commending "Mr. Pecksniff and his daughters, to your tender regard. I have a kind of liking for them, myself." *Letters of Dickens,* III, 414.

8. Cf. W. D. Howarth, *Molière: A Playwright and His Audience* (Cambridge: Cambridge University Press, 1982), p. 198: "If Molière had been writing entirely in the farce tradition, the discomfiture of the impostor [Tartuffe] would have been marked by the ritual *coups de bâton.*"
9. See Paul Benichou, *Man and Ethics: Studies in French Classicism* (New York: Anchor, 1971), pp. 224–229. This is a translation of Benichou's *Morales du grand siècle* (1948).
10. Johnson, *Charles Dickens,* II, 1137; I, 481–483.
11. Michael Steig, *"Martin Chuzzlewit:* Pinch and Pecksniff," *Studies in the Novel,* 1 (1969), 181. Steig further writes, "It is almost as though in this novel Dickens is unconsciously revealing *himself* as the supreme confidence man" (p. 187).
12. Molière, *Oeuvres complètes,* I, 754. In Pecksniff's adoption of the principle, he enforces silence on Mary Graham by threatening to speak to old Martin Chuzzlewit about her interest in young Martin.
13. Robert M. McCarron, "Folly and Wisdom: Three Dickensian Wise Fools," *Dickens Studies Annual,* 6 (1977), pp. 40–56, is one of the few critics to touch on the "traditional" role of Pinch as a fool. See also Miller, *Charles Dickens,* p. 122.
14. The difference is partly accounted for by the English novel's preference of false courtship to adultery, when it comes to portraying sexual vagaries: see Ruth Bernard Yeazell, "Podsnappery, Sexuality, and the English Novel," *Critical Inquiry,* 9 (1982), 339–357.
15. Dickens makes much of his unrequited passion throughout the novel, and today's readers may react incredulously to the masturbatory language of the following passage, in which Pinch's organ seems transformed as the god Priapus: "When she spoke, Tom held his breath, so eagerly he listened; when she sang, he sat like one entranced. She touched his organ, and from that bright epoch even it, the old companion of his happiest hours, incapable as he had thought of elevation, began a new and deified existence" (24.395).
16. Letter to H. K. Browne, [June 1844], *Letters of Dickens,* IV, 140.
17. See the Clarendon edition, p. 601n3. Dickens's pen also hesitated over thirty-one and thirty-three.
18. Kincaid, *Dickens and the Rhetoric of Laughter,* pp. 154–155.
19. Ian Watt, "Oral Dickens," *Dickens Studies Annual,* 3 (1974), 168. Watt's case for an oral Dickens has to be weighed against the belief of another distinguished critic that the novelist "belonged to the Freudian 'anal type' ": see Humphry House, *The Dickens World,* 2nd ed. (1942; rpt. London: Oxford University Press, 1961), pp. 202–203. For Pecksniff's performance in both departments, see his famous "grace after meat" (8.124).
20. According to the *O.E.D.,* "pecker" was slang in Dickens's time for a large eater, but it could also mean a small hoe for planting seed. The entry cites Dickens himself, in a letter of 1857, for the expression "keep your pecker up." Though the expression supposedly means keep your head high, it

was very likely schoolboy slang for a more special bravado, as it is today.

21. Probably Thomas Cleghorn, in *North British Review*, 3 (1845), 72. George H. Ford, *Dickens and His Readers: Aspects of Novel Criticism since 1836* (Princeton: Princeton University Press, 1955), p. 48, gives the reference.

22. Robert M. Polhemus, *Comic Faith: The Great Tradition from Austen to Joyce* (Chicago and London: University of Chicago Press, 1980), pp. 108–110. A number of critics have called attention to unintended self-parody in the novel, and each is able to cite different passages in evidence: see Marcus, *Dickens*, pp. 219–220; Barbara Hardy, *The Moral Art of Dickens* (London: Athlone, 1970), pp. 117–119; and A. E. Dyson, *The Inimitable Dickens: A Reading of the Novels* (London: Macmillan, 1970), pp. 86–87.

23. Miller, *Charles Dickens*, pp. 104, 137. "Breasts" in the quotation from Mrs. Gamp is a manuscipt reading restored by the Clarendon edition.

III. *Hypocrisy and Copyright*

1. Forster, *Life of Dickens*, I, 274, 296.

2. Albert J. Guerard, *The Triumph of the Novel: Dickens, Dostoevsky, Faulkner* (New York: Oxford University Press, 1976), pp. 245–250.

3. *The Speeches of Charles Dickens*, ed. K. J. Fielding (Oxford: Clarendon, 1960), pp. 21, 24–25. In Hartford he insinuated that if there had been an international copyright agreement, Scott "might have lived to add new creatures of his fancy" to those he had already given to the world by his novel writing. See also the few sentences in Dickens's New York speech, p. 28.

4. See Forster, *Life of Dickens*, I, 196–197, 214–215; and *Letters of Dickens*, III, 212–215, 221–224. For a history that puts these efforts in perspective, see James J. Barnes, *Authors, Publishers and Politicians: The Quest for an Anglo-American Copyright Agreement, 1815–1854* (London: Routledge, 1974).

5. Sidney P. Moss, *Charles Dickens' Quarrel with America* (Troy: Whitston, 1984), samples some virulent attacks on Dickens by Americans, but these date from after his visit and are responses to his real and supposed writings about the country. On the copyright question, Moss believes that "in all probability . . . Dickens did not go forth as a missionary, but became one in America" (p. 65).

6. To Jonathan Chapman, 22 February 1842, *Letters of Dickens*, III, 76–77.

7. See Forster, *Life of Dickens*, I, 25, 33.

8. Forster, *Life of Dickens*, I, 195.

9. To John S. Bartlett, 24 February 1842, *Letters of Dickens*, III, 79.

10. Printed circular, 7 July 1842, *Letters of Dickens*, III, 259.

11. Cf. K. J. Fielding, "*American Notes* and some English Reviewers," *Modern Language Review*, 59 (1964), 527–537. Fielding accepts Dickens's word that he did not go to America "to engage in the copyright controversy" (p. 534).

12. *Edinburgh Review*, 76 (1843), 500–501.
13. To the *Times*, 15 January 1843, *Letters of Dickens*, III, 423–424. See also his letters of the following week to Macvey Napier and Lord Brougham, III, 429–432.
14. Quoted in *Letters of Dickens*, III, 430n1.
15. James Spedding, *Reviews and Discussions: Literary, Political, and Historical* (London: Kegan Paul, 1879), pp. 270–276.
16. Cf. Polhemus, *Comic Faith*, p. 99.
17. Norman and Jeanne Mackenzie, *Dickens: A Life* (Oxford: Oxford University Press, 1979), p. 135.

IV. *Chuzzlewit Madness*

1. Hardy, *The Moral Art of Dickens*, pp. 117–118.
2. Ibid., p. 115.
3. Harry Stone, "Dickens's Use of His American Experiences in *Martin Chuzzlewit*," *PMLA*, 72 (1957), 464–478.
4. Forster, *Life of Dickens*, I, 293.
5. See W. Glyde Wilkins, *Charles Dickens in America* (London: Chapman and Hall, 1911), pp. 139–147, 241–242.
6. See Gerald G. Grubb, "Dickens's Western Tour and the Cairo Legend," *Studies in Philology*, 48 (1951), 87–97. Wilkins, *Charles Dickens in America*, pp. 1–2 and 210–211, uncritically repeats these stories.
7. Meckier, "Dickens Discovers America," p. 268.
8. Forster, *Life of Dickens*, I, 294.
9. See Johnson, *Charles Dickens*, II, 1101–14, 1142–46, and the headnote to "Sikes and Nancy" in *Charles Dickens: The Public Readings*, ed. Philip Collins (Oxford: Clarendon, 1975), pp. 465–471.
10. Cf. Johnson, *Charles Dickens*, I, 195–204; and Michael Slater, *Dickens and Women* (London: Dent, 1983), pp. 77–102.
11. Kathleen Tillotson, *Novels of the Eighteen-Forties* (1954; rpt. London: Oxford University Press, 1961), p. 157.

V. *Paradise Lost*

1. Curran, "The Lost Paradises of *Martin Chuzzlewit*," pp. 51–67.
2. Cf. *Paradise Lost*, ed. Merrit I. Hughes (New York: Odyssey, 1962), III.682–685.
3. Forster, *Life of Dickens*, I, 273; cf. Clarendon edition of *Martin Chuzzlewit*, appendix A, p. 834.
4. Polhemus, *Comic Faith*, pp. 93–94, discusses a possible play on "chisel" in the name "Chuzzlewit," but while this possibility brings out the idea of cheating it does not complement the oral connotations of "Pecksniff."
5. Cf. Curran, "The Lost Paradises of *Martin Chuzzlewit*," p. 59.

6. Cf. *Paradise Lost,* II.344–385. It is just possible that Beelzebub is an ancestor of the Sweezle family.
7. Cf. Marcus, *Dickens,* pp. 253–255.
8. The best general account is Mircea Eliade, *The Myth of the Eternal Return,* trans. Willard R. Trask (New York: Pantheon, 1954).
9. A. Bartlett Giamatti, *The Earthly Paradise and the Renaissance Epic* (Princeton: Princeton University Press, 1966), p. 359.
10. Harold Bloom, "The Internalization of Quest Romance," *The Ringers in the Tower: Studies in Romantic Tradition* (Chicago: University of Chicago Press, 1971), pp. 13–35.
11. The classic studies are Henry Nash Smith, *The Virgin Land: The American West as Symbol and Myth* (Cambridge: Harvard University Press, 1950), esp. bk. 3, and R. W. B. Lewis, *The American Adam: Innocence, Tragedy, and Tradition in the Nineteenth Century* (Chicago: University of Chicago Press, 1955). Leo Marx, *The Machine in the Garden: Technology and the Pastoral Ideal in America* (New York: Oxford University Press, 1964), pp. 36–46, calls attention to the contradictory images of America as garden and wilderness that go back to the sixteenth century.
12. "Experience," in *The Collected Works of Ralph Waldo Emerson,* III (Cambridge: Harvard University Press, 1983), pp. 37, 49.
13. See Johnson, *Charles Dickens,* I, 93; II, 958–959. Dickens himself was separated from his wife in 1858.
14. Preface to *The Last Essays of Elia,* in *Complete Works and Letters of Charles Lamb* (New York: Modern Library, 1935), p. 135.

VI. *Dickens as Dombey*

1. Forster, *Life of Dickens,* I, 289.
2. Tillotson, *Novels of the Eighteen-Forties,* pp. 162–163.
3. Marcus, *Dickens,* pp. 213–268.
4. Forster, *Life of Dickens,* II, 19.
5. See Patten, *Charles Dickens and His Publishers,* pp. 182–197.
6. Ada B. Nisbet, "The Mystery of *Martin Chuzzlewit,*" in *Essays Critical and Historical Dedicated to Lily B. Campbell* (Berkeley: University of California Press, 1950), pp. 201–216.
7. Forster, *Life of Dickens,* II, 20–21. The second two ellipses in the passage are Forster's.
8. Charles Dickens, *Dombey and Son,* ed. Alan Horsman (Oxford: Clarendon, 1974), ch. 8, pp. 93–94. Further citations are from this edition and will be given by chapter and page in parentheses.
9. Philip Collins, *Dickens and Education* (1963; rpt. London: Macmillan, 1965), pp. 201–202. If Paul can be thought of as Lear's Fool, after the fifth number his place is taken by a Cordelia, his sister Florence.
10. Clarendon edition, appendix B, p. 840.
11. Forster, *Life of Dickens,* II, 19.

12. Cf. Louise Yellin, "Strategies for Survival: Florence and Edith in *Dombey and Son*," *Victorian Studies*, 22 (1979), 297–319. Nina Auerbach writes of the masculinity of Edith in "Dickens and Dombey: A Daughter After All," *Dickens Studies Annual*, 5 (1976), 108–111.
13. See Forster, *Life of Dickens*, II, 34.

VII. *Dombey as King Lear*

1. Tillotson, *Novels of the Eighteen-Forties*, pp. 170–171.
2. See Alexander Welsh, "The Allegory of Truth in English Fiction," *Victorian Studies*, 9 (1965), 7–28.
3. See Paul Schlicke, "A 'Discipline of Feeling': Macready's *Lear* and *The Old Curiosity Shop*," *Dickensian*, 76 (1980), 79–80; and Jerome Meckier, "Dickens and *King Lear*: A Myth for Victorian England," *South Atlantic Quarterly*, 71 (1972), 75–90.
4. For comparison of *The Old Curiosity Shop* with other adaptations of King Lear, see my "King Lear, Père Goriot, and Nell's Grandfather," in *Literary Theory and Criticism: A Collection of Essays in Honor of René Wellek*, ed. Joseph P. Strelka (Bern: Peter Lang, 1984), pp. 1405–25.
5. John Butt and Kathleen Tillotson, *Dickens at Work* (London: Methuen, 1957), p. 103.
6. *King Lear*, III.iv.28–36. Quotations from Shakespeare are from *The Riverside Shakespeare*, ed. G. Blakemore Evans (Boston: Houghton Mifflin, 1974).
7. For the importance of the family for Shakespeare, see Rosalie L. Colie, "Reason and Need: *King Lear* and the 'Crisis' of the Aristocracy," in *Some Facets of "King Lear": Essays in Prismatic Criticism*, ed. Rosalie L. Colie and F. T. Flahiff (London: Heinemann, 1974), pp. 185–219.
8. Thomas McFarland, "The Image of the Family in *King Lear*," in *On "King Lear,"* ed. Lawrence Danson (Princeton: Princeton University Press, 1981), pp. 91–118.
9. Victor Hugo, *William Shakespeare*, trans. Melville B. Anderson (Chicago: McClurg, 1887), pp. 244–249.
10. A. C. Bradley, *Shakespearean Tragedy* (1904; rpt. New York: Meridian, 1955), pp. 252–253.
11. Since I have discussed the allegory of death in *The City of Dickens* (1971; rpt. Cambridge: Harvard University Press, 1985), pp. 150–212, I have given only a brief idea of it here.
12. Miller, *Charles Dickens*, pp. 148–150.
13. Cf. Barbara Everett, "The New King Lear," *Critical Quarterly*, 2 (1960), 325–339. The standard work on the belief system of the play is William R. Elton's *"King Lear" and the Gods* (San Marino: Huntington Library, 1966).
14. Freud, "The Theme of the Three Caskets" (1913), *Standard Edition*, XII,

301. For the background of these views, see Erik H. Erikson, *Insight and Responsibility* (New York: Norton, 1964), pp. 178–185.

15. Simone de Beauvoir, *The Second Sex,* trans. H. M. Parshley (1952; rpt. New York: Vintage, 1974), p. 187.

16. Chesterton, *Charles Dickens,* p. 122.

17. De Beauvoir, *The Second Sex,* p. 167.

18. See the memorandum preserved with the manuscript of the novel, Clarendon edition, appendix B, p. 849.

19. Marcus, *Dickens,* pp. 298–300.

20. Cf. Yellin, "Strategies for Survival," pp. 304–305.

21. Charles Dickens, *Christmas Books* (London: Oxford University Press, 1954), pp. 76, 71, 151.

22. Quoted by Ford, *Dickens and His Readers,* p. 58.

VIII. *A Novelist's Novelist*

1. Hugo's play *Le Roi s'amuse* dates from 1832; Verdi's *Rigoletto* was produced just a year after *Copperfield* was completed, in 1851.

2. For a brief summary of these maneuvers, see *The City of Dickens,* pp. 171–174, 207–209. Martin Meisel, *Realizations: Narrative, Pictorial, and Theatrical Arts in Nineteenth-Century England* (Princeton: Princeton University Press, 1983), pp. 302–321, expounds the iconography of the daughter figure and points out that the prison setting derives more immediately from Nahum Tate than from Shakespeare.

3. Charles Dickens, *David Copperfield,* ed. Nina Burgis (Oxford: Clarendon, 1981), ch. 1, p. 8. Further citations are from this edition and will be given by chapter and page in parentheses.

4. Sylvia Manning, "Masking and Self-Revelation: Dickens's Three Autobiographies," *Dickens Studies Newsletter,* 7 (1976), 69–70.

5. Robert F. Fleissner, *Dickens and Shakespeare: A Study in Histrionic Contrasts* (New York: Haskell, 1965), pp. 149–160, picks up six more unmistakable allusions to *Hamlet* in *Copperfield,* three of them attributable to Micawber; but he presents no persuasive case for their importance. William A. Wilson, "The Magic Circle of Genius: Dickens's Translations of Shakespearean Drama in *Great Expectations,*" *Nineteenth-Century Fiction,* 40 (1985), 154–174, is able to make a somewhat stronger case for the significance of *Hamlet* in the later novel.

6. Forster, *Life of Dickens,* II, 98–104.

7. K. J. Fielding, "Dickens and the Past: The Novel of Memory," in *Experience and the Novel,* ed. Roy Harvey Pearce (New York: Columbia University Press, 1968), p. 114.

8. Jerome H. Buckley, "The Identity of David Copperfield," in *Victorian Literature and Society: Essays Presented to Richard D. Altick,* ed. James R. Kincaid and Albert J. Kuhn (Columbus: Ohio State University Press, 1983), p. 237.

9. Forster, *Life of Dickens*, II, 77.
10. To D. M. Moir, 17 June 1848, *Letters of Dickens*, V, 341.
11. William C. Spengeman, *Forms of Autobiography: Episodes in the History of a Literary Genre* (New Haven: Yale University Press, 1980), pp. 119–132.
12. See *The City of Dickens*, pp. 73–85; and Walter Houghton, *The Victorian Frame of Mind* (New Haven: Yale University Press, 1957), pp. 242–262.
13. See John Sutherland, *Thackeray at Work* (London: Athlone, 1974), pp. 45–55.
14. Philip Collins, *Charles Dickens: David Copperfield* (London: Arnold, 1977), p. 40.
15. Miller, *Charles Dickens*, pp. 155–158.
16. Welsh, *The City of Dickens*, pp. 180–183; Erikson, *Childhood and Society*, pp. 247–251, and *Young Man Luther*, pp. 115–119.
17. Barry Westburg, *The Confessional Fictions of Charles Dickens* (Dekalb: Northern Illinois University Press, 1977), pp. 104–106.
18. Avrom Fleishman, *Figures of Autobiography: The Language of Self-Writing in Victorian and Modern England* (Berkeley: University of California Press, 1983), pp. 214–218, argues that "Agnes's prose becomes the conduit by which Dickens brings the spiritual autobiography tradition to bear on his personal situation."
19. Forster, *Life of Dickens*, I, 32.
20. Miller, *Charles Dickens*, p. 151. See also John P. McGowan, "*David Copperfield:* The Trial of Realism," *Nineteenth-Century Fiction*, 34 (1979), 1–19.
21. Cf. Garrett Stewart, *Death Sentences: Styles of Dying in British Fiction* (Cambridge: Harvard University Press, 1984), p. 80.
22. Stanley Tick, "The Memorializing of Mr. Dick," *Nineteenth-Century Fiction*, 24 (1969), 142–153. See also Spengeman, *Forms of Autobiography*, pp. 126–132.
23. Forster, *Life of Dickens*, II, 77.
24. Sylvère Monod, *Dickens the Novelist* (Norman: University of Oklahoma Press, 1968), pp. 302–303, and E. Pearlman, "David Copperfield Dreams of Drowning," *American Imago*, 28 (1971), 394, emphasize the similarity of names as between the hero and heroine, rather than the heroine's father. Pearlman suggests that the relative stability of "field" contrasts with the association between Steerforth and the sea.
25. Forster, *Life of Dickens*, II, 90.

IX. *Women Passing By*

1. Forster, *Life of Dickens*, II, 109.
2. F. R. and Q. D. Leavis, *Dickens: The Novelist* (London: Chatto and Windus, 1970), pp. 85–86. John Lucas, *The Melancholy Man* (Brighton: Harvester, 1980), pp. 194–198, gives a very good account of Dora.

3. Monod, *Dickens the Novelist*, pp. 323–325. The French version of this book appeared in 1952.

4. To Mrs. Winter, 10, 15, and 22 February 1855, *The Letters of Charles Dickens*, ed. Walter Dexter, 3 vols. (London: Nonesuch Press, 1938); quotations at II, 626, 629. This is the only time I cite the Nonesuch edition of the letters, which bears the same title as the Clarendon edition. The three letters to Maria Winter are important for recalling the ambition of the young Dickens—"It is a matter of perfect certainty to me that I began to fight my way out of poverty and obscurity, with one perpetual idea of you" (II, 628)—and their ambiguous account of the autobiographical fragment—"A few years ago (just before Copperfield) I began to write my life, intending the manuscript to be found among my papers when its subject should be concluded. But as I began to approach within sight of that part of it [his love for Maria], I lost courage and burned the rest" (II, 633). There is some confusion here: did he first write and then burn or merely "approach within sight" of his first love and burn some blank sheets?

5. Philip Collins, "*David Copperfield*: 'A Very Complicated Interweaving of Truth and Fiction,' " *Essays and Studies*, n.s. 23 (1970), 81–84. The complaint about Catherine Dickens's "weak hand" dates from 1858: see *The Heart of Charles Dickens: As Revealed in His Letters to Angela Burdett-Coutts*, ed. Edgar Johnson (Boston: Little, Brown, 1952), p. 361. Collins's opinion that Agnes was modeled on Mary Hogarth receives some general support from Forster's summary of his friend's "Personal Characteristics" at the end of the *Life*: "What he said on the sixth anniversary of the death of his sister-in-law, that friend of his youth whom he made his ideal of all moral excellence, he might have said as truly after twenty-six years more; for in the very year before he died, the influence was potently upon him. 'She is so much in my thoughts at all times, especially when I am successful, and have greatly prospered in anything, that the recollection of her is an essential part of my being, and is as inseparable from my existence as the beating of my heart is' " (II, 402). This is obviously an idealized Mary Hogarth, who has become a specular figure not unlike Agnes in the novel.

6. The fullest account of Dickens's relation to his wife is Slater, *Dickens and Women*, pp. 103–162. Phyllis Rose's account, in *Parallel Lives: Five Victorian Marriages* (New York: Knopf, 1984), pp. 145–191, looks back on the marriage in light of the separation of 1858.

7. Hardy, *The Moral Art of Dickens*, p. 131.

8. George H. Ford, "David Copperfield," in *The Dickens Critics*, ed. George H. Ford and Lauriat Lane, Jr. (Ithaca: Cornell University Press, 1961), pp. 349–356; Robin Gilmour, "Memory in *David Copperfield*," *Dickensian*, 71 (1975), 30–42.

9. Monroe Engel, *The Maturity of Dickens* (Cambridge: Harvard University Press, 1959), p. 156.

10. Forster, *Life of Dickens*, II, 197.

11. The argument of the following paragraphs first appeared in *Yale Review*, 71 (1981), 151–156.

12. Cf. Monod, *Dickens the Novelist,* pp. 358–360.
13. To [William Brown], 11 January [1848], *Letters of Dickens,* V, 231–232.
14. To Miss Burdett Coutts, 14 January 1848, ibid., V, 234.
15. To William Brown, 6 November 1849, ibid., V, 638–639.
16. For other examples see *The City of Dickens,* p. 224.
17. The leaflet is reprinted as appendix D, *Letters of Dickens,* V, 698–699.
18. To Miss Burdett Coutts, 26 August and 28 October 1847, ibid., V, 152, 179.
19. To Miss Burdett Coutts, 3 November 1847, ibid., V, 182.
20. To Miss Burdett Coutts, 7 November 1848, ibid., V, 436.
21. Appendix D, ibid., V, 699.
22. Cf. Ruth F. Glancy, "Dickens and Christmas: His Framed-Tale Themes," *Nineteenth-Century Fiction,* 35 (1980), 53–72; and Westburg, *The Confessional Fictions of Charles Dickens,* pp. 53–67.
23. Dickens, *Christmas Books,* p. 332.
24. See above, Chapter 8, note 10.
25. The essay most often cited is Gwendolyn B. Needham, "The Undisciplined Heart of David Copperfield," *Nineteenth-Century Fiction,* 9 (1954), 81–107.
26. See Collins, ed., *Charles Dickens: The Public Readings,* p. 217.

X. *Perfection of English Mirth*

1. Harry Stone, *Dickens and the Invisible World: Fairy Tales, Fantasy, and Novel-Making* (Bloomington: Indiana University Press, 1979), pp. 193–278. The quotation is from p. 272.
2. Monod, *Dickens the Novelist,* p. 307.
3. Hardy, *The Moral Art of Dickens,* p. 132.
4. T. A. Jackson, *Charles Dickens: The Progress of a Radical* (New York: International, 1938), p. 119.
5. E.D.H. Johnson, *Charles Dickens: An Introduction to His Novels* (New York: Random House, 1969), p. 97.
6. Alexander A. Parker, *Literature and the Delinquent: The Picaresque Novel in Spain and Europe, 1599–1753* (Edinburgh: Edinburgh University Press, 1967), argues that the picaresque hero is originally a middle-class youth but delinquent and absent from his family.
7. Hardy, *The Moral Art of Dickens,* p. 130.
8. Forster, *Life of Dickens,* II, 78. The Clarendon edition of the novel reprints the memoranda of names as appendix B, pp. 753–755.
9. Monod, *Dickens the Novelist,* p. 302.
10. Cf. Welsh, *The City of Dickens,* pp. 130–135. Such demonic characters can be read, without tracing their provenance back to the novelist, as figments of the hero's desires or fears.
11. 2 Samuel 11:2–12:25.
12. Though Heep and Steerforth are linked in the hero's dreams; see Pearlman, "David Copperfield Dreams of Drowning," pp. 392–393, 396–397.

13. On the class implications, see especially Lucas, *The Melancholy Man,* pp. 183–193.
14. Matthew 6:25–34 and Luke 12:22–31.
15. Forster, *Life of Dickens,* I, 32. For the Victorian resonance of this idea of forgiveness, see Welsh, *The City of Dickens,* pp. 110–117.
16. See the Clarendon edition, p. 233n2.
17. Forster, *Life of Dickens,* II, 105.
18. Ross H. Dabney, *Love and Property in the Novels of Dickens* (London: Chatto and Windus, 1967), p. 73. Chesterton, *Charles Dickens,* p. 268, charges that "when Dora dies recommending Agnes we know that everything is wrong, at least if hypocrisy and artificiality and moral vulgarity are wrong."
19. Especially Sylvère Monod in *Dickens the Novelist,* pp. 275–369, and Leavis in *Dickens,* pp. 34–117. Few critics, whatever their reservations, are unimpressed by the novel.
20. Angus Wilson, *The World of Charles Dickens* (1970; rpt. Harmondsworth: Penguin, 1972), p. 216.
21. Forster, *Life of Dickens,* II, 106.
22. Ibid., II, 106–108.
23. Ibid., II, 107.
24. See also the comments in his chapter "Dickens as a Novelist," ibid., II, 277.
25. Garrett Stewart, *Dickens and the Trials of Imagination* (Cambridge: Harvard University Press, 1974), pp. 115–116.
26. Forster, *Life of Dickens,* II, 99–104.
27. Stewart, *Dickens and the Trials of Imagination,* pp. 138–141. Stewart claims that Micawber's "self-conscious phrasing, which turns up repeatedly in his talk, is a parody of David's own verbal wariness and humility" (p. 140).
28. Hutter, "Reconstructive Autobiography," p. 10.
29. Mackenzie, *Dickens,* p. 210.
30. See above, Chapter 1, note 19.

XI. *Young Man Copperfield*

1. Avrom Fleishman, *Figures of Autobiography,* p. 207, suggests that the treatment of the mother as a child comes about as "the best excuse . . . for maternal inadequacy."
2. Spengeman, *Forms of Autobiography,* pp. 119–132.
3. Hutter, "Reconstructive Autobiography," p. 7; Robert L. Patten, "Autobiography into Autobiography: The Evolution of *David Copperfield,*" in *Approaches to Victorian Autobiography,* ed. George P. Landow (Athens: Ohio University Press, 1979), pp. 273–278.
4. Forster, *Life of Dickens,* I, 25; for a fuller quotation see Chapter 1 above.
5. Ibid., I, 25.
6. For an essay on the control exerted by Dickens over his autobiography,

see Jean Fergusson Carr, "Dickens and Autobiography: A Wild Beast and His Keeper," *ELH,* 52 (1985), 447–469.

7. J. Hillis Miller, "Three Problems of Fictional Form: First Person Narration in *David Copperfield* and *Huckleberry Finn,*" in *Experience and the Novel,* ed. Roy Harvey Pearce (New York: Columbia University Press, 1968), p. 33; and Miller, *Charles Dickens,* p. 157.

8. Robert E. Lougy, "Remembrance of Death Past and Future: A Reading of *David Copperfield,*" *Dickens Studies Annual,* 6 (1977), 87, suggests that the drowning of Ham and Steerforth "moves primarily toward a recognition of his own death that David can no longer conceal or evade."

9. Erikson, *Young Man Luther,* p. 83.

10. Ibid., pp. 264–265.

11. Ibid., p. 73.

12. Ibid., pp. 69–70.

13. Letter of 5 October 1893, quoted by Ernest Jones, *The Life and Work of Sigmund Freud,* 3 vols. (New York: Basic Books, 1953–1957), I, 174; also p. 104.

14. I have especially in mind the work of social historians, such as William J. McGrath's *Freud's Discovery of Psychoanalysis: The Politics of Hysteria* (Ithaca: Cornell University Press, 1986). The inspiration of this work can be said to be the chapter on Freud in Carl E. Schorske, *Fin-de-Siècle Vienna: Politics and Culture* (New York: Vintage, 1981), pp. 181–207, but in a real sense also Erikson is the one who has taught us to see Freud against the background of his times.

15. The dependence of psychoanalysis on narrative is now frequently urged. Donald P. Spence, *Narrative Truth and Historical Truth: Meaning and Interpretation in Psychoanalysis* (New York: Norton, 1982), perhaps goes furthest in seeing the analytic narrative as fiction. Though Spence calls on literary theory, he does not see the history of the novel as relevant to his argument.

16. Frank J. Sulloway, *Freud, Biologist of the Mind: Beyond the Psychoanalytic Legend* (New York: Basic Books, 1979).

17. Letter of 15 October 1897, *The Complete Letters of Sigmund Freud to Wilhelm Fliess, 1887–1904,* trans. and ed. Jeffrey Moussaieff Masson (Cambridge: Harvard University Press, 1985), p. 272.

18. D. W. Winnicott, *Playing and Reality* (New York: Basic Books, 1971), p. 144; Hutter, "Reconstructive Autobiography," p. 10, cites Winnicott.

XII. *Expectations*

1. Cf. Philip Collins, Letter to *Times Literary Supplement,* 18 May 1973, pp. 556–557.

2. Leavis, *Dickens,* pp. 35–43, 68–71.

3. Mark Spilka, *Dickens and Kafka: A Mutual Interpretation* (Bloomington: Indiana University Press, 1963), pp. 150–195.

4. Forster, *Life of Dickens,* II, 62; see also *Letters of Dickens,* V, 611n.
5. See George Katkov, "Steerforth and Stavrogin: On the Sources of *The Possessed,*" *Slavic and East European Review,* 27 (1949), 469–488.
6. N. M. Lary, *Dostoevsky and Dickens: A Study of Literary Influence* (London: Routledge, 1973), pp. 135–136, believes that Stepan Verkhovensky derives from William Dorrit as well as Wilkins Micawber.
7. Forster, *Life of Dickens,* II, 284–285.
8. Jerome H. Buckley, *Season of Youth: The Bildungsroman from Dickens to Golding* (Cambridge: Harvard University Press, 1974), pp. 43–46.
9. Forster, *Life of Dickens,* I, 32.
10. Charles Dickens, *Great Expectations* (London: Oxford University Press, 1953), ch. 14, p. 101. Subsequent references are given by chapter and page in parentheses.
11. Julian Moynahan, "The Hero's Guilt: The Case of Great Expectations," *Essays in Criticism,* 10 (January 1960), 60–79.
12. Forster, *Life of Dickens,* II, 287–288.
13. Erikson, *Young Man Luther,* p. 68.

Index